Thinking with Adorno

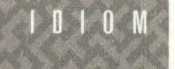 INVENTING WRITING THEORY

Jacques Lezra and Paul North, series editors

Gerhard Richter

Thinking with Adorno

THE UNCOERCIVE GAZE

FORDHAM UNIVERSITY PRESS · NEW YORK · 2019

Fordham University Press gratefully acknowledges financial
assistance and support provided for the publication of this book
by Brown University.

Copyright © 2019 Fordham University Press

All rights reserved. No part of this publication may be reproduced,
stored in a retrieval system, or transmitted in any form or by any
means—electronic, mechanical, photocopy, recording, or any
other—except for brief quotations in printed reviews, without the
prior permission of the publisher.

Fordham University Press has no responsibility for the persistence or
accuracy of URLs for external or third-party Internet websites referred
to in this publication and does not guarantee that any content on such
websites is, or will remain, accurate or appropriate.

Fordham University Press also publishes its books in a variety of
electronic formats. Some content that appears in print may not be
available in electronic books.

Visit us online at www.fordhampress.com.

Library of Congress Cataloging-in-Publication Data available online at
https://catalog.loc.gov.

Printed in the United States of America

21 20 19   5 4 3 2 1

First edition

CONTENTS

	Introduction: The Art of Reading	1
1.	Adorno and the Uncoercive Gaze	17
2.	Buried Possibility: Adorno and Arendt on Tradition	39
3.	The Inheritance of the Constellation: Adorno and Hegel	70
4.	Judging by Refraining from Judgment: Adorno's Artwork and Its *Einordnung*	95
5.	The Literary Artwork between Word and Concept: Adorno and Agamben Reading Kafka	115
6.	The Artwork without Cardinal Direction: Notes on Orientation in Adorno	131
7.	False Life, Living On: Adorno with Derrida	144
	Conclusion: A Kind of Leave-Taking	161
	Acknowledgments	167
	Notes	169
	Index	203

Thinking with Adorno

INTRODUCTION

The Art of Reading

Let us begin with an interruption, an interruption that will have marked a beginning even as it also marks the end of a life, so that the acts of beginning and ending no longer appear as mere oppositional poles in the world of thought and experience. When, in spring 1969—only months before his unexpected death in August of that same year—Theodor W. Adorno is interviewed at length by the influential German news magazine *Der Spiegel*, the reporter commences the conversation by alluding to the tensions between Adorno and the student movement that recently had escalated and caused the philosopher to cancel his lecture course at the University of Frankfurt. "Professor Adorno," the journalist begins, "two weeks ago, the world still seemed in order." At which point Adorno interrupts him by interjecting: "Not to me [*Mir nicht*]."[1]

Adorno's dry "*Mir nicht*" here cannot be reduced to a kind of Frankfurt School version of Melville's Bartleby, who remains in our literary consciousness as the voice of the "I would prefer not to." After all, what on one level can be taken as a witty retort by an embattled philosopher in the less-than-reflective environment of the public arena appears on another level as the subtle expression of one of his abiding theoretical commitments. For Adorno, there can be no genuine thinking, and certainly no thinking that shows itself responsible to the rigors of what he names a negative dialectics, that does not also attempt to take into account the genealogy of

I

the present, the archive of human suffering that continues to haunt us, and the historical inheritance of the demand *to think*. Such thinking would always have to catch up with its own historical unfolding, the hidden paths and passageways that came before—in other words, the often invisible traces of past thinking and experience that have conspired to make a thinking what it is now. It is as if in the moment at which critical thought attempted to confront its own having-become-ness, it had to come to terms with Faulkner's well-known dictum that the "past is never dead. It's not even past."[2] Yet precisely in relating to its own undead past—a past that has neither simply passed nor resides in the past, but rather has passed on and is alive at the same time—and in attempting to give an account of itself to itself, this thinking is eminently future-directed. Just as for the Heidegger of "Was heißt denken?" we are still not thinking, for Adorno the thinking that may call itself genuine is *still to come*. Whatever it will have been, it is a thinking that also thinks against itself and, always dissatisfied with its own premises and movements, calls upon the one who thinks to reimagine what such inherited terms as *critique, world, dialectic, progress, culture,* or, as so often in Adorno, "after Auschwitz," might demand of us. Such thinking could not deny its own disaster, the fact that the catastrophe that it wishes to theorize has always already occurred and, in fact, continues today. In response to any theoretical point of view that postulates thinking in relation to a prelapsarian world or to an imagined former state of achieved reconciliation, Adorno can only answer: *Mir nicht.*

An altogether different kind of thinking thus appears to be required. What such a mode of thinking might entail is the topic of this book. My study attempts to give an account of the ways in which Adorno, beyond the confines of any of the particular subject matters on which he so often trains his critical gaze (among them, prominently, questions of aesthetics and cultural criticism, epistemology, the philosophy of history, moral and political philosophy, musicology, and literary theory), teaches us how to read, how to relate the texts and topics that concern us most urgently at any given moment to other texts and topics, how to question, and how to fashion a genuinely open yet uncompromisingly vigilant *comportment* toward the objects of one's inquiry.

For Adorno himself, attempting to ascertain what such a comportment toward the objects of one's inquiry and one's intellectual and artistic creativity might entail was a lifelong task. One thing that it entails is the demand to take seriously the wish not to decide, at least never prematurely. Let us consider a concrete example. In addition to being a philosopher, sociologist, musicologist, political theorist, and literary and cultural critic of the first rank, Adorno was also a gifted musician. His composition teacher Alban Berg, of Second Viennese School fame, writes in 1925 to the young Adorno about his concerns that the latter's strong attachment to theoretical work in such areas as philosophy, art history, and sociology might infringe upon his work in musical composition: "The question as to whether your musical creation (I mean your composing), which I value so highly, will suffer is a fear that befalls me whenever I think of you. For, one thing is clear: Since you are someone who only knows how to go all out (thank God!), one day you will have to decide between Kant *or* Beethoven."[3] It is no accident that Berg, whom Adorno unfailingly addresses as "Dear Master and Teacher" in their correspondence, underlines the "or," because from his perspective the path of Adorno's intellectual and creative trajectory cannot accommodate any other preposition, least of all the "and." Yet Adorno went on to become what he himself called "a thoroughly theoretical human being," thus appearing to have chosen Kant—that is, the path of the concept—without ever renouncing or abandoning Beethoven, the path of art, creativity, and the aesthetic. In 1968, one year before Adorno's death, the book that he published on Berg and his music (*Berg: Master of the Smallest Transition*) could hardly have been created in the way that it was if Adorno had heeded the call of Berg's "or" because he never would have become the thinker that he was. The preface to this late book on Berg, who had died prematurely in 1935, already reveals something of the ambivalence and the struggle that characterized Adorno's decision not to decide between music and philosophy, art and the concept, once and for all, as Berg had implored him to do: "On the occasion of a longer separation, Alban Berg wrote the author a postcard quoting Hagen's passage from *Götterdämmerung*: 'Sei treu' ('Be faithful'). It is the author's dearest wish not to have fallen short of that—without, however, allowing his passionate gratitude to encroach upon the autonomy his teacher and friend fostered in him musically."[4] At times, one may remain more faithful to one's master and teacher precisely by not following him—that is, by exercising the autonomy and freedom that this same master and teacher also has instilled in one to retain the upper hand over some of his other precepts. In the case of an especially powerful and transformative teacher, the traces of this struggle belong to an unmasterable past of the self and continue throughout the trajectory of a thinking being up until the end. If Adorno was unable or unwilling to accede to his master and teacher's demand of the "or," his decision to tarry within the difficult and open-ended orbit of the "and" placed him in the position of a perpetual outsider whose intellectual being was never comfortably settled, never fully at home in any one particular discipline or domain of the mind. On the contrary, the difficulties that came with rejecting Berg's "or" forever sensitized Adorno to the more general question of just *how to relate* to the work of the mind and to the objects with which it engages. Refusing to take for granted this or that stable demarcation line in his intellectual and aesthetic comportment, Adorno articulated a creative, probing, shifting, and restlessly vigilant relation to the world. As he formulates this stance in *Minima Moralia: Reflections from Damaged Life*, the major text from his middle period, "Freedom would be not to choose between black and white, but to abjure such prescribed choices [*aus solcher vorgeschriebenen Wahl herauszutreten*]."[5]

In recent years the older scholarship on Adorno has been supplemented by fresh perspectives on a number of key aspects of his multifaceted oeuvre, providing us with heterogeneous new vistas onto Adorno's concerns.[6] My particular aim in the present book, however, is to probe the very strategies of Adorno's reflections, the incommensurate and singular manner in which his ways of thinking self-consciously work to forge a dynamic relationship between thought and the objects of its inquiry, a critical and intimate process by which thinking—and, by extension, the thinking of thinking—first comes to constitute itself.

At the beginning of his most significant and conceptually sustained book of philosophy, *Negative Dialectics*, Adorno recounts a remark addressed to him in 1937, some three decades earlier, by his friend and former mentor Walter Benjamin. "One must," Benjamin said after having read a text by Adorno, "traverse the ice-desert of abstraction [*Eiswüste der Abstraktion*] in order conclusively to reach concrete philosophizing."[7] Given that Benjamin's trenchant remark remained with Adorno for so many years, one may wonder what it is in the experience of this ice-desert that continues to shape our engagement not only with Adorno's concepts—the elements of his "concrete philosophizing"—but also with his particular style of thinking and the language in which his concepts come to pass. The constellation of words and strategies of reflection that we so intimately connect with the signature, even the singularity, of Adorno's thinking continues to make him one of the few figures in the critical field whom we can never do without.

Contrary to widely held belief, Adorno considered problems of language, and issues of presentation (*Darstellung*) more generally, to be of the highest significance for his theoretical enterprise, even—and especially—in those textual precincts where this enterprise may appear to be concerned exclusively with the development of concepts or with the generation of propositional truth claims. Although he never composed a fully developed treatise exclusively devoted to the topic, he does emphasize, at key moments throughout the various periods of his thought, the problem of language as such as well as the intricate imbrication of conceptual production with its linguistic or textual dimension. There are, to be sure, Adornean statements in canonical works, such as this one from *Minima Moralia*, in which he explicitly emphasizes the role that language and textuality play in our critical understanding: "History does not merely touch on language, but takes place in it [*ereignet sich mitten in ihr*]."[8] Yet there also are little-known but equally significant formulations in which he stresses the importance that language, textuality, and questions of presentation play in his intellectual orbit. For instance, in his Bar Harbor notebook, which is named after Adorno's vacation home in Maine and which he kept during much of the time of his exile in the United States, he writes: "That the violence of the facts has become such a horror that any theory, even the true kind, looks like a ridicule of that horror—this is burned as a sign into the very organ of theory, language."[9] To confront such violence by means of a theory that would strive to do justice to the urgency and complexity of what it seeks to confront requires us to turn to language itself. Language emerges as a form of genuine historicity and critical potentiality—indeed, as the very "organ" of theory. And as Adorno, having returned from his exile, unequivocally states in his 1960/61 Frankfurt lecture course *Ontologie und Dialektik*, "philosophy that is not a philosophy of language cannot be imagined at all today [*Philosophie, die nicht Sprachphilosophie ist, kann heute eigentlich überhaupt gar nicht vorgestellt werden*]."[10] Adorno is fully aware, of course, that such critical attention to language and issues of presentation in the context of conceptual work may create suspicion. It causes irritation on the part of those who seek the apparent immediacy and transparency that go hand in glove with the view of language that regards it exclusively along the lines of the most familiar and comfortingly conventional lines. As he observes in the thought-image "Morality and Style" from *Minima Moralia*: "Regard for the object, rather than for communication, is suspect in any expression: anything specific, not taken from pre-existing patterns, appears inconsiderate, a symptom of eccentricity [*Eigenbrödlerei*], almost of confusion [*fast der Verworrenheit*]." By contrast, "rigorous formulation demands unequivocal comprehension, conceptual effort, from which people are deliberately discouraged."[11] Yet it is precisely our regard for the singularity and particularity of the object—or idea, concept, phenomenon—under investigation at any critical moment that should propel us to seek modes of expression and presentation that break with the prescriptions of the expected and conventional. What is required of critical thought is a different and open relationship to the unanticipatable challenges and potentialities of language itself. My principal aim in this book is not to reconstruct something like Adorno's philosophy of language or theory of presentation. Rather, I seek to illuminate and submit to scrutiny some of the heterogeneous ways in which his refractory view of language, along with the particularities of his style of thinking, reading, and writing that this view sponsors, make themselves felt in the concrete praxis of specific moments and conceptual movements in his theoretical work.

I am guided by the following premises: *What* Adorno says cannot be separated from *how* he says it. By the same token, *what* he thinks cannot be isolated from *how* he thinks it. But these premises are not mere iterations of the more or less classical question of what constitutes a philosophical "style," important as it undoubtedly is. A central aim of this book, rather, is to demonstrate that these basic yet far-reaching assumptions teach us how to think *with* Adorno—which is to say, alongside him in the ice-desert of abstraction and in the variegated contexts and concrete constellations in which his writing is examined here. These contexts and constellations range from aesthetic theory to political critique, from the problem of judgment to that of inheriting a tradition, from Hegel to Kafka, from the work of art to the question of leading a right life within a wrong one, and beyond.

Thinking with Adorno: The Uncoercive Gaze suggests, then, that we begin to think with Adorno when we engage his textual production in a way that does not merely reconstruct this or that development of a concept. Rather, to think with Adorno also means to accept the invitation to learn what he calls "the art of reading." One might say that the stratagem that Adorno expresses in his "Skoteinos, oder wie zu lesen sei" ("Skoteinos, or, How to Read") with regard to Hegel is equally applicable in his own case: "The art of reading him [*Die Kunst, ihn zu lesen*] should take note of where something new begins. . . . At every moment one needs to keep two seemingly incompatible maxims in mind: painstaking immersion in detail, and free detachment [*die minutiöser Versenkung und die freier Distanz*]."[12] Thinking with Adorno by learning to engage in the art of reading requires a special attentiveness to the singularity of his language and mode of thinking, to the eruption of an idiomaticity that cannot be reduced to preexisting categories and labels provided by the already available programs of explanation and designation. What this art of reading requires of us is our constant attention to the refractory detail that does not quite fit into the larger structure in which it occurs and, at the same time, an abiding respect for the greatest possible freedom, even detachment, from the confined space of this detail and its immediate contexts. Thinking while reading—that is, thinking-reading—we give ourselves over to a singularity and its idiomatic requirements while also insisting on the possibility of the experience of freedom itself. What thus animates this book is the desire to think with Adorno precisely by developing an Adornean art of reading, a *Kunst des Lesens*. This art of reading would extend not only to Adorno's texts (the art of reading Adorno) but also, through our engagement with Adorno, to the critical praxis of reading in a more general sense (the art of reading as such).

In what way, then, must the art of reading (with), and thinking (with), Adorno take account of the ways in which the "how" and the "what" of Adorno's writing and thinking are so intimately intertwined? What is it that makes the how and the what something more than mere manifestations of certain idiosyncrasies of writing and thinking? What is it, in other words, that ties them to the heart of Adorno's intellectual enterprise? The answer to these questions cannot lie in the construction of a "literary Adorno" or of an Adorno who refuses to respect the residual difference between word and concept, literature and philosophy, rhetoric and logic. Rather, this study wishes to make vivid the notion that answers to these questions may be found by turning to what the mature Adorno, in his programmatic yet often-overlooked "Notes on Philosophical Thinking," calls the "uncoercive gaze upon the object" ("der gewaltlose Blick auf den Gegenstand").[13] This uncoercive, or "violence-free," gaze—explored at length in chapter 1—names a way of relating to an object of critical analysis that is marked by a specific kind of comportment. The gaze moves close to the object, lingers with it, tarries with it, and struggles to decipher the singularities, idiomaticities, and nonidentities that are lodged within it, whether the object is an idea, a thought, a concept, a text, a work of art, an experience, a musical composition, a film, a photograph, or a problem of political or sociological theory. Adorno's uncoercive gaze refuses to imprison an object in the straitjacket of preformed assumptions of reading and interpretation. Rather, this mode of gazing needs to be reinvented each time it is cast upon a new object so as to affirm that object's idiomaticity and singularity. The uncoercive gaze, in short, seeks to establish a productive critical intimacy with the object that respects that object's primacy, what Adorno calls "der Vorrang des Objekts." As we will see in detail, through the uncoercive gaze, thinking, for Adorno, "snuggles up to an object" ("einem Objekt sich anschmiegen").[14] This critical strategy of clinging to and nestling against the object bespeaks the felt contact between thinking and the object such that it allows the latter to tell us something that we did not already know or suspect to be the case.

If Adorno's practice of the uncoercive gaze provides part of the title for the present book, it is because what is most productive in reading Adorno must be based on an investigation of the specific ways in which the uncoercive gaze relates to its subject matter differently with each new act of thinking. With each new critical reflection, thought snuggles up to its object, whose qualities and demands are always singular, in an unanticipated way. No prescriptive philosophical system emerges from this uncoercive gaze, no systematic outline of propositional reasoning. Rather, the variegated acts of thinking that are at work here coalesce around a concept of truth that is constellative in nature, with a deep affinity for the idea of the constellation. As Adorno stresses in "Notes on Philosophical Thinking," employing a trope that takes up the strong elective affinity between thinking and the constellation that traverses so many of the sentences across his corpus, "truth is a constantly evolving constellation [*Wahrheit ist werdende Konstellation*]" rather than "something running continuously and automatically." Like Adorno's own collection, *Stichworte*, or *Catchwords*, in which he included his "Notes on Philosophical Thinking," my chapters thus remain mindful of their own residual allusion "to the encyclopedic form that, unsystematically, presents what the unity of experience crystallizes into a constellation."[15] This constellative form suggests, among other things, "that no philosophical thinking of quality allows of concise summary [*sich resümieren läßt*]" and that it "does not accept the usual scientific distinction between process and result," just as "Hegel, as is known, conceived truth as process and result in one." From this perspective, "philosophical thoughts that can be reduced to their skeleton or their net profit are of no worth."[16] The book therefore may be said to perform what Adorno calls "intermittences" of thinking, in which what is at stake are the particular contours of the uncoercive gaze that Adorno, and we with him, cast each time upon the objects at hand. The book thus works to exemplify ways of snuggling up, under an uncoercive gaze, to its objects. The critical intimacy that it wishes to call into presence touches its subject matter with a double gesture: each of the chapters in this book investigates how Adorno's thinking itself stages elements of the uncoercive gaze in relation to a particular object, while each chapter also works to cast its own uncoercive gaze on Adorno's thinking.

In performing this double gesture, the chapters do not proceed from an a priori truth claim about Adorno's philosophy as such, an examination of his position in the history of Western philosophy, or the idea that he could be reduced to a facile category or convenient label, some "-ism." This is not to say that Adorno could not be tied to any of the theoretical currents of his time or to a broader discursive episteme. On the contrary, as the following chapters make clear, he is always engaged in actual or ghostly dialogue with a number of significant discourses outside of his own idiomatic orbit. In order to appreciate the subtlety and import of Adorno's texts one must always also learn how to relate them effectively to other texts and contexts. The problem is that any label, once affixed to him like a bar code on a consumer product, is normally meant to "cash out"—in the language of today's corporate university—his concepts. Yet Adorno's concepts are not pre-written checks that await only a countersignature to turn them into ready money, nor do they amount to a pile of playing chips ready to be converted into currency in a casino of concepts. Such an instrumentalist desire to "cash out" stands in contrast to Adorno's own guardedness with regard to philosophical thoughts that are meant to yield "net profit." By contrast, therefore, the chapters of this book each proceed from a circumscribed problem, local issue, or specific textual difficulty. In so doing, they also engage with Adorno's admonition "that one should not just up and start thinking, but rather think of something [*daß man nicht drauflosdenken soll, sondern an etwas*]" and that for "this reason texts to be interpreted and criticized are an invaluable support for the objectivity of a thought [*Zu interpretierende und zu kritisierende Texte stützen darum unschätzbar die Objektivität des Gedankens*]."[17] The critical intimacy of the uncoercive gaze cannot be achieved without the perpetual engagement with a text, a phrase, or a rhetorical figure that necessarily suffuses a conceptual argument.

The chapters that follow therefore wish to take Adorno's invitation to think "an etwas" seriously. Taken together, they attempt to think *with* him, which is to say, both next to him—in the sense of alongside him—and through him, which is to say, *by means of* him, by virtue of what *his* thinking enables *us* to think in other contexts and with regard to a variety of critical concerns. This double "with-ness" plays itself out across a variety of different themes and problems, each time in singular circumstances, yet with an eye toward casting an uncoercive gaze upon each object, problem, experience, or idea. One might say that the book consists of interconnected case studies that revolve around Adorno's particular gesture of thinking and his singular mode of engagement with a number of key theoretical problems that coalesce under the general concept of the uncoercive gaze. The chapters of this book can be read in a linear and cumulative fashion, but they also can be read independently—or even in alternate sequences determined by a particular reader's individual intellectual interests—with profit.

Chapter 1 develops in detail Adorno's concept of the uncoercive gaze as the primary mode of reflective engagement with his objects of thinking. Proceeding from an explication of his conviction that the kind of thinking that philosophy performs cannot be performed without also considering its relation to questions of language, this chapter sets the stage for our understanding of the uncoercive gaze. It engages with the idea that, as *Negative Dialectics* argues, "presentation is not a matter of indifference to philosophy, or external to it, but immanent to its idea [*warum der Philosophie ihre Darstellung nicht gleichgültig und äußerlich ist sondern ihrer Idee immanent*]."[18] This textual moment of presentation, I suggest, also raises the question as to the possible relationships between Adorno's own idiom, a self-consciously adopted theoretical German, and the trajectory of speculative thought as such. As this chapter demonstrates, one of the seminal realms in which these concerns with the relation of philosophical thought and questions of presentation are addressed is that of the uncoercive gaze. By refusing to submit to the dictates of an obscene and transfixed *Hinstarren*—a mere staring—at the object, Adorno's uncoercive gaze eschews the critical violence that attends to the moment in which a thinker or writer works to superimpose onto the object this or that set standard of measurement, premise, agenda, or assumption that, as *a priori* ossified modes of relating to the object, only ends up by missing a certain *critical intimacy* with the object—and thus its productive primacy, its critical *Vorrang*.

The six remaining chapters act as critical case studies in which Adorno's understanding of the uncoercive gaze is set to work in a variety of specific contexts. I pursue the uncoercive gaze along various avenues and in variegated modulations, although different paths and other case studies also would have been possible. After all, the uncoercive gaze as Adorno attempts to think it can never be reduced to a dogmatic, uncritical, or overly narrow set of principles. On the contrary, this gaze always receives its inspiration and future direction from the objects themselves and from the singular requirements that their each-time-unique formation issues to the critic, without thereby rendering the specific operations of the gaze arbitrary or whimsical. Another way to put this is to say that the singular beauty and rigor of the uncoercive gaze demands to be rearticulated, relearned, even reinvented each time the critic's gaze is cast on the irreducibly idiomatic confrontation with a specific text, image, idea, work of art, theoretical problem, historical formation, or cultural episteme. (Adorno, like his early mentor Benjamin, was an undeniable master at casting such a micrological gaze at the object world.) One might even say that part of the very uncoerciveness that constitutes the uncoercive gaze resides precisely in its refusal to be coerced—or to self-coerce—into conforming to a closed program of critical operations that could be taught, learned, and practiced as though it came from a book of recipes or from a philosopher's intellectual instruction manual.

In order to deepen our understanding of the role of the "with" in this book's title, *Thinking with Adorno*, it is important to note that it is not only we who think with Adorno. Rather, Adorno himself emerges as a thinker who always thinks *with others*—that is, he casts his uncoercive gaze at the object precisely while at the same time standing in conversation with other thinkers and writers. In other words, when Adorno is in critical dialogue with his object of study, he also is in constant and interminable dialogue with a vast number of intellectual interlocutors, some of whom are long-deceased historical figures who inhabit Adorno's mind as significant spectral voices, whereas others are empirical interlocutors with whom he shared an actual lifeworld. Many of the case studies in *Thinking with Adorno* therefore exhibit an *Adorno in dialogue*, whether with philosophical forerunners in the German tradition such as Kant and Hegel, with writers such as Kafka, with contemporaries such as Benjamin and Arendt, or—in a ruptured temporality that becomes thinkable, in part, by means of Adorno's own strategies of reflection—with philosophical "heirs" and their critical voices that will have succeeded him, such as those of Derrida and Agamben. Because no uncoercive gaze is ever merely identical to itself, a Cartesian consciousness present-to-self or a self-contained version of the Leibnizian windowless monad that is content to rest in itself, there can be no uncoercive gaze—that is, no thinking *with* Adorno—that is not always also a hospitable thinking and a probing practice of the "with." With Adorno, one might say, there is no "thinking with" without an abiding emphasis on the with, even in those cases when the with is also, and even primarily, an against.

Chapter 2, the longest of the book, explores instances of the uncoercive gaze in Adorno's thinking of tradition in relation to that of his allegedly antipodal contemporary, Hannah Arendt. As I argue in this chapter, Adorno's and Arendt's respective thinking of the difficult concept of tradition is itself in constant dialogue with that of Benjamin, a mutual friend over whose intellectual legacy the two would often quarrel. But rather than follow the tradition of much of the existing scholarship by merely positing Benjamin as the symbolic point of division between the irreconcilable projects of Adorno and Arendt, I wish to suggest that, for all their differences, the two also can be said to be inextricably interconnected in that both of their reflections on the concept of tradition powerfully engage with Benjamin's thinking of this problem. Especially in Adorno's often-overlooked 1966 essay "On Tradition" and in Arendt's *Between Past and Future*, their two conceptions of thinking tradition crystallize into conceptual rigor. Whereas Adorno ultimately develops a concept of tradition that affirms the critical potential of the traditional paradoxically by dismantling it through the movement of a dialectical negativity, Arendt engages the thinking of tradition by examining a number of experiential gaps in our modern thinking of temporality. The two ways of conceptualizing tradition, each in their unique way and each in unique response to Benjamin's provocations, both hinge on the hidden aporetic structure that powerfully traverses any thinking of tradition in the modern age.

Whereas chapter 2 interrogates practices of the uncoercive gaze by focusing on Adorno's reading of the concept of tradition in relation to Arendt and Benjamin, chapter 3 devotes itself to the complex relation between Adorno and Hegel via the question of inheritance and the constellative form itself. To refine our understanding of Adorno's critical gesture of the uncoercive gaze in relation to certain aspects of Hegelian thought, this chapter focuses in particular on Adorno's understanding of Hegel's masterful early work, the *Phenomenology of Spirit* (1807), a text without which Adorno's practice of negative dialectics would hardly be graspable. By focusing on the question of an uneasily "inherited" intellectual tradition—an inheritance with which it is ultimately impossible fully to come to terms and which continues to remain something of an unhealed wound—Adorno's uncoercive gaze here is exposed and enriched in terms of its genealogical and historical substrata. In works such as *Hegel: Three Studies*, Adorno not only grapples with the "with" when he thinks "with Hegel"; he also theorizes his own intellectual project in terms of a spectral inheritance, a legacy that is enigmatic and demands to be interpreted always one more time, rather than being taken for granted as a stable system of precepts, dialectical or otherwise. As I also argue in this chapter, learning how to inherit Hegel and Hegelian modes of thought—along with the very idea of an uncoercive gaze—is inseparable from the fundamental question of how to read philosophically, a question that Adorno formalizes in terms of the concept of the ancient Greek *skoteinos:* that which is covered with darkness.

While chapter 1 lays the groundwork for our understanding of Adorno's practice of reading and writing through an extended exposition of the uncoercive gaze, and chapters 2 and 3 offer case studies of the uncoercive gaze in relation to what might be called two differently modulated legacies of reflection (tradition and inheritance, respectively), the following three chapters shift the focus of our attention to examples of the uncoercive gaze within the realm that occupies a central part of Adorno's way of thinking and being in the world: the work of art. These three case studies of the uncoercive gaze in explicit relation to questions of art and aesthetic theory commence with chapter 4, which focuses on Adorno's understanding of the category of judgment. Proceeding from Adorno's apodictic interpretation of a poem by the German Biedermeier writer Eduard Mörike, this chapter reconstructs what it might mean for Adorno to argue for the critical practice of judging by refraining from judgment. Mörike's children's poem, "Mousetrap Rhyme," is the only poem that Adorno chooses to quote in its entirety in his *Aesthetic Theory*. His surprising choice reveals the ways in which the uncoercive gaze can never be reduced to a set of ideological operations or *a priori* correspondences but rather must confront, in the space of the work of art, the question of its judgment—and the typically unspoken premises and presuppositions of any judgment—always one more time. Here, the uncoercive gaze—itself a critical art—fastens upon the artwork in a way that allows art to become world without reducing the art to the condition of being merely that which already is the case, or that which already claims to be world. The artwork, when engaged by an uncoercive gaze, keeps alive the singular form of judgment as judgment without judging, in which the ultimate arrest of judgment remains deferred in virtue of another judgment, based on a future critical engagement, one that is always still to come.

Chapter 5 moves our attention from the question of judgment as it emerges in Adorno's interpretation of Mörike to his engagement with the literary artwork of a later German-language writer, Kafka—and in particular his unfinished novel *The Trial*. This chapter investigates another set of problems with which the uncoercive gaze must contend when it fastens upon a work: the relationship of speculative thought to the work of art and the ways in which the chasm between literal and figurative speech bears upon that relationship. I examine the ways in which Adorno confronts a seminal problem in the philosophical interpretation of art: Without the intervention of theoretical or philosophical discourse, the conceptual dimension of an artwork would remain incomprehensible. But if the commentator succeeded fully in articulating and interpreting the conceptual truth content of the artwork, this success also would have made the artwork itself superfluous. After all, what the artwork represents and achieves in its singular way could be replaced by discursive logic. One of the themes that a reading of *The Trial* therefore should emphasize is the very way in which a literary text both calls for philosophical interpretation and resists such interpretation at the same time. This double gesture of calling forth and resisting philosophical interpretation, while shared by all great literary works, is staged by each work in specific ways that are idiomatic and singular to the particular text. One problem that arises out of this constellation concerns the question about the relationship between the literal and the figurative nature of a text's rhetorical operations. If Kafka's novel, by causing the relation between the literal and the figural to enter a space of indeterminacy, enacts something of what Adorno calls "a sickness of all signification [*eine Krankheit alles Bedeuten*]," no reading of Kafka—at least no reading informed by the sensibilities of the uncoercive gaze—can afford to ignore the precise conceptual terms of this sickness. Finally, to cast Adorno's reflections on Kafka into sharper relief, I also consider them in relation to (and distinction from) Giorgio Agamben's recent interpretation of *The Trial* as Kafka's commentary on the imbrication of law and slander.

Chapter 6 marks a transition from the uncoercive gaze as it finds expression in Adorno's consideration of Kafka to the problem of orientation, understood both as an intellectual phenomenon and as a problem to be considered in relation to the work of art. This chapter adds another case study to our examination of Adorno's critical practice of the uncoercive gaze by complicating the concept of orientation and supposed "cognitive maps" provided by the artwork and by theoretical discourse. Tracing Adorno's abiding engagement with the problem of orientation back to Kant's essay on what it might mean to orient oneself in thinking, I interrogate how Adorno's engagement with the problem of orientation, and the attendant specter of disorientation, inflects a broader set of concerns that traverse his writings throughout its various periods.

Chapter 7, finally, casts an uncoercive gaze at the relation between Adorno and Derrida, with special emphasis on the problem of desiring to live a right life inside of a wrong one. The relation between Adorno and Derrida—often overshadowed by an unfortunate series of prejudicial polemics, premature demarcations, and habitual resistances on the part of some Adorneans as well as some Derrideans—can, in today's critical climate, finally begin to come into more serious and sustained focus in which fruitful cross-illuminations become possible. Tracing a set of uneasy couplets—including thinking and thanking, the prize and the price, and false life in relation to living on—this chapter augments, with the strategic help of suggestive Derridean concepts such as *sur-vivance* as well as remarks delivered by Derrida on the occasion of being awarded the Adorno Prize, our understanding of the stakes of Adorno's uncoercive gaze by returning to a vexing statement. This statement has fascinated his readers ever since 1951, when it appeared in his *Minima Moralia*: "Es gibt kein richtiges Leben im falschen"—meaning "There is no right (or correct) life within (or inside of) a wrong (or false) one"—which in the standard English translation is rendered, rather problematically, as "Wrong life cannot be lived rightly." As we will see, how precisely one chooses to translate Adorno's apodictic sentence has significant and far-reaching implications. What emerges here, I wish to suggest, is an uncoercive gaze—indeed, a form of life—in which our critical task is no longer defined by the need to establish and subsequently maintain at all cost a distinction between a right life and a presumably wrong one, but rather by an engagement with the very forms of survival that promise, ever so fleetingly and intermittently, the experience of life as lived, fragile life.

It is perhaps not entirely inappropriate, finally, to compare the gesture of thinking that is at stake in *Thinking with Adorno: The Uncoercive Gaze* to the thought of another thinker, one who died about a century before Adorno's death, Henry David Thoreau. Most of the sentences that constitute my book were written in close geographical proximity to Thoreau's New England home in Concord, Massachusetts, and to Walden Pond, where he lived, thought, and wrote in a lakeside cabin for two years. In a journal entry from December 31, 1837, after an autumn in which he filled his journal with reflections on such topics as thinking, nature, ancestry, peculiarity, revolutions, frozen mist, homesickness, heroes, and, above all, Goethe, we find the following remarkable passage:

> As the least drop of wine tinges the whole goblet, so the least particle of truth colors our whole life. It is never isolated, or simply added as treasure to our stock. When any real progress is made, we unlearn and learn anew what we thought we knew before. We go picking up from year to year and laying side by side the *disjecta membra* of truth, as he who picked up one by one a row of a hundred stones, and returned with each separately to his basket.[19]

To be sure, the American transcendentalist is separated from the European thinker of negative dialectics by more than time, space, and idiom. And yet, Thoreau's image appears strikingly relevant here. If there is any amount of truth that makes itself felt in our thinking and experience, it does not come to us in the form of a stable possession. The truth that counts, the truth that catches us unawares, comes to inflect all that we assumed we already knew as a secure staple of our being in the world. There can be no systematicity to this process, as the learning and unlearning of our assumptions retains an aleatory and unpredictable element. This is, in part, why both Thoreau and Adorno are rigorously anti-systemic thinkers. Transformative learning and thinking can hardly be measured in terms of so-called learning outcomes of the kind that many university administrators in the English-speaking world—under pressure from the global market ideologists and their relentless neoliberal imposition of "metrics" onto all aspects of academic life and, in fact, onto all human affairs—now increasingly insist that students and their teachers mindlessly abide by. It is thus no accident that Adorno reminds us of how, "when all actions are mathematically calculated, they also take on a stupid quality."[20] And as Thoreau suggests, learning is not simply a process that can be implemented to achieve a preestablished goal; because it always exposes us to the contingency of what we think we already know, to learn always also means to unlearn. We are, rather, collectors of certain elements that will enter the unexpected constellation opened each time anew by an uncoerced practice of learning and thinking. Like Thoreau's collector of stones, who lays side by side the *disjecta membra*—the dispersed fragments—the Adorno who emerges from the pages of this book teaches us how to relate to the scattered remains of critical thought itself, to the surviving fragments of a reading and writing that come to pass in the luminous orbit of Adorno's uncoercive gaze.

CHAPTER ONE

Adorno and the Uncoercive Gaze

Anyone who has immersed himself for any length of time in the labyrinthine and often refractory world of texts signed by Adorno is confronted with a singular mode of formulation and argumentation. Whatever else may be said about Adorno's inimitable way of thinking and writing, it is immediately recognizable. If one were to tear out a random page from each of several hundred scholarly books in German, including one book by Adorno, throw these pages in the air, and allow them to land on the ground in an aleatory way, one always would be able to identify with certainty the one page of German prose that had been written by Adorno. One could even allude to the musicological realm of the acoustic that was so central to Adorno's thinking in speaking of a signature "Adorno sound." From his typical movements between hypotactical and paratactical sentence constructions, via his transformative evocations of the tropes of German Idealism, to his well-known preference for deferring self-reflexive pronouns, Adorno's singular ways of mobilizing and engaging the German language does not readily lend itself to translation into other idioms, even into related Germanic languages such as English. Adorno himself is very aware of the intricate imbrication of his thinking with the German language. For instance, in a letter dated September 1, 1955, that he wrote from Frankfurt to Siegfried Kracauer in New York, Adorno reminds his older friend and colleague "that what is most decisive in what someone like us has to say can be said by us only in German. We can write English, at best, like the others; like ourselves, only German [*daß das Entscheidende, was unsereins zu sagen hat, von uns nur auf deutsch gesagt werden kann. Englisch können wir allenfalls so schreiben wie die anderen, so wie wir selbst nur deutsch*]."[1] And ten years later, in his 1965 essay "On the Question: 'What Is German?,'" in which Adorno meditates on what propelled him to move back, after World War II, from his American exile to Germany, the country of the perpetrators, he confesses that a central reason for returning, in spite of everything, was the German language itself, in which the essential features of his movements of thinking are lodged:

> The decision to return to Germany was hardly motivated by a merely subjective need, or homesickness, as little as I deny having had such sentiments. An objective factor also made itself felt. It is the language. Not only because one can never express one's intention so exactly, with all the nuances and the rhythm of the train of thought in the newly acquired language as in one's own. Rather, the German language also apparently has a special elective affinity with philosophy and particularly with its speculative element that in the West is so easily suspected of being dangerously unclear, and by no means completely without justification. Historically, in a process that finally needs to be analyzed seriously, the German language has become capable of expressing something in the phenomena that is not exhausted in their mere thus-ness, their positivity and givenness. This specific quality of the German language can be most graphically demonstrated in the nearly prohibitive difficulty of translating into another language philosophical texts of supreme difficulty such as Hegel's *Phenomenology of Spirit* or his *Science of Logic*. German is not merely the signification of fixed meanings; rather, it has retained more of the power of expression—more in any case than would be perceived in the Western languages by someone who had not grown up in them and for whom they are not second nature.[2]

Adorno continues by arguing that "whoever remains convinced" that "the mode of presentation [*Darstellung*] is essential to philosophy" will be "disposed to the German language." For him, "the native German will feel that he cannot fully acquire the essential aspect of presentation or of expression in the foreign language" because if "one writes in a truly foreign language, then whether it is acknowledged or not, one falls under the spell of wanting to communicate, to say it in such a way that others can understand." To which Adorno juxtaposes a contrasting linguistic experience: "In one's own language, however, if one says the matter as exactly and uncompromisingly as possible, one may hope through such unyielding efforts to become understandable as well." Although Adorno concedes that he is unable to decide whether "this circumstance is specific to German or whether it affects far more generally the relationship between each person's native language and a foreign language," he does emphasize the peculiarity of German by stressing the "impossibility of conveying without violence not only high-reaching speculative thoughts but even particular, quite precise concepts such as those of *Geist* [spirit, mind, intellect], *Moment* [moment, element, aspect], and *Erfahrung* [experience], including everything with which they resonate in German." What, from a conceptual perspective, might be called "a specific, objective quality of the German language" pertains to the philosophical thought that can be produced within it.[3] This perspective on the special philosophical status of German is one that Adorno shares, in spite of all the differences between them, with Heidegger, for whom ancient Greek and German are the languages in which Being can come to be thought.

But this "metaphysical excess" of German also comes at a price. As Adorno cautions, no one "who writes in German and who knows how much his thoughts are saturated with the German language should forget Nietzsche's critique" that a "self-righteous German profundity [*selbstgerechte deutsche Tiefe*] was ominously in accord with suffering and its justification."[4] If there is a negative dialectic between, on the one hand, the apparent elective affinity of the German language with speculative philosophy and, on the other hand, a certain tendency toward delusion and intellectual self-righteousness, the implications of this dialectic are never far from Adorno's own textual production. On the contrary, this negative dialectic binds the thinker to the very objects that his discourse wishes to illuminate. The result is a pellucid and rigorous German prose that nevertheless pushes against the limits of conventional hermeneutic understanding.

In Adorno's self-conscious critical "models" (as he would often refer to his work), the thinking of philosophy is inseparable from its always specific formulation in language, which is why "presentation is not a matter of indifference to philosophy, or external to it, but immanent to its idea [*warum der Philosophie ihre Darstellung nicht gleichgültig und äußerlich ist sondern ihrer Idee immanent*]," as we read in *Negative Dialectics*.[5] This moment of presentation cannot be separated from the language in which it was first thought, especially if that language may be considered, rightly or wrongly, to hold a special relationship to speculative thought itself. Elsewhere in *Negative Dialectics*, Adorno thus emphasizes that any attempt to eradicate in philosophical thinking a consideration of the language in which philosophical ideas are thought and written is doomed to failure—a sign of the reification of mind itself. For him, "to abolish language in thought is not to demythologize thought" because the "rhetorical element is on the side of content."⁶ After all, through its "dependence—patent or latent—on texts [*sei's offenbare, sei's latente Gebundenheit an Texte*], philosophy admits that which the ideal of method leads it to deny in vain: its linguistic nature [*ihr sprachliches Wesen*]."⁷ If rhetoric therefore "presents in philosophy that which cannot be thought except in language," it is because it belongs to those "postulates of presentation [*Postulaten der Darstellung*]" through which "philosophy differs from the communication of already known and fixed contents."⁸ Adorno thus urges philosophy to untether itself from the misguided desire to regard the language in which it is thought, written, and spoken as more or less transparent, unproblematic, and wholly subservient to the conceptual content in which it is interested at any given moment.

Taking into account the imbrication of Adorno's works with their linguistic or textual nature is not to suggest that Adorno should be seen as a literary author rather than as a philosopher and critical theorist, nor is it to assume a pragmatist view of the Rortian kind that the particular discourse that we name philosophy is, in the end, nothing more than "a kind of writing." On the contrary, although Adorno self-consciously wrestles with the linguistic modes of presentation that impose themselves on him, down to the very fibers of his prose, his texts have significant philosophical and conceptual arguments to make. These important arguments, however, are not indifferent to the particular ways in which they are cast linguistically or to the manner in which their linguisticality may work to disrupt the conceptual labor that they set out to perform. Rather, the relationship of rhetoric and logic, language and argument, draws attention to itself as an abiding and irreducible conceptual concern—and therefore ultimately as a central concern of philosophical thought itself.

This perspective illuminates why readers who are attentive to the rhetorical structure of Adorno's philosophical writings have remarked that his prose "breathes in German," where "its ductus is freer" and where the "exquisiteness of its word choice—the Parnassian face of a negative Reason—gives it a lustrous obscurity," something that "marks precisely its origin in Europe—in Germany" and that, even "with the best will in the world, is lost in translation."⁹ Perhaps it is no accident that, when one encounters Adorno in a language other than the original German, one has the eerie sense, no matter how adroit the rendering, that the text is "dubbed rather than translated."¹⁰ Whether this marked singularity is admired or ridiculed, made the object of imitation or of resistance, one thing is clear: *What* Adorno says and thinks cannot be separated from *how* he says and thinks it. The moment of presentation (*Darstellung*) is integral to the thought itself. Samuel Weber, one of Adorno's earliest American translators—in both the literal and the figurative senses—puts it as follows in his 1967 introduction to Adorno's essay collection *Prisms*, "Translating the Untranslatable": the "specificity of Adorno's thought is inseparable from its articulation," so "conceptual concreteness may be measured by the density with which thought and articulation permeate each other."[11] Adorno's emphasis on the inter-permeation of thought and its articulation not only places the thinker within the German tradition of writers such as Hegel, Nietzsche, Benjamin, and many others, but it also challenges us to concretize the specifically Adornean contours of an experience of thinking and writing that may still hold out previously unsaturated critical potentialities.

There is no question about the continued relevance of these reflections on the relationship between Adorno's arguments and his methods of engagement, his *Auseinandersetzung*, with the German language. Yet in order to think the possibilities of Adorno's thought more fully, I wish to proceed not merely by adding another layer of commentary on the idiosyncrasies of Adorno's writing style or his relationship to philosophical German as such but rather by supplementing the existing sphere of rhetorical analysis with an account of Adorno's transformative yet refractory idea of philosophical thinking itself. The singularity of his writing and thinking cannot be explained by stylistic features of his German prose style alone (although it certainly does play out in that sphere as well); it is, rather, inextricably intertwined with his *comportment* toward philosophical thinking as such, including the *specific manner of relating to his objects of study and his attitude or stance toward the unfolding of conceptual problems*. In other words, to begin to appreciate what is seminal and irreducible in Adorno's writing and thinking, the question of how he reconfigures the idea of philosophical thinking itself needs to be cast into sharper relief. In keeping with Adorno's understanding of philosophical activity and in an attempt not to remain deaf to the rigorous demands that this understanding places on critical practice, no viable reading of Adorno may reduce his thinking to any kind of rigid system, unchanging method, or stable orthodoxy. It is possible nevertheless to attempt to specify some of the more persistent contours, rhythmic patterns, and characteristic features of this thinking.

To this end, I wish to linger with his inexhaustibly rich but often-overlooked late essay "Notes on Philosophical Thinking" ("Anmerkungen zum philosophischen Denken"), a first version of which was broadcast as a radio address for *Deutschlandfunk* on October 9, 1964, appearing in print for the first time in *Neue Deutsche Hefte* in October 1965. Whereas other essays by Adorno that exhibit a certain "programmatic" character have received attention in the scholarship on Adorno—especially the 1931 "The Actuality of Philosophy" ("Die Aktualität der Philosophie") and the 1962 "Why Still Philosophy?" ("Wozu noch Philosophie?"), but also the "Theses on the Language of the Philosopher" ("Thesen über die Sprache des Philosophen"), which Adorno did not date but which his editor Rolf Tiedemann maintains were written "without doubt also in the early thirties"—the "Notes on Philosophical Thinking" are typically neglected.[12] This remarkable text, dedicated to Herbert Marcuse on the occasion of his seventieth birthday, contains the mature Adorno's pivotal, if underappreciated, reflections on what philosophical and theoretical thinking requires of the one who wishes to engage in it with rigor and stringency. The essay's significance in Adorno's corpus is further underscored by the fact that it was written at the same time as his philosophical magnum opus, *Negative Dialectics*, and its published version appeared in the same year in which Adorno delivered the seminal lecture course on negative dialectics (1965–1966) in Frankfurt. As such, it may be regarded as a highly condensed distillation of the movements of thought that are at work in his larger engagements with a negatively dialectical philosophy and cultural criticism. It is thus hardly an accident that in June 1969, he accords this text the following significance in the introduction to this essay collection *Stichworte*, or *Catchwords*, which would appear the fall of that same year, shortly after his unexpected death in August: "The 'Notes on Philosophical Thinking' offer reflection upon the procedure that can provide an introduction to the content of thought [*Die 'Anmerkungen zum philosophischen Denken' bieten eine Reflexion der Verfahrungsweise, die ins Gedachte einleiten mag*]."[13] According to the gesture of thought encoded in this sentence, it is as if learning to read the reflections offered in the sentences that constitute this particular essay provided one with an intimation of how to approach all of Adorno's sentences. What comes to be thought in these sentences, or what addresses itself in these sentences to that which has been thought elsewhere, *das Gedachte*, opens onto a particular kind of analysis. This analysis serves as an *Einleitung*, a "leading-into" what has been thought—which is to say, it shows the path or opens up a way toward what has been thought, tracing the movements by which what has been thought, *das Gedachte*, came to be thought *in this particular way*.

When the published English translation provides "content of thought" for Adorno's phrase *das Gedachte*, the translator is rightly aware of the difficulty that attaches to *das Gedachte* beyond this or that stable piece of content: "'Content of thought' cannot convey the density of Adorno's expression *das Gedachte*, which is the substantivized past participle of the verb 'to think' (*denken*) but also of the verb 'to remember, be mindful of' (*gedenken*); the interrelationship between these two actions is central to the argument of *Dialectic of Enlightenment* and Adorno's philosophy of nature."[14] One might add that we also should be mindful of the key role that *das Gedachte* plays in the respective projects of thinkers such as Heidegger and Adorno's friend Benjamin, both of whom self-consciously employ this term as well. In the case of Adorno, one could say that *das Gedachte*, as that which has been thought and that which has been made the object of an act of mindfulness and remembrance, refers both to his own acts of thinking—its very formation as that-which-has-been-thought—and to his thinking of thinking as such—that is, to his understanding of the modalities of thinking pursued by the kind of philosophical thought that is worthy of its name.

The relationship to *das Gedachte* that philosophical thinking is meant to pursue is elusive on at least two counts: first, in that it demands to be reinvented each time it turns to a new and different object and, second, in that it itself resists being cast into a descriptive or normative formulation. Adorno thus begins his essay with a striking image in part to illustrate the position from which his reflections on philosophical thinking emanate: "If one is obliged to say something about philosophical thinking, stopping in midstride as it were, and not wanting to slip into the arbitrary, then one should confine oneself to just a single aspect."[15] What, one may ask, would it mean to interrogate philosophical thinking precisely "in midstride"? Does Adorno mean to suggest that such thinking only ever can be thought about when one is actually in the process of engaging in it? Or does the locution "in midstride" rather imply that when one finds oneself engaged in the process of thinking philosophically, the question of the very status of this thinking tacitly imposes itself on the one who thinks? Or does this trope rather suggest that ongoing philosophical thinking, a thinking that is alive and going somewhere—that is, taking a step or stride somewhere—requires suspension in mid-activity, a kind of freeze-frame, in order for the one who thinks to gain insight into its procedures and movements? In that case, thinking about thinking could be thought to take place precisely in the moment when it has left the place from which it set out but has not yet arrived at a new position—that is, when it has departed but now finds itself in the no-man's-land between origin and arrival, between the point of its former situatedness and the as-yet-unattained (and perhaps as-yet-unknown) point toward which it strives and strides.

If one wished to emphasize this particular aspect of philosophical thinking, one could place this moment into a constellation with other Adornean moments in which the time and space *between* two points becomes the sphere of engaged philosophical reflection and conceptual meditation. One is reminded, for instance, of the famous rhetorical image in the final sentence of *Negative Dialectics*—written at the same time as the "Notes"— in which Adorno evokes the "solidarity of such thinking with metaphysics in the moment of its fall [*Solches Denken ist solidarisch mit Metaphysik im Augenblick ihres Sturzes*]"[16] or the luminous passage in *Aesthetic Theory* in which artworks set out to depart from the empirical world in order to create and reach another world, another Adornean "midstride" moment (discussed more fully in chapter 4).[17] For Adorno, thinking philosophically about thinking philosophically thus cannot be accomplished from a position of secured knowledge or a priori conceptual stability; if it can be done at all, it happens *en passant*, in midstride, in mid-sentence, on one's way elsewhere, in the middle of things, *in medias res*.

A further perspective on Adorno's richly textured opening sentence emerges when one turns from the published English translation to the original German. There, the sentence begins: "Soll man, gleichsam auf einem Beine stehend, etwas über philosophisches Denken sagen. . . ."[18] In German, Adorno's image is even more peculiar than in its translation. The phrase "gleichsam auf einem Beine stehend," which is quite justifiably rendered as "stopping in midstride as it were," literally means "as if standing on one leg" or "standing on one leg, as it were." Adorno's original phrasing does not explicitly deploy the imagery of stopping or of finding oneself suspended while taking a step, although it is possible to interpret the phrase "gleichsam auf einem Beine stehend" to refer to the moment in a stride when one leg is in the air, while the other leg is still on the ground to provide the moving body with balance. Were one to take seriously, which is to say literally, Adorno's trope of standing on a single leg, rather than on two, one could also interpret this figure to suggest the absence of movement and, by extension, even the absence of the interruption of that movement—that is, without the stopping that the English translation hears in it. *Auf einem Beine stehen*, standing on one leg, in German also implies a precarious instability, a moment at which one's powers of balance and skill are tested because one can tip over very easily. For instance, children will often play games involving *auf einem Beine stehen* in order to determine who among them can perform a number of difficult tasks under similarly challenging conditions. *Auf einem Beine stehen* also is used in German in counterdistinction to *auf zwei Beinen stehen*, to stand on two legs, which refers to a place of solidity and stability, whereas a related form, *auf eigenen Beinen stehen*, to stand on one's own legs, is the German locution, together with its close relative *auf eigenen Füßen stehen*, to stand on one's own two feet, for autonomy, self-reliance, and self-determination.

Auf einem Bein kann man nicht stehen, one cannot stand on one leg alone, is a German idiomatic expression that suggests the importance of ensuring that one keeps more than one option open to oneself, especially with regard to earning a living, and it is simultaneously a German *Trinkspruch*, a saying by means of which one invites someone (or oneself) to have another drink. *Auf einem Bein kann man nicht stehen* is also akin to the English clause "a bird never flew on one wing." If Adorno, at the beginning of the essay, finds himself standing on one leg, he will have to probe just how much he can accomplish in this awkward position, just how much he will be able to say and think about philosophical thinking. Standing on one leg, the other either suspended in midstride or simply lifted in the air, he will think about thinking, knowing at the same time that this enterprise may be a foolish attempt, perhaps doomed from the very beginning. Thinking about philosophical thinking while standing on only one wobbly leg—perhaps because one has chosen to assume this position or perhaps because this position happens to be where one inevitably finds oneself whenever one sets out to make thinking the very subject of thinking—may belong to the domain of those who, like Adorno, "sensed that whatever one accomplishes in life is little other than the attempt to catch up with one's childhood [*die Kindheit einzuholen*]" and in this way to begin to learn to relate to "what is specifically mine."[19]

Partly because of the difficulties of standing on one leg, or of being suspended in midstride, Adorno's reflections on philosophical thinking thus wish "only to impart a few things I believe I have observed in my own thinking [*nur einiges mitteilen, was ich am eigenen Denken glaube beobachtet zu haben*]."[20] This wish to share, report, communicate, or im-part (*mitteilen*) certain aspects of the experience of a thinking while standing on one leg implies that a difference can be made, at least in principle, between *what* is thought and *how* the *what* is thought, between the alleged content of thinking and the procedure of thinking. Adorno concedes that this premise or assumption stands in opposition to Hegel's insight, which Adorno nevertheless calls "unsurpassed," that one of the tasks of dialectical philosophical thought is to sublate the false distinction between the what and the how of thinking—that is, to correct the error of a bad abstraction not merely by arguing against it but precisely by developing a form of philosophical thought in which the tacit fissure between thought and content is no longer operative. If Adorno nevertheless allows himself to indulge, at least for the time being, the idea that the how and the what of philosophical thinking could be kept apart, it is not because he simply wishes to rebel against Hegel or to reject his conceptual stance but rather because he sees the—however problematic—distinction in question as necessary from the point of view of diagnosing, and then working to undo, certain intellectual tendencies that foster the reification of thinking in the contemporary critical field. In particular, the kind of thinking that he calls into question exemplifies the ways in which the reason-based, liberation-oriented form of Enlightenment thought tacitly turns against itself. As "it became autonomous," Adorno therefore argues, "and developed into an apparatus, thinking also became the prey of reification and congealed into high-handed method. Cybernetic machines are a crude example of this." These machines "graphically demonstrate to people the nullity of formalized thinking abstracted from the contents insofar as such machines perform better than thinking subjects much of what used to be the proud achievement of the method of subjective reason."[21] The thinking, in other words, that was once considered to be the domain of the reflective, autonomous subject has become formalized in the manner of machine-like algorithms that perform versions of what is already assumed to be the case—that is to say, of the existing status quo and its implicit parameters of what to think and how it is acceptable to think. Here, the remnants of the thinking subject have become degraded and an "imperfect replica" of the machines they are encouraged to emulate. But, by contrast, Adorno's point of departure is the articulation of another kind of thinking, a genuine—and genuinely critical—thinking that is still to commence:

> Philosophical thinking begins as soon as it ceases to content itself with cognitions that are predictable and from which nothing more emerges than what had been placed there beforehand. The humane significance of computers would be to unburden the thinking of living beings [*das Denken der Lebendigen*] to the extent that thought would gain the freedom to attain a knowledge that is not already implicit.[22]

The kind of thinking that Adorno thus wishes to pursue is at odds with the kind of philosophical thinking that reaffirms the logic and substance of that which precedes it. In this context, the point of thinking-machines such as the computer would not be to provide an exemplary model according to which philosophical thinking should fashion itself, in an ongoing effort to become ever-more machine-like, predictable, and largely self-contained. Instead, such machines would be seen as mere instruments that take on some of our menial tasks and quotidian cognitive requirements so that genuine thinking may learn to open onto the experience of freedom that is required to pursue the unpredictable paths of thought in the emphatic sense. If any knowledge is attained on the paths of this new thinking, wherever these paths may lead, it can only be the sort of knowledge that is not already implied by that which is the case anyway or by the expectations of the totality of a given set of (often unconscious) assumptions and modes of knowing that obtain in a certain time and space, which is to say, in what in a Foucauldian register might be called an *episteme*. One might say that this, for Adorno, would be the true thinking of *die Lebendigen*, the thinking of and by the living, if such a thing exists, whether the living are standing on one leg or two.

Yet how can one begin to understand this thinking of and by the living, this living thinking, this thinking on the far side of what already is implicit? Taking seriously Kant's refusal simply to identify the concept of thinking as spontaneity, in the *Critique of Pure Reason*, with conscious activity, Adorno points out that even for Kant the "definitive, constitutive achievements of thinking" are "not the same acts of thought within the already constituted world," and their "fulfillment is hardly present to self-consciousness."[23] If, according to Adorno's understanding, the *Critique of Pure Reason* already is a *Phenomenology of Spirit* "in the sense in which Hegel later entitled his analysis of consciousness, a *Phenomenology of Spirit*," this is so because no "objectivity of thinking as an act would be possible at all if thinking in itself, according to its own form, were not bound to what is not itself properly thinking: this is where one must seek and work out what is enigmatic in thinking [*was an Denken zu enträtseln wäre*]."[24] One can interpret Adorno's statement as saying that, for thinking to come into its own, to become that which it is, it must rely on what is not thinking, on a residue of otherness to thinking that always also attaches to an act of thinking. Thinking thinking therefore also requires thinking nonthinking. Yet, according to the path of thinking that Adorno pursues, this negative dialectic does not result, through a Hegelian sublation, in some ultimate identity of thinking and nonthinking. Rather, as a form of nonidentity, it retains the otherness and particularity of nonthinking within the very act of thinking, keeping alive in thought that which within thinking does not yet think but, in the form of an otherness, nevertheless makes thinking, including the thinking of thinking, possible in the first place.

To open up to the aspect of thinking that also resists thinking, the part of thinking that is tacitly nonthinking, would mean to affirm the view that thinking, as a gesture of critical philosophy, fastens not merely upon an idea or matter external to it—an idea, a view, a practice, or a state of affairs to be criticized—but also upon *itself*. To register the urgency of this (partial) self-directness of genuine thinking, Adorno therefore emphasizes that any "adequate philosophical thinking is not only critical of the status quo and its reified replica in consciousness [*seinem dinghaften Abguß im Bewußtsein*] but is equally critical of itself," so that the one who "thinks philosophically hardens intellectual experience by the same logical consistency whose antithesis he wields."[25] For thinking to be something other than a form of mere repetition, even if negatively, of that which is the case, it is not enough to depart from the forces of reification that leap from the object to the consciousness that criticizes it by submitting it to sustained scrutiny. It is no accident that Adorno returns to an observation that he had made in his introductory essay to the writings of Benjamin, that "Benjamin once alluded" to the idea that "to every respectable thought belongs a respectable portion of stupidity as well [*zu einem ordentlichen Gedanken gehöre eine ordentliche Portion Dummheit dazu*]."[26] The point, however, in referring to Benjamin's dictum is not to excise from genuine thinking the element of stupidity that also comes with it, the way a butcher chops off unwanted elements from a choice piece of prime meat, but rather to submit to scrutiny the tension between thinking and forms of nonthinking—the usually repressed conditions of thinking and knowledge—that makes genuine thinking what it is.[27] Thinking therefore must also subject itself to criticism; it must actively seek to make itself the target of its own critique. Taking up a trope that, in various formulations, also animates other seminal works such as *Minima Moralia*, *Negative Dialectics*, and *Aesthetic Theory*, Adorno thus affirms a kind of thinking that also thinks *against itself*, or, more precisely, that makes the act of thinking against itself one of the conditions of possibility for genuine thinking in the first place. Such thinking does not exhaust itself in self-preservation, in fending off that which threatens to enter it from an elsewhere—that is, from the provenance of a distant otherness that is to be kept at bay. Rather, this thinking is *exposed* thinking, a form of thought that, by admitting into itself its own criticizability, does not take its own self-identity for granted.

One particular form that this nonidentity of thinking assumes is that of *Nachdenken*. The German language differentiates, when speaking of thinking, between *Denken* and *Nachdenken*. Attempting to mark something of the difference between these two words and concepts for thinking, the English translation of Adorno's essay provides "thinking" for *Denken* and "reflective thinking" for *Nachdenken*, even though the English cannot fully capture all the nuanced semantic work that the prefix and preposition "nach" (after) performs in *Nachdenken*. Well aware that Heidegger also had meditated on the "nach" in *Nachdenken*, Adorno asserts that, even if one is not a devotee of Heideggerean philology, one still must not "disavow that reflective thinking, as opposed to thinking, linguistically refers to the idea of philosophical construction as one of reconstruction."[28] It is especially difficult here to render in English the conceptual movement of Adorno's argument as it unfolds in his mobilization of different German words and concepts that share "nach," "Zug," and "Vollzug," when he says that one "wird sich doch nicht die Erinnerung daran verbieten, daß Nachdenken, gegenüber Denken, sprachlich auf die Idee philosophischen Vollzugs als eines Nachvollzugs verweist."[29] As the English translator of the text correctly points out, "Adorno plays on the ambiguity of the preposition and verbal prefix *nach*, which can mean (among much else) 'after' in the temporal and spatial senses. So *denken* 'to think' but *nachdenken* 'to reflect deeply upon.'" And *Vollzug*, itself the "nominalization of the verb vollziehen," which means "to perform, to carry out," signifies "action, performance." *Nachvollziehen*, in turn, means "'to comprehend'" or to "'understand something that has occurred as though one had done it oneself,' from which Adorno coins the analogous noun *Nachvollzug*, here translated as 'reconstruction.'"[30] The constellation of *Nachdenken*, *Vollzug*, and *Nachvollzug* that Adorno here constructs points to the significance of the idea that the acceptance or afterlife of a philosophical idea is too often predicated upon its having been translated, by a move of facile thinking, into a mere instantiation, after the fact, of what could have been understood as a matter of received common sense, that is, "understood" as if anyone at all could have uttered the idea. *Nachdenken*, one might say, in this model threatens to degenerate into idle repetition of what was always already implied—it can merely be *nachvollzogen*, understood as if it were a commonly shared and therefore, in principle, already articulated and available experience of thinking. But the point, rather, is to find in *Nachdenken*—conceived not as a shortcut to achieved, commonsense understanding but rather as a reflective, creative, and incommensurable activity—an opportunity to extricate one's thinking from the mere "convention of received thought," the "Convenu des Vorgedachten."[31] The *Vorgedachte* is not merely received thought but literally the pre-thought or that which someone else thinks for me, in front of me, and in my stead (as in "Ich lasse mir etwas vordenken"). It is to be broken open through genuine, nonossified *Nachdenken*. *Vordenken* versus *Nachdenken*: genuine thinking detaches itself from the pre-thought in order to chart new territory in the reflective engagement with an object, experience, or idea to come—which is to say, to come after, *nach*.

Whereas the thinking that is tied to the concept of identity is concerned, by convention, with eliminating disturbances and deviations from methodological prescriptions—that is, with safeguarding against and eradicating any aberrations from its established norms—the thinking of thinking that Adorno's thinking strives to unfold is explicitly hospitable to such disturbances of its norms. His strategy is thus to identify moments that disrupt, interrupt, and disturb thought, viewing in such disturbances not mere embarrassments or obstacles to be overcome but conditions of possibility for genuine thought to unfold. The specific name that Adorno bestows on these disturbances is "intermittences." From Adorno's perspective, to "think philosophically means as much as to think intermittences, to be interrupted by that which is not the thought itself [*Philosophisch denken ist soviel wie Intermittenzen denken, gestört werden durch das, was der Gedanke nicht selber ist*]." As a result, in "emphatic thinking the analytic judgments it unavoidably must use become false. The force of thinking, not to swim with its own current, is the strength of resistance to what has been previously thought."[32] Emphatic or genuine thinking in the Adornean sense thus names the mode of thought that registers the ways in which it allows itself to become affected, even interrupted, by what is not already included in it. This genuine thinking consists neither in a defensive gesture of fending off nor in an acquisitive gesture of appropriation, in which what is different from the thought that is being unfolded is made to conform to its precepts, but rather in an attitude that also honors what resists it.

One might say, then, that Adorno here thinks a version of the thought that, in *Negative Dialectics* and elsewhere, he terms the nonidentical. It is nonidentity that, by preserving the ways in which it remains at odds with the assumed identity or self-identity of a thought, makes itself felt in the reality of emphatic thinking as an aleatory element, a wild card of incommensurability and otherness that introduces risk and tension into the act of thinking. Yet without taking this risk, there can be no freedom and no autonomy in thinking—and ultimately no truth. In an epigrammatically condensed formulation from *Minima Moralia*, Adorno avers that "only those thoughts are true which do not understand themselves."[33] In light of our discussion here, this sentence does not embody a plea for ignorance or for a facile lack of understanding but rather marks the result of a courageous struggle with the nonidentical in which thought drives itself forward precisely by confronting the otherness that keeps interrupting it, contradicting it, and talking back at it. To think the nonidentity of philosophical thinking is to think thinking in terms of its multiple intermittences and ruptures, its vulnerability and exposedness to, but also its hospitality and nonaggression toward, that which disturbs it and which remains irreducibly other to it.

From the outset of thinking thinking, even the nonidentity of thinking, along the lines that Adorno develops, it must be made clear that genuine thinking cannot be subsumed under any method or under any concept of method. To the extent that "thinking should not reduce itself to method," any truth that such thinking may yield is not to be regarded as "the residue [*der Rest*] that remains after the subject has been eradicated."³⁴ Thinking must, rather, "incorporate all innervation and experience into the contemplation of the subject matter [*in die Betrachtung der Sache*] in order, according to its ideal, to vanish within it [*in ihr zu verschwinden*]."³⁵ Philosophical thinking, once it opens onto the experience of contemplation in a critical and sensitive manner, is thus no longer a discourse on method, to employ Descartes' formulation, but rather a kind of self-delivery into the sphere of its subject matter and its requirements. This self-delivery is nothing to be frightened of, according to Adorno's logic, but rather a harbinger of a possible bliss, happiness, and good fortune to come. To be sure, Adorno points out, during his years in American exile he learned that the "Americans have their own pejorative expression of this: *armchair thinking*, the behavior of one who comfortably sits in an easy chair like a friendly and superfluous grandfather enjoying his retirement."³⁶ Yet what is at stake in the philosophical thinking developed here is not the superfluousness of a grandfatherly armchair thinking, which basks in its passivity and presumed self-satisfied irrelevance, but the most active actualization of the possibilities of thinking itself, a thinking that relates to an experience of *Glück* whose "calmness retains something of that happiness" which "the conventional notions of thinking finds unbearable."³⁷ This thinking, for all its negativity, is thus a thinking of the future, and of as-yet-unsaturated potentialities to come, for which no method has as yet been scripted.

These potentialities, however much they seem to resist premature codification, are tied in Adorno's thinking to a moment of happiness not because they provide a picture of what could be or because they could transcend a relentless emphasis on the kind of unyielding negativity in which, from Adorno's perspective, genuine thinking must be rooted. Rather, the potentialities of philosophical thinking in the Adornean sense cannot be thought in separation from their basis in desperation. "Philosophy's power of attraction, its happiness [*ihr Glück*]," Adorno avers, "is the fact that even the desperate thought [*der verzweifelte Gedanke*] conveys something of this certainty about what has been thought [*Gewißheit des Gedachten*], a final trace [*Spur*] of the ontological proof of God, possibly its ineradicable core [*das Unauslöschliche an ihm*]."³⁸ Genuine thinking would proceed from the cognition that thinking out of desperation is also an affirmation, just as writing a pessimistic book of philosophy is an optimistic act, because true pessimists would never have begun to think or to write in the first place, as Maurice Blanchot and others will have taught us. The certainty of what has been thought, the "Gewißheit des Gedachten," does not signify the infallibility of what has been thought but rather the fact that thought has come to pass, the *that* of true thinking, not its *what*.

In his attempt to make this point vivid, Adorno refers to the ontological proof of God, first developed by the medieval Benedictine monk Anselm of Canterbury, the Catholic theologian and philosopher for whom the existence of God can be deduced from the fact that the human being is capable of thinking something that in itself cannot be exceeded, which is to say, it has been endowed by God with the special capability of thinking the existence of the highest being. As such, the highest being, merely by being thought, is affirmed in its existence. While Adorno's perspective is certainly not a theological one, he nevertheless does mobilize in his argument the post-secular afterness of the ontological proof of God, something that lingers in, as he writes, its *Spur* or trace.[39] Yet here it is not a transcendental signified that makes itself felt but rather a fallible, exposed, vulnerable, nonself-identical thinking, a form of reflection that has engaged in genuine thought and that can hardly be canceled or eradicated once it has been thought. What is perhaps inextinguishable in it is the very fact of its having been stringently and rigorously thought, and, as such, it cannot be revoked. To be sure, Adorno is enough of a Freudian not to wish to repress Freud's laconic reminder, in *Civilization and Its Discontents*, that "the intention that the human being should be 'happy' is not included in the plan of Creation."[40] Still, the one who has dared to think in this way experiences a certain moment of *Glück*, however momentary and elusive, a rare instance of happiness or sense of fortune in the shadow of catastrophe and in the face of all that mitigates against thinking—and against happiness. This experience of thinking, and this experience of experience itself, is ultimately tied not to negative theology but to negative dialectics.

The thinking that is to be thought here, in excess of any positive method, feels itself responsible for articulating a certain dimension that is not normally available to critical insight or to the positive scientific disciplines, what, in the essay we have been reading, Adorno refers to as "die positiven wissenschaftlichen Disziplinen."[41] The focus, within the philosophical thinking that is to be thought, on a critical reflection of experience is not concerned with mobilizing any empirical concept of experience in order to insert the achieved data into a statistical method or model but rather with capturing, in the act of thinking, something of the singularity and specificity of an experience. If, therefore, "philosophical thinking continually attempts to express experiences [*Erfahrungen auszudrücken*]," it does so not by reinserting experience into empiricist models of explanation but rather by "assuring oneself" of an "experience by reflecting on a problem autonomously yet always remaining in the closest contact with the problem in its given configuration [*autonom und doch im engsten Kontakt mit dem jeweils vorgezeichneten Problem über es reflektiert*]."[42] One could argue that what is at stake is not the processing of experiential data in the empiricist sense but rather a careful reconsideration of the very category of experience, whose difficulty, elusiveness, and resistance to hermeneutic understanding are a shared trope in the larger orbit of the early Frankfurt School. Here, the "Notes on Philosophical Thinking" enter not only an implied syntactical relation with Benjamin's "Experience and Poverty" and his reflections on the waning of experience in "The Storyteller" but also with Kracauer's meditation on the fraught category of experience in his Weimar essays, such as "Those Who Wait," "Boredom," and "Farewell to the Linden Arcade," not to mention Adorno's own "Scientific Experiences of a European Scholar in America."[43] For Adorno, any rigorous reflection on experience strives to do justice to the unsublatable dialectical tension obtaining between, on the one hand, the need for autonomy, or self-law-giving, in the thinking of experience and, on the other hand, the importance of allowing that autonomous thinking to unfold in close proximity, in felt critical contact, with its respective objects and their singular requirements and demands.

To appreciate the specific nature and implications of this thinking (of) thinking, it is necessary to cast into sharper relief the particular ways in which Adorno's thought relates to its object. After all, the thinking of thinking that he performs hinges on the specific relationship of thought to what he here, in the essay we have been reading as well as in many other places across his far-reaching oeuvre, names *Vorrang des Objekts*, a "preponderance of the object" or "primacy of the object." One thinks especially of the crisp section devoted to the primacy of the object in part 2 of *Negative Dialectics*, "Negative Dialectics: Concepts and Categories."[44] Yet even when he does not explicitly speak of the primacy of the object by name, Adorno will evoke this very primacy in the critical act itself. One thinks, among many other key places in his corpus, of the trenchant passage in the final thought-image of *Minima Moralia*, in which "what matters to thinking" is to gain "perspectives without arbitrariness and violence, wholly from one's felt contact with the objects [*ganz aus der Fühlung mit den Gegenständen heraus*]."[45] Although the primacy of the object assumes various tonalities and differently inflected modulations across Adorno's corpus, in the "Notes on Philosophical Thinking" it emerges with a particular vividness and elegance:

> There is hardly a stronger argument for the fragile primacy of the object [*Vorrang des Objekts*] and for its being conceivable only in the reciprocal mediation of subject and object than that thinking must snuggle up to an object [*daß Denken einem Objekt sich anschmiegen muß*], even when it does

not yet have such an object, even intends to produce it. . . . Despite the Copernican turn, and thanks to it, Kant inadvertently confirms the primacy of the object.[46]

What exactly does thinking do, one might wonder, when it "snuggles up" to an object? Why choose this phrase? Adorno's German term *anschmiegen*, like the somewhat more quotidian, home-spun phrase "snuggling up" in English, conjures images of intimacy, proximity, and closely felt contact that bespeaks a certain tenderness. It is hardly an accident that Adorno, in a letter to Gershom Scholem from March 14, 1967—only two years after "Notes on Philosophical Thinking" was published—speaks of this tenderness in direct terms, emphasizing that "what I, in the immanently epistemological discussion, call the primacy of the object" should indeed be conceptualized as "something indeed very tender [*sehr zart*]," "namely only within dialectics, not as a crude assertion [*nicht als krude Behauptung*]."[47] This tenderness suggests not a false familiarity borne out of a merely mimetic impulse but a strategic clinging to and a nestling against. For thinking to engage in this *Anschmiegen* to an object implies that, while the former sees itself as fundamentally distinct from the latter, it takes its shape and form from the object; rather than simply speaking about the object—or, as German would have it, "over" the object, as in "über ein Objekt sprechen"—thinking takes its sense of direction and purpose from it. The object, once it comes into clear view, teaches thinking how to proceed, how to reinvent itself, how to allow the one who thinks to become a careful and caring reader of the object and, by extension, of the object world in which this particular object is situated. To be sure, thinking may be, following the Copernican turn in Western philosophy, accustomed to relinquishing something of the world because of the cognitive inaccessibility of the *Ding an sich*, the thing-in-itself, as Kant refers to it, an inaccessibility that makes thinking focus on problems related to the cognitive representation of entities or issues in the mind—that is, of how the mind presents something to itself—rather than on the object that is external to a subject's cognitive faculties. And yet, for Adorno's thinking of thinking, it is only by seeking contact with the very object that is to be the focus of a critical act of thinking—that is, by self-reflexively snuggling up to the object—that thinking can become something other than an expression of that which, before and during the act of thinking, was already implied and tacitly anticipated.

To appreciate more fully the ways in which the primacy of the object conditions the thinking of thinking in this key passage, it is important to note the specification that Adorno's if-clause adds to our understanding of the act of snuggling up to an object. After all, we are told that this act of snuggling up to the object is to occur "even when it does not yet have such an object, even intends to produce it." But how would this be possible? In what sense can thinking be expected to snuggle up to an object that does even exist yet? And how could thinking be said to produce or create the very object against which it snuggles up, when the potentiality of thinking, its capability of performing this or that action, precisely depends on its having snuggled up to its object already? What Adorno seems to be suggesting is that even in cases when thinking does not yet have the contours of a firm object before it, its proclivity for snuggling up to its object will provide it with an intuition, or at least a preliminary insight, regarding the contours and eventual requirements of that which will need to be thought, that which has created a certain need in thinking. As he avers at the end of *Negative Dialectics*, "the need in thinking is what makes us think."[48] One can take the Adorno of the "Notes" to mean that, even if the precise shape of that need initially remains diffuse, thinking will seek preliminary contact with it in order to learn how to relate to it and finally to read it, more fully and rigorously. It is as if Adorno wished to preserve, one might say, the possibility of thinking thinking as an act that does not merely, or not exclusively, depend on its contact with an object—which, of course, in the case of thinking, can also be an idea or a concept—that already exists and that has been waiting, as it were, for an analytic gaze to fasten upon it. Rather, thinking, when thought in the rigorous and open-ended sense proposed here, is in principle capable of generating an intimate relation to an object in the broad sense (a thing, idea, experience, problem, or concept) that has not yet fully revealed itself to the one who thinks. It is in the snuggling up performed by the act of thinking that the contours, logic, and special interpretive and analytic requirements of the object come into ever-sharper focus. This is not to suggest that Adorno would fully share the view of Deleuze and Guattari that "philosophy is the discipline that involves *creating* concepts."[49] Adorno is too historical a thinker to subscribe to such as view, for the creation of concepts can also work to obliterate the history—Nietzsche would call it, more precisely, the genealogy—of the very concept upon which an act of thinking fastens. Nevertheless, there is, in Adorno's understanding of the act of thinking as an intimate snuggling up to the object, an element of creation, the generation of an idea or a singular sphere of reflection without which thinking would not be capable of attaining results that are not already either implicit or else pre-understood—and therefore not in need of understanding.

One may begin to understand more concretely what Adorno's specific thinking of thinking entails if one connects the act of snuggling up to the object to the different modalities of *gazing* upon this very object in the critical act. To the extent that the thinking of thinking that Adorno is after "can no more be reduced to a psychological process than to timelessly pure, formal logic," thinking is "a mode of comportment [*eine Verhaltensweise*], and its relation to the subject matter with which it comports itself [*die Beziehung zu dem, wozu es sich verhält*] is indispensable."[50] The *Verhaltensweise*, the mode of comportment or way of relating, that is in question here can best be interrogated by focusing on the ways in which different kinds of gazing relate to their objects. In particular, two different forms of the gaze, *der Blick*, come into focus. The first kind of gaze is the enemy of that which is required by thinking: the "active moment of the thinking comportment [*aktive Moment des denkenden Verhaltens*]," which bears the name "concentration."[51] This active moment of thinking "mediates the exertions of the ego through what is opposed to it."[52] It is with this active, concentrated comportment toward thinking that the first kind of gaze clashes. This first kind of gaze thus deserves to be named "der abgelenkte Blick," the distracted gaze:

> Hostile to thought is avidity, the distracted gaze out past the window that wants nothing to escape it [*Denkfeindlich ist die Gier, der abgelenkte Blick zum Fenster hinaus, der möchte, daß ihm nichts entgehe*]; theological traditions such as the *Talmud* have warned of it. The concentration of thought bestows upon productive thinking a quality the cliché denies it. Not unlike so-called artistic inspiration, it lets itself be directed, to the extent that nothing distracts it from the matter at hand.[53]

The distracted gaze out the window, the gaze that wants to take in too much, the insatiable gaze that wishes to survey everything and to allow for the loss of nothing, is the enemy of concentrated, active thought. Thinking is active only when it knows how to bring a gaze to limit itself, to constrain its purview in the name of the cause of thinking. Even though Adorno does not mention Hegel in this passage, we might say that his reflections on the distracted gaze relate back to a passage in Hegel's *Encyclopedia of the Philosophical Sciences*. There, evoking Goethe, Hegel makes a point similar to Adorno's:

> Someone who wants to do something great [*Wer etwas Großes will*] must know, as Goethe says, how to limit himself [*zu beschränken wissen*]. By contrast, someone who wants everything in fact wants nothing and accomplishes nothing. There are a lot of interesting things in the world: Spanish poetry, chemistry, politics, music. All of that is very interesting, and one

cannot blame anybody who takes an interest in them. However, if as an individual one wants to achieve something in a particular situation, one must stick to something determinate and not split up one's power in various directions [*muß man sich an etwas Bestimmtes halten und seine Kraft nicht nach vielen Seiten hin zersplittern*].[54]

Like Adorno's critique of the distracted gaze that fatefully wishes to include everything and to miss nothing, Hegel's mobilization of Goethe's exhortation serves to emphasize the necessity of thinking to limit itself—to constrain itself to one matter, the matter at hand. The distracted gaze out the window that wishes to take all in is to be interrupted in order for genuine thinking to unfold. This interruption does not imply that curtains are to be drawn before the window or that the one who thinks retreats from the world of lived experience into a solipsism and single-mindedness in which he succumbs to the delusion of assuming that his thinking is not affected by the forces of history, politics, and the variegated issues of the day that circulate through his community and his entire lifeworld. This is also why eschewing the distracted gaze is precisely not to be misunderstood as a procedure "for transforming reflective thinking into a form of indirect practical activity; that would only foster, from a societal perspective, the repression of thinking."[55] If one were to assign thinking the function of indirect practical activity, or as a mere preparation for a later praxis, one would implicitly subject it to a practice-based precensorship, in which thinking were only legitimate to the extent that it is translatable, even if only indirectly, into praxis. Seeking in advance such an instrumentalizing link between thinking and practical activity would rob thinking of the very freedom and autonomy it seeks to think into presence; abstaining from seeking such a link sets the stage for the possibility of genuine thinking having unexpected, transformative effects on the world, even if these are not implied, predictable, or necessary for thinking to come into its own. In order slowly and carefully to work its way through these force fields, genuine thinking requires a concentrated, nondistracted relationship to the object to which it can forge a thoughtful, intimate, and critical comportment.

The second form of the gaze that Adorno develops belongs precisely to such a comportment. In contrast to the first gaze (the distracted gaze), this other gaze is situated not in hurried distraction or restless window-gazing, but in patience and deceleration, a special kind of critical intimacy. It is here, in relation to the second gaze, that what is to be thought first offers itself to thinking:

> The subject matter opens us to patience, the virtue of thinking. The saying, "genius is diligence [*Genie sei Fleiß*]," has its truth not in a slavish drudgery but rather in this patience toward the subject matter. The passive connotation of the word "patience" expresses well the nature of this comportment [*Verhaltensweise*]: neither zealous bustling about nor stubborn obsession but rather the long and uncoercive gaze upon the object [*weder emsiges sich Tummeln noch stures sich Verbohren, sondern der lange und gewaltlose Blick auf den Gegenstand*].[56]

While *der abgelenkte Blick*, the distracted gaze, loses itself and any critical potentiality in its hopeless search for a totality that it can never take in, it is *der lange und gewaltlose Blick auf den Gegenstand*, the long and uncoercive gaze upon the object, that intimates how true thinking may proceed. The uncoercive gaze embodies the specific comportment of thinking (through) the primacy of the object because it enables the one who thinks to snuggle up to the object by tarrying with it, by lingering with its singularities, its idiomaticities and differences. One might say that there obtains a marked difference between the uncoercive gaze that Adorno evokes here and the kind of staring that he, in his 1960–1961 lecture course on *Ontologie und Dialektik*, associates with a certain mode of ontology. There is, for Adorno, a kind of ontologico-philosophical gaze that "one can hardly term a thinking any longer" but rather "a kind of manically fascinated staring [*manisch-fasziniertes Hinstarren*]."[57] In that case, the actual work of thinking threatens to surrender to a riveted, quasi-hypnotized staring at an object or a concept. But the uncoercive gaze is not a transfixed staring, a fierce glare. As opposed to any kind of cold *Hinstarren*, *der gewaltlose Blick*, the uncoercive gaze, which is also a nonviolent, violent-free, or, most literally, violent-less (*gewalt-los*) gaze, comes to pass in the moment—or *Augenblick*, blink-of-the-eye—in which that same gaze strives to learn from the singular and as yet nonimplied and unverifiable object. It rejects violence, *Gewalt*, in that it does not seek to superimpose upon the object a variety of standards and assumptions that are alien to it. The lingering, intent, and focused gaze is not a cold stare at the other; it seeks and invites the other into an intimate critical communion because it sees in the very otherness of the object upon which it fastens its ownmost conditions of possibility. The uncoercive gaze is the steady, intent, and attentive mode of comportment through which, in critical intimacy, genuine thinking honors the productive primacy of the object by snuggling up to it. This is where philosophical thinking would have to begin.

CHAPTER TWO

Buried Possibility

Adorno and Arendt on Tradition

For their often unbridgeable theoretical differences and personal antipathies, their mutual nonreception and their sometimes vehement struggle over the legacy of other thinkers' intellectual enterprises (especially that of Walter Benjamin), Adorno and Hannah Arendt share an intense engagement with the concept of tradition. As German-Jewish contemporaries, Adorno and Arendt came of age in the same intellectual and cultural milieu—that of Weimar Republic Germany—and both philosophers escaped the National Socialist's state-sponsored industrial killing by seeking exile in the United States.[1] Perhaps what has been suggested with regard to Arendt, namely that her "life and thought were passionately linked to core predicaments of the modern Jewish experience" and deserve to be read as part of the "extraordinary history of post-emancipation German-Jewish intellectuals and their wider engagement with the imperatives of German culture and its later great breakdown," is not an inappropriate way of framing Adorno's life and thought as well.[2] Although Arendt chose to remain in the United States after World War II while Adorno returned to his native Frankfurt, both thinkers accompanied the reconstruction of postwar German culture with a critical eye and a series of decisive theoretical interventions.

One might say that, for both heterogeneous thinkers, the personal and intellectual experience of the rise of German fascism, of exile, and of the

Shoah marked the occasion for reflecting on the conditions of possibility for relating to a German and Western tradition within the *episteme* that Adorno famously termed "after Auschwitz." If Adorno's statement in the section of *Negative Dialectics* entitled "Meditations on Metaphysics"—that a "new categorical imperative has been imposed by Hitler upon unfree mankind: to arrange their thoughts and actions so that Auschwitz will not repeat itself, so that nothing similar will happen"—can give rise to a new form of reflection, this new thinking cannot be considered in isolation from the concept of tradition, a tradition that has created certain high points of human achievement and at the same time failed to prevent the rupture of civilization that is marked by the Shoah.[3] In the summer of 1950, Arendt writes in the final paragraph of her preface to *The Origins of Totalitarianism*: "We can no longer afford to take that which was good in the past and simply call it our heritage, to discard the bad and simply think of it as a dead load which by itself time will bury in oblivion. The subterranean stream of Western history has finally come to the surface and usurped the dignity of our tradition." To which she resolutely adds a concluding statement with which Adorno would hardly disagree: "This is the reality in which we live. And this is why all efforts to escape from the grimness of the present into nostalgia for a still intact past, or into the anticipated oblivion, are vain."[4] The task of thinking tradition after its fall thus embodies, for both Arendt and Adorno, one of the most urgent challenges of the present. If the inherited concept of tradition can be defined succinctly as a "discursive construct of beliefs and conventions based on the presumption of historical continuity in the transmission of inherited patterns across generations"—that is, as "a normative mode of knowledge through which an image of society's relationship to time is understood and through which ascribed linkages to the past are conceived as sources of authority for institutions and actions in the present"—then the question as to how to relate to tradition in modernity can no longer be taken for granted.[5] In this case, how to live and think in a time and space whose relation to tradition has become tenuous and elusive assumes particular urgency.

In thinking through this urgent and uneasy relation, it behooves us to recall the essential importance of the concept of tradition for all thought and experience. In *The Dominion of the Dead*, Robert Pogue Harrison puts it well when he reminds us of our fundamental relation to the legacy of our predecessors: "Our basic human institutions are authored, always and from the very start, by those who came before. The awareness of death that defines human nature is inseparable from—indeed, it arises from—our awareness that we are not self-authored, that we follow the footsteps of the dead."[6] This "necrocratic" disposition can be articulated as follows:

> Whether we are conscious of it or not we do the will of our ancestors: our commandments come to us from their realm; their precedents are our law; we submit to their dictates, even when we rebel against them. Our diligence, hardihood, rectitude, and heroism, but also our folly, spite, rancor, and pathologies, are so many signatures of the dead on the contracts that seal our identities. We inherit their obsessions; assume their burdens; carry on their causes; promote their mentalities, ideologies, and very often their superstitions; and often we die trying to vindicate their humiliations. Why this servitude? We have no choice. Only the dead can grant us legitimacy. Left to ourselves we are all bastards. In exchange for legitimacy, which humans need and crave more than anything else, we surrender ourselves to their dominion. We may, in our modern modes, ignore or reject their ancient authority; yet if we are to gain a margin of real freedom—if we are to become "absolutely modern," as Rimbaud put it—we must begin by first acknowledging the traditional claims that such authority has on us.[7]

If Harrison proceeds to investigate what he calls the "humic foundations of our life world," by which he means foundations "whose contents have been buried so that they can be reclaimed by the future," he does so by focusing on the practice of burying the dead as a way both to achieve closure and to claim for oneself the place—a ground "humanized" through the corpse—in which one's dead are interred.[8] The many secular afterlives of the dead can be investigated in terms of the categories of place and dwelling, as Harrison does, but also in the less concrete and more elusive realm of an intellectual tradition that holds sway over us, even when that tradition appears remote or ruptured. There can be no thought and no experience without a visible or invisible mediation by the dead who predate us and against whose ideas, laws, practices, premises, and modes of being in the world we measure ourselves.

Adorno and Arendt, each in their own singular ways, are fully attuned to the dominion of the dead and to the fundamental thinking of tradition to which it gives rise. Although the internally variegated concept of tradition, alongside related notions such as inheritance, legacy, and transmission, is never far from the respective archives of Adorno's and Arendt's thinking—including, for instance, Adorno's relation to Hegelian thought as a problem of inheriting a tradition (as we shall see in chapter 3) or Arendt's account of totalitarianism in relation to its break with tradition as well as her frequent reflections on the question of tradition in the fragments of her *Denktagebuch*, the "thought-diary" she kept from 1950 until 1973—I will focus my discussion here on two specific texts in which the concept is treated with sustained focus and explicit urgency. They are the pivotal first chapter or "exercise," as Arendt preferred to say, of her first collection of philosophical essays, *Between Past and Future*: "Tradition and the Modern Age," and Adorno's 1966 essay "On Tradition" ("Über Tradition"), later included in his essay collection *Ohne Leitbild. Parva Aesthetica*. By placing Arendt's and Adorno's thinking of tradition into a constellation, my aim is to show that Arendt develops a critical concept of tradition that attends to the historical, intellectual, and experiential gap in our modern thinking of temporality, whereas Adorno's concept of tradition pivots on a negatively dialectical gesture of thinking in which the value and potentiality of tradition are affirmed precisely by repudiating the concept of tradition itself. Taken together, these concepts of tradition work to cross-illuminate the aporetic structure of tradition and the hidden critical possibilities emerging from this very structure.

Before we turn to these two texts by Arendt and Adorno, it will be instructive first to bring the two thinkers of tradition together in the critical terrain of their shared relation to Benjamin, a writer and mutual friend whose legacy also divides them. The intense intellectual and personal friendship between Benjamin and Adorno—sometimes difficult and fraught, as their extensive correspondence amply reveals—lasted until Benjamin's suicide in 1940. The simultaneous friendship between Benjamin and Arendt, though more indirect and mediated, was intimate enough for Benjamin personally to entrust Arendt, shortly before his death, with carrying the handwritten manuscript that would come to symbolize his intellectual legacy, the "Theses on the Philosophy of History," into safety in the United States.[9] To be sure, the disparate interpretations of Benjamin's thinking starkly demarcates a line between, on the one side, Adorno and the members of the early Frankfurt School, and, on the other, Arendt, who insisted that, without "realizing it, Benjamin actually had more in common with Heidegger's remarkable sense for living eyes and living bones that had sea-changed into pearls and coral . . . than he did with the dialectical subtleties of his Marxist friends."[10] And it certainly behooves us not to underestimate or to minimize the deep tensions between Arendt and Adorno that emerged, in part, as a result of their heterogeneous relations to Benjamin, tensions that Gershom Scholem lucidly records when recalling a conversation with Arendt from as early as 1938: "Hannah Arendt had a profound aversion [*tiefgehende Abneigung*] to the circle around the Institute, particularly Horkheimer and Adorno," an aversion that "was mutual" and that often centered on her uncharitable interpretation of "the

Institute's conduct toward Benjamin."[11] Yet what I wish to provide here, before we turn to Arendt's and Adorno's own theses on tradition, is not the staging of an arm-wrestling match between the two thinkers over Benjamin's legacy but rather a preparatory analysis of Arendt's and Adorno's differently modulated and discretely accented relation to Benjamin's mobilization of tradition that simultaneously, as we shall see, animated their own.

In section 3, entitled "The Pearl Diver," of her capacious, if idiosyncratic, introductory essay on Benjamin—first written in German and later included, in an English version, both as the introduction to Benjamin's essay collection *Illuminations* and in Arendt's *Men in Dark Times*—Arendt insists on the centrality of the thinking of tradition to Benjamin's project. She writes that insofar "as the past has been transmitted as tradition [*Sofern Vergangenheit als Tradition überliefert ist*], it possesses authority; insofar as authority presents itself historically, it becomes tradition. Walter Benjamin knew that the break in tradition and the loss of authority which occurred in his life-time were irreparable, and he concluded that he had to discover new ways of dealing with the past." To which Arendt adds: "In this he became a master when he discovered that the transmissibility of the past had been replaced by its citability and that in place of its authority there had arisen a strange power to settle down, piecemeal, in the present and to deprive it of 'peace of mind,' the mindless peace of complacency [*gedankenlosen Selbstzufriedenheit*]."[12] She thus focuses in her interpretation of Benjamin on those aspects of his work that speak to a decisive break in the thinking of tradition, a moment in which the authority of what has been transmitted calls itself into question. As we shall see, this idea of a fundamental break in the concept and function of tradition also will be decisive for her own development of the notion of tradition. In Arendt's understanding of Benjamin's project, a broken tradition cannot be mended, and this very irreparability calls for a rethinking of the past that does not content itself with the precepts provided by available historical models. If a past is not merely transmissible as tradition, it now enters a realm of citability ("Zitierbarkeit"), in which it can be alluded to, or invoked, indirectly—that is to say, always in an elsewhere and at another time—but no longer relied upon as the stable gesture of a historically reliable handing-down. Those who find themselves in the postlapsarian state of a tradition in ruins must learn to become especially sensitive readers of citation.[13]

Arendt locates concrete examples of citability that, from the perspective of tradition, have replaced the transmissibility of the past, in such variegated Benjaminian practices as the idiomatic use of citation in his own works, his conflicted relation to the tradition of Judaism, his obsession with Kafka's literary challenge to the tradition of handed-down truths, his interpretive engagement with the problem of translation, and his theoretical reflections on, as well as concrete habits of, collecting such seemingly marginal cultural objects as children's books and books written by the mentally ill. Even Benjamin's peculiar choice of scholarly subject matter—the less-than-illustrious literary period of the German Baroque—illustrates, for Arendt, his particular way of relating to a broken tradition. As she argues, "Benjamin's choice, baroque in a double sense, has an exact counterpart in Scholem's strange decision to approach Judaism via the Cabala—that is, that part of the Hebrew literature which is untransmitted and untransmissible in terms of Jewish tradition, in which it has always had the odor of something downright disreputable."[14] For Arendt, nothing "showed more clearly" the ways in which "there was no such thing as a 'return' either to the German or the European or the Jewish tradition than the choices of these fields of study" because it "was an implicit admission that the past spoke directly only through things that had not been handed down, whose seeming closeness to the present was thus due precisely to their exotic character, which ruled out all claims to a binding authority."[15] It is thus only when the end of transmissibility has made itself felt in thinking that the citability of the past emerges to structure one's critical relation to tradition.

Arendt pays such close attention to the Benjaminian practices of citing and collecting because they stage the need to come to terms with the ways in which thinking can and must relate to a past (and, by extension, a futurity) without having any recourse to tradition available to guide it. Benjamin's figure of the collector, for instance, does not merely follow the trajectories of a handed-down tradition but relates to the (often marginal and culturally unsanctioned) objects of his passion in unpredictable ways. Whereas tradition, Arendt argues, "puts the past in order, not just chronologically but first of all systematically in that it separates the positive from the negative, the orthodox from the heretical, that which is obligatory and relevant from the mass of irrelevant or merely interesting opinions and data," the passion of the collector pulls thought and experience in a rather different direction. After all, the "collector's passion . . . is not only unsystematic but borders on the chaotic, not so much because it is a passion as because it is not primarily kindled by the quality of the object—something that is classifiable—but is inflamed by its 'genuineness,' its uniqueness, something that defies any systematic classification."[16] Whereas "tradition discriminates, the collector levels all differences," even in cases in which tradition itself may be the field of collection.[17] The special force field to which Arendt points in this connection is one in which the "heir and preserver unexpectedly turns into a destroyer [*verwandelt sich so der Erbe und Bewahrer in einen Zerstörer*]," inciting a certain rebellion against the traditional and the classifiable that makes itself felt even in the impulse to preserve and to protect for the future.[18] This Benjaminian double gesture of preserving and destroying, lamenting the loss of tradition while also furthering it, is precisely what attracts Arendt to Benjamin's thinking. Indeed, she will allow it to exert a decisive influence on her own account of the problem of tradition.

As with Arendt, Benjamin is never far from Adorno's vigilant thinking of tradition and the uncoercive gaze he casts upon it, albeit in different terms. In 1966, the same year in which he publishes his essay "On Tradition," Adorno includes in his *Negative Dialectics* a concentrated and apodictic meditation on the concept of tradition that pivots to a significant degree on Benjamin. In the section "Tradition und Erkenntnis" ("Tradition and Cognition"), Adorno criticizes certain tendencies in contemporary mainstream philosophy that exclude the thinking of tradition altogether. "The hitherto dominant philosophy of the modern age," he points out, "wishes to eliminate the traditional moments of thinking, dehistoricize the contents and import of thought, and assign history to a special, fact-gathering branch of science."[19] This dehistoricization of thinking, which disregards the tradition in which it nevertheless stands, endorses the supposedly transhistorical and timeless nature of its logical operations, while regarding the historical and tradition-related dimensions of every thought as merely the aberrant expression of superstition. Although humans had "every reason to criticize authority" that was based on the "ecclesiastically institutional traditions," a critique that had as its purpose the enabling of human beings to make use of their own capacity for free and nondogmatic critical thought, this repression of the historical and the traditional has assumed a sinister underbelly.[20] According to Adorno, a wholesale rejection of tradition and history amounts to an ill-advised "critique" through which philosophers "misconceived that tradition is immanent in cognition itself, that it serves to mediate between its objects," and to disregard this historical or tradition-based aspect of knowledge is to "distort the objects" by means of a "stabilizing objectification."[21] This gesture is fatal because "cognition as such, even in a form detached from substance, takes part in tradition as unconscious remembrance [*unbewußte Erinnerung*]; there is no question that could simply be posed in which knowing of past things is not preserved and spurred onward."[22] In other words, even when modes of cognition believe themselves to be far removed from the tradition out of which they flow—they may contest or reject it—something of their own genealogy, the contexts of their genesis, remains inscribed in them. To illustrate his argument, Adorno points to Husserl's insistence, in his late work, on the idea of an inner historicity ("innere Historizität") in which thinking cannot remain merely formal or self-referential but also is interwoven with content and, by extension, with the history of that content—its tradition. In other words, there can be no thinking of time without that which is actually in it. Every thought, every idea, no matter how fervently it wishes to see itself as autonomous and as removed from the contingencies of time and space, has a history. This history ineluctably binds it to a tradition with which it must struggle to come to terms.

In the undialectical striving for autonomy from tradition, Adorno sees an unwitting expression of a latently or openly bourgeois consciousness seeking to compensate for its own mortality and finitude by insisting on absolute traditionlessness, which is to say, a supposed timelessness. At this crucial point of the argument, he refers to Benjamin by suggesting: "Benjamin innervated this when he strictly foreswore the ideal of autonomy and submitted his thought to tradition [*sein Denken einer Tradition unterstellte*]—although to a voluntarily installed, subjectively chosen tradition that is as unauthoritative as it accuses autarkic thought of being."[23] Adorno, like Arendt, thus identifies in Benjamin a key element in the modern thinking of tradition. The specifically Adornean reading of Benjamin on tradition insists on a negatively dialectical movement, according to which Benjamin calls into question the idea of autonomy of philosophical thinking from such dimensions as tradition and rhetoric in a way that still preserves the tension between thought and tradition. For Benjamin, tradition is not something that could simply be left behind in the name of a supposed autonomy; tradition also needs to be reconfigured, reinterpreted, which is to say reread, reinstalled always one more time. Thinking unfolds in relation to a nonfixed, dynamic conception of tradition that is not based on authority or handed-down doctrine but on an active engagement with the tradition of tradition itself. This is also why, for Adorno, a critical appreciation of Benjamin's complex relation to tradition may help us to broaden what could be seen as the "overly narrow initial questions in the *Critique of Pure Reason*," namely "how a thinking obliged to relinquish tradition might preserve and transform tradition."[24] In other words, by learning to read Benjamin on tradition, we might articulate how Kantian and post-Kantian critique could begin to relate to the tradition in which it is inscribed and with which it simultaneously breaks. Such a learning how to read would bind the understanding of tradition and its breaks to the interminable question of exegesis and interpretation. Here, philosophy's methexis in tradition would only be a determined negation of tradition. Philosophy is founded on the texts it criticizes [*Sie wird gestiftet von den Texten, die sie kritisiert*]. They are brought to it by the tradition they embody, and it is in dealing with them that the conduct of philosophy becomes commensurable with tradition. This justifies the move from philosophy to interpretation [*Übergang von Philosophie an Deutung*], which exalts neither what is interpreted [*das Gedeutete*] nor the symbol into an absolute but seeks what is said to be true there where thought secularizes the irretrievable *Ur*-image of scared texts [*wo der Gedanke das unwiederbringliche Urbild heiliger Texte säkularisiert*].[25]

For Adorno, philosophical thinking thus relates to the tradition in which every act of thinking is inscribed by attending to the very texts that enable critical reflection in the first place. To show itself responsible to a tradition, or to a broken tradition in ruins, philosophical thought must realize that it is based on a restless and ever-vigilant interpretation and reinscription of the texts that make thinking what it is. With Benjamin, Adorno emphasizes the textual and linguistic nature that characterizes any close and attentive relation between critical thought and the tradition. Although the active and sensitive interpretation of texts that underlies this relation to the tradition has broken with the scene of exegetical reading that informs the biblical tradition, it also keeps alive certain elements of that tradition in a radically secularized way. Such secularized textual exegesis, however, is no longer performed in the service of some putative transcendental signified or of the absolute (from the Latin *absolvere*, to detach or untie), but rather in the name of rebinding the critical act into the texts that first made it possible, what Benjamin himself in his preparatory notes for the *Arcades Project* once called "the image that is read," which is to say, "the image of the Now of recognizability," which "bears to the highest degree the stamp of that critical, dangerous moment that lies at the ground of all reading."[26] Any negatively dialectical thinking of the tradition would have to take into account this critical and dangerous moment that calls for an act of emphatic and patient reading.

We are now in a position to examine more closely, first, Arendt's own understanding of tradition, which, like Adorno's, takes its point of departure in Benjamin. If Étienne Balibar's assessment is right that Arendt belongs to those thinkers "who never wrote the same book twice," never even composing "two successive books from the same point of view" because she allowed "herself to become transformed by the writing itself," this does not mean that there is no continuity in her thinking or that the "permanence of certain crucial questions" do not remain "the horizon of the philosophical quest, and even account for its variations."[27] Focusing on her thinking of tradition in one particular text, "Tradition and the Modern Age," in order to query her thinking of tradition more generally, is thus an interpretive gesture that locates, in an exemplary site, the conceptual impulses of a thought that permeates, in a variety of tonalities and modulations, her oeuvre as a whole. This text on the concept of tradition in modernity, which Arendt wrote in English, had its origin in lectures for the Gauss Seminars in Criticism that she delivered at Princeton University in October and November 1953; its core concern with the thinking of tradition would never leave her.[28]

As Arendt sets out to specify the political and experiential determinations and overdeterminations of our being in the world, she also works to concretize our understanding of a certain "gap between past and future," as the subtitle of the preface to *Between Past and Future* reads. The difficulty and provocation of thinking this gap informs, directly or indirectly, the entirety of her work, and it is no accident that she herself considered the text in which the gap is first addressed at length and in the context of a thinking of tradition, *Between Past and Future*, her best book.[29] The gap of which Arendt speaks is not to be confused simply with the moment of the present, the contemporary situatedness of an experience, being, or act of thinking that is neither already a matter of the past nor as yet the matter of a time to come. What she has in mind, rather, is a consideration of the ways in which the Now-Time of our political and epistemological situatedness reveals a certain empty space, a space of reflection in which the tradition of a past and its relation to an unnamed futurity can no longer be taken for granted but must become the object of thinking and questioning. Following the great challenges to the notion of tradition in the movements of modernization that characterize the eighteenth and nineteenth centuries, as well as the subsequent fundamental rupture of tradition in the twentieth century marked by the Shoah and its aftermath, tradition presents itself more than ever as a question mark and as a demand for sustained interpretive engagement with it. This, for Arendt, is an especially difficult demand because "we seem to be neither equipped nor prepared for this activity of thinking, of settling down in the gap between past and future." And she continues by providing reasons for this assessment:

> For a very long time in our history, actually throughout the thousands of years that followed upon the foundation of Rome and were determined by Roman concepts, this gap was bridged over by what, since the Romans, we have called tradition. That this tradition has worn thinner and thinner as the modern age progressed is a secret to nobody. When the thread of

tradition finally broke, the gap between past and future ceased to be a condition peculiar only to the activity of thought and restricted as an experience to those few who made thinking their primary business. It became a tangible reality and perplexity for all; that is, it became a fact of political relevance.[30]

The tradition that once could be relied upon for guidance and orientation has left us in a position of vulnerability and exposedness. The modern age, what in German is called "Neuzeit" or "new time," is a time in which not only a new thinking is required but also one in which time itself must be thought anew. Part of this rethinking requires that the gap between past and future, the gap that we inhabit and inherit, must itself be the locus that gives rise to thinking. Such thinking is, according to Arendt's conception, not confined to philosophers and critical theorists; on the contrary, it becomes a general condition and as such emerges as a thoroughly urgent political concept. It is worth noting that this point is so salient to her that she takes it up again in her final work, *The Life of the Mind*, where, in volume 1—devoted to the very question of thinking—she emphasizes again that the gap between past and future has put so much pressure on our thinking and being that it is "no longer a part of the 'history of ideas' but of our political history, the history of the world."[31]

It is thus no accident that *Between Past and Future* commences with a quotation from the French writer René Char: *"Notre héritage n'est précédé d'aucun testament*—'our inheritance was left to us by no testament,'" which suggests, among many other things, that the inheritance and legacy of the tradition that is handed down to us needs to be reread and reinterpreted because no testament and no instruction manual will teach us how to understand it.[32] Tradition not only hands something down to us, a stable content to be consumed or appropriated, but it also asks us to learn how to read it, to interpret it without guidance and without quite knowing how. The Western tradition itself cannot guide us in how to read it and how to become proper heirs of its legacies; it requires a new kind of thinking. Yet Arendt's own reflections on the question of tradition are not meant as pragmatic solutions to the problem of how to bridge the gap between past and future by reconceptualizing the concept of tradition itself. In keeping with her preferred model, the "exercise" that also is encoded in the subtitle of the book in which her reflections on tradition occur, *Between Past and Future: Eight Exercises in Political Thought*, she provides "exercises" whose "only aim is to gain experience in *how* to think; they do not contain prescriptions on what to think or which truths to hold." To which she adds: "Least of all do they intend to retie the broken thread of tradition or to invent some newfangled surrogates with which to fill the gap between past and future," because their "concern is solely with how to move in this gap—the only region perhaps where truth will eventually appear."[33] Learning how to relate to tradition through certain exercises in thinking thus always also entails learning to move within a gap. The strategy that Arendt pursues is therefore not predicated upon the conception of a movement that pulls the one who thinks out of a predicament but rather installs him ever more firmly in it, which is to say, allows him to navigate, within the space of the gap in which he is situated, the vagaries and vicissitudes of tradition ever more vigilantly.

In order to generate a thinking of the gap that confronts tradition as such—which one could call the tradition of tradition, tradition *as* tradition—it may be strategically useful first to interrogate a certain strand within a tradition. The specificity of a tradition can then be placed into conceptual relation with the concept of tradition as such, and the two conceptual poles may illuminate each other reciprocally. This, perhaps, is one of the reasons why Arendt embarks on her examination of tradition by focusing on a particular tradition, the tradition of political thought. Her motivation for doing so cannot be reduced to her often-expressed wish not to be considered a philosopher but rather a political theorist; it is rather grounded in the requirements of thinking the complex tradition itself.[34] This specific Western tradition, she reminds us, "had its definite beginning in the teachings of Plato and Aristotle" and, in her view, "came to a no less definitive end in the theories of Karl Marx."[35] Although the state of human affairs in the cave allegory of *The Republic* is cast by Plato in terms of a need to leave behind darkness and deception so that the "clear sky of eternal ideas" may be viewed, Marx's model, Arendt emphasizes, locates the truth of philosophical inquiry not in some space outside of human affairs but rather within them, within our particular modes of living together. Yet, according to Arendt's account, this shift from the Greek beginning of the tradition of political thought to its supposed Marxian end necessitates a reflection on the very concepts of beginning and end within the conceptual orbit of thinking (a) tradition. She therefore avers:

> The beginning and the end of the tradition have this in common: that the elementary problems of politics never come as clearly to light in their immediate and simple urgency as when they are first formulated and they receive their final challenge. . . . Only beginning and end are, so to speak, pure or unmodulated; and the fundamental chord therefore never strikes its listeners more forcefully and more beautifully than when it first sends its harmonizing sound into the world and never more irritatingly and jarringly

than it still continues to be heard in a world whose sounds—and thought—it can no longer bring into harmony. A random remark which Plato made in his last work: "The beginning is like a god which as long as it dwells among men saves all things" . . . is true of our tradition; as long as its beginning was alive, it could save all things and bring them into harmony. By the same token, it became destructive as it came to its end—to say nothing of the aftermath of confusion and helplessness which came after the tradition ended and in which we live today.[36]

Arendt thus argues that the beginning and the end of a tradition disclose a problem or state of affairs—here, the political as such—more clearly and more palpably than does an ongoing tradition, a tradition-saturated way of being in the world in which one finds oneself and in which one is not normally on the lookout for the causes of beginnings and ends or for ways of relating to what certain beginnings and ends may have to teach one about this or that aspect of a tradition. It is thus in the moment of a certain rupture, marked precisely by the terms "beginning" and "end," that tradition enters most forcefully into our orbit of thinking. The thought of tradition, we might say, is always dislocated in time and space, the thought of a time that, as Shakespeare's Hamlet has it, is "out of joint." If Plato, as Arendt enlists him here, invokes the simile of a beginning being like a divinity, and if he relates this god-likeness of the beginning to a certain redemptive quality, it is because a beginning typically harbors potentiality and promise, the salutary prospect of a world yet to be created. Yet the felt end or loss of tradition, embodied in the postlapsarian condition in which thinking finds itself today, offers no such promise. It relates to tradition after the end of tradition; its art, perhaps, is the art that is still created after Hegel's pronouncement of the end of art; and its general perspective is one of afterness, with which it must constantly grapple. If there is no "Hegelian dialectic between continuity and discontinuity in Arendt's work because the contradiction is not sublated," as Agnes Heller reminds us, we could say it is because Arendt refuses to inscribe continuity and discontinuity, main modes of the concepts of tradition, into the linearity and homogeneity of any single historical narrative.[37] Tradition resides, rather, as Arendt puts it in her 1946 review essay on Hermann Broch's novel *The Death of Vergil*, in an "empty space," in which the continuity of historical and personal experience, the unfolding itinerary of one's being between the "no-longer" and the "not-yet," cannot be taken for granted anymore.[38]

To concretize the difference between the beginning of the tradition of political theory and its end, Arendt's strategy is to emphasize Marx's appropriation of these two poles under the sign of a post-Hegelian inflection. The utopian element in Marx's political thought appears as such only if one neglects the perspective that it also works "to reproduce the political and social conditions of the same Athenian city-state which was the model of experience for Plato and Aristotle, and therefore the foundation on which our tradition rests."[39] Marx's predictions thus break with tradition and at the same time tacitly reproduce certain assumptions and premises within it; the ending that they augur also marks the reinscription of a beginning, a silent survival, under altered conditions, of elements that obtained at the beginning of the tradition of political philosophy. Arendt's argument in relation to Marx is that the "hold which the tradition had over him" was not fully visible to him, which unwittingly led him to an interpretation of his times "in terms and concepts having their origin in an altogether different historical period."[40] Nevertheless, the special quality of Marx's political philosophy, which also marked the ending of the tradition, rests on the particular imbrication of two modes of relating to tradition, namely, "the perception of certain trends in the present which could no longer be understood in the framework of the tradition, and the traditional concepts and ideals by which Marx himself understood and integrated them."[41] One might say that it is through the double perspective of taking on the tradition, both in the sense of resisting it and showing oneself responsible to it, that Arendt's Marx—even when she is critical of him, as she often can be—sheds light on the transformative aspects of thinking tradition.

These two imbricated modes of relating to the tradition illuminate, in Arendt's account, the idea that "Marx's own attitude to the tradition of political thought was one of conscious rebellion," in which he "challenges the traditional God, the traditional estimate of labor, and the traditional glorification of reason."[42] What is more, the tradition of "philosophy from Plato to Hegel was 'not of this world,' whether it was Plato describing the philosopher as the man whose body only inhabits the city of his fellow men, or Hegel admitting that, from the point of view of common sense, philosophy is world stood on its head, a *verkehrte Welt*." But Marx, by contrast, issues a "challenge to tradition" by locating the labor of conceptual analysis precisely in the "world of human affairs," among those inhabitants of the material world seeking guidance and inspiration in their search for freedom and justice.[43] One way of glossing the specificity of Arendt's argument is to point out that, according to the logic of her narrative, Marx could have issued a challenge to tradition only by also being thoroughly informed by, and fully saturated with, the same tradition. A formidable challenge to tradition, even a rebellion against it, can be articulated only when the central features of that tradition already are so well understood and internalized by a thinker that, even by breaking with tradition, he also affirms it. That is to say, by not following in ways that already are specific and germane to it, he also issues a tacit affirmation of the very tradition he criticizes. If Arendt is right that Marx "tried desperately to think against the tradition while using its own conceptual tools," a productive predicament arises.[44] By employing, one could say, the very tools and premises of what he criticizes precisely in order to criticize it, the critic's gesture of departure from what is criticized also unwittingly ties him ever more closely to the most important elements in that which he criticizes. It is out of this simultaneous departure from, and affirmation of, the tradition, that the thinking of tradition itself gains innovative impulses, that is, remains alive in the first place.

Yet to identify, as Arendt does, the productive predicament of taking on the tradition should not suggest any kind of automatism, in which a critic of and in the tradition simply could employ this relation as a recipe or program to be followed in the critical act or in the service of this or that preestablished political agenda. Such an assumption would presuppose an awareness of the workings of tradition that cannot simply be taken for granted. Arendt thus reminds us that "this tradition, its hold on Western man's thought, has never depended on his consciousness of it."[45] On the contrary, Arendt's argument depends on the assumption that it is not necessary to presuppose conscious awareness of the forces of tradition when one wishes to analyze the ways in which tradition has worked to inflect the thinking and behavior of those who dwell in its long shadow. She suggests, however, that two specific moments can be identified as historical exceptions to this generally unconscious relation between the human being and tradition. Arendt thus points, first of all, to the moment "when the Romans adopted classical Greek thought and culture as their own spiritual tradition and thereby decided historically that tradition was to have a permanent formative influence on European civilization."[46] This moment was so decisive because prior to "the Romans such a thing as tradition was unknown; with them it became and after them it remained the guiding thread through the past and the chain to which each new generation knowingly or unknowingly was bound in its understanding of the world and its own experience."[47] As Arendt was undoubtedly aware, the Greeks had no concept, word, or mode of being that was equivalent to the Latin term used by the Romans: *traditio* or "handing down."[48] It is worth noting that here she implicitly follows the epistemo-genealogical conception of her teacher Heidegger, for whom the fateful transition from ancient Greek to Roman culture, and thus from the Greek tradition to a Latin context that was not prepared for it, defines some of the core tensions inherent in Western metaphysical thought.[49] Arendt's unique inflection of this general model consists in her argument that the Roman appropriation of ancient Greek tradition was not just one episode in the history of tradition, one form of taking on tradition among others; it was in fact the foundational moment and primal scene of the idea of assuming, possessing, and conforming to the perceived precepts of tradition.[50] One could even go so far as to claim that, within the Western world, this Roman moment embodied the invention of the very concept of "tradition."

The other historical point in Western culture that is particularly saturated with an intense consciousness of relating to tradition is, in Arendt's account, the period of Romanticism. It is here, with the Romantics, that "we again encounter an exalted consciousness and glorification of tradition."[51] One should be mindful of the fact that this turn of argument also connects Arendt's understanding of the place of Romanticism in the thinking of tradition implicitly to Benjamin's, for it is hardly by chance that in her essay on Benjamin, Arendt quotes his statement that Romanticism functioned as the "last movement that once more saved tradition."[52] Although it could be objected at this point that the discovery or rediscovery of antiquity by the Renaissance marked an equally momentous encounter with tradition, it needs to be pointed out that for Arendt this moment rather marked an "attempt to break the fetters of tradition" precisely by returning to "the sources themselves to establish a past over which tradition would have no hold."[53] In that case, tradition was turned against tradition in an attempt to gain the possibility of a certain freedom in relation to the sway of tradition. The Romantics, by contrast, self-consciously worked to "place the discussion of tradition on the agenda of the nineteenth century," at a time when the world was beginning to change in such fundamental ways that the very idea of a tradition, or the notion of taking recourse to the precepts and resources of a tradition as a self-evident good, no longer could be taken for granted.[54] One way of conceptualizing the state of affairs that Arendt attempts to describe is to say that prior to the Romantics and the nineteenth century, the new had to justify itself vis-à-vis the old and the established in order to gain acceptance; now the epistemic situation was shifting the other way: the old had to justify its continued existence and acceptance in light of the sheer newness of the new, which, even prior to having proved itself or having demonstrated its alleged superiority over the old, lays claim to cultural and ideological dominance and preference.

But to say, as Arendt does, that the tradition has come to an end and that "the break in our tradition is now an accomplished fact" that cannot be reversed is not the same as to suggest that the tradition therefore no longer has any sway over our consciousness. On the contrary, as she is careful to argue, "it sometimes seems that this power of well-worn notions and categories becomes more tyrannical as the tradition loses its living force and as the memory of its beginning recedes; it may even reveal its full coercive force only after its end has come and men no longer even rebel against it."[55] It is, in other words, precisely in those moments when the tradition has ceased to be seen as a force to contend with as the ultimate measuring stick against which contemporary thoughts and actions should be compared, that it silently and invisibly holds us in its grip. Among the lessons to be learned, in Arendt's account of tradition, from the historical example of thinkers such as Kierkegaard, Marx, and Nietzsche—the three philosophers to whom most of the second part of her text is dedicated—is thus an appreciation of their exemplary status as thinkers on the cusp of a tradition that is about to be lost irretrievably yet continues to haunt us. If Kierkegaard, Marx, and Nietzsche "are for us like guideposts to a past which has lost its authority," it is because they were great critics of a tradition who "were still held by the categorical framework of the great tradition."[56] Pointing to their immediate predecessor, Hegel, Arendt writes:

> The thread of historical continuity was the first substitute for tradition; by means of it, the overwhelming mass of the most divergent values, the most contradictory thoughts and conflicting authorities, all of which had somehow been able to function together, were reduced to a unilinear, dialectically consistent development actually designed to repudiate not tradition as such, but the authority of all traditions. Kierkegaard, Marx, and Nietzsche remained Hegelians insofar as they saw the history of past philosophy as one dialectically developed whole; their great merit was that they radicalized this new approach toward the past in the only way it could still be further developed, namely, in questioning the conceptual hierarchy which had ruled Western philosophy since Plato and which Hegel had still taken for granted.[57]

According to Arendt's account, Hegel's theoretical model of historical continuity came to occupy the place that was vacated by an absent tradition. From this perspective, Kierkegaard, Marx, and Nietzsche all can be seen as both furthering and breaking with the Hegelian system that had insinuated itself, through its historicity, into the empty space of tradition. One could say that, like Hegel, they each generated what Jean-François Lyotard would much later name a "master narrative" to explain the totality of a historical development—be it a subversive transition from doubt to belief, be it a critique of political economy, be it the transvaluation of all values—while simultaneously attempting to part in decisive ways with the traditional conceptual hierarchies and premises operative in the tradition of Western metaphysics.

By the same token, Arendt locates within this very rupture a subtle yet decisive movement of "turning." This general turning of and within the tradition is one of the names that can be bestowed on the "images and similes of leaps, inversion, and turning concepts upside down," whether it concerns Kierkegaard's "leap from doubt into belief," Marx's turning of Hegel "right side up again," or Nietzsche's inverted Platonism and his transvaluation of all values.[58] It is important to register, however, that in Arendt's account of tradition the turning she identifies not only allows her to place three transformative thinkers of the tradition, for all their individual distinctiveness, into special syntactical relation. After all, her argument mobilizes the figure of turning also to describe a key movement by which tradition itself operates:

> The turning operations with which the tradition ends bring the beginning to light in a twofold sense. The very assertion of one side of the opposites—*fides* against *intellectus*, practice against theory, perishable life against permanent, unchanging, suprasensual truth—necessarily brings to light the repudiated opposite and shows that both have meaning and significance only in this opposition. Furthermore, to think in terms of such opposites is not a matter of course, but is grounded in a first great turning operation on which all others ultimately are based because it established the opposites in whose tension the tradition moves.[59]

The first or foundational turning-about that called tradition into presence was, according to Arendt's account, the parable of the cave in Plato's *Republic*, where the chains of the cave dwellers are broken through a special kind of "turning," through which the images and the worlds of the cave dwellers are radically reinterpreted in favor of the clear sky of eternal ideas. Yet the account and function of a turning operation in tradition simultaneously emphasize the ways in which the tradition relies on an often invisible connection between two opposite poles, two opposites that condition each other and in whose simultaneous distinction and mutual dependence a thinking of tradition unfolds. For, according to Arendt's reflections, elements in and of a tradition acquire meaning only in direct relation to their supposed other, their excluded opposite. The latter may include the supposedly nontraditional or a-traditional element, a form of thinking and acting that has been rejected as false or other, or an idea that is believed to have been contradicted and discredited by its opposite and thus no longer can lay claim to any validity. Tradition, according to this model, proceeds not through moments of affirmed identity but rather through difference, which is to say a difference that retroactively produces all effects of positive identity. It is as though Arendt's turn of argument about the reliance of tradition on the thinking of repressed or disarticulated opposites prefigures Jacques Derrida's later analyses of the fateful working of binary oppositions in the canonical thought pattern of Western metaphysics as well as his interpretive engagements with what he calls the "logic of supplementarity," in which a term, concept, or idea assumes significance only in terms of its actual or implied differential comparison with its opposite, its other. For Arendt, there can be no thinking of tradition that does not strive to come to terms with the logic of repressed binary oppositions that, since *The Republic*, make any tradition what it is.

It is this conceptual framework that propels Arendt to argue that Kierkegaard, Marx, and Nietzsche not only serve as prime exemplars of a powerful challenge to tradition but that they each also tacitly embody particular excesses to the very challenges they issue. That is to say, the "significance of Kierkegaard's, Marx's, and Nietzsche's challenges to the tradition—through none of them would have been possible without the synthesizing achievement of Hegel and his concept of history—is that they constitute a much more radical turning-about than the mere upside-down operations" of various binary oppositions would seem to suggest.[60] The "turning-about" that we witness at work in these thinkers "goes to the core of the matter; they all question the traditional hierarchy of human capabilities, or, to put it another way, they ask again what the specifically human quality of man is; they do not intend to build systems or *Weltanschauungen* on this or that premise."[61] Instead of presupposing a model of human consciousness as the dogmatic basis for a form of ideology, Marx, like Kierkegaard and Nietzsche, worked to preserve the actual question mark as to what makes the human what it is at the center of his theoretical reflections and his engagement with the tradition. If Marx through his political thought participated in "turning the tradition upside down within its own framework, he did not actually get rid of Plato's ideas, though he did record the darkening of the clear sky where those ideas, as well as many other presences, had once become visible to the eyes of men."[62] To disrupt the tradition thus always also means to reflect on the residual attachment of one's thinking to that which it believes to have repudiated, overcome, or even brought to an end. Taking on the tradition, in the double sense of the phrase, here means not to outwit tradition or simply to supersede it with the new, but critically to record and analyze the ways in which one's view of the genealogical fibers of the tradition has become increasingly occluded and disarticulated. Like Marx's concerned accounts of the fateful darkening of Plato's clear sky, our reading of tradition must thus begin with the ways in which its elements continue to exert a more or less unacknowledged influence over our thinking and being, even as its workings are the targets of an ongoing erasure by the supposedly new, which claims to have no tradition and no historico-genealogical ballast.

Let us now perform another kind of turning, as we shift our attention from Arendt to Adorno. Toward the end of his 1969 essay "Resignation," published shortly before his death in August of that same year, Adorno makes a statement that is anything but self-evident. Responding to the charges brought against him and other members of the early Frankfurt School that, for all their revolutionary acts of thinking, they somehow seem "resigned" in the face of the status quo and the urgent need for actual political praxis, Adorno reflects on the relation among thinking, resignation, and resistance. After developing a concept of emphatic thinking that refuses to be reified by a praxis-driven precensorship or a premature utopianism, Adorno invokes an "open thinking," a thinking that points beyond itself ("Offenes Denken weist über sich hinaus").[63] To specify this open thinking, he then writes the following:

> Prior to all particular content, thinking is actually the force of resistance, from which it has been alienated only with great effort. Such an emphatic concept of thinking admittedly is not secured, not by the existing conditions, nor by ends yet to be achieved, nor by any kind of battalions. Whatever has once been thought can be suppressed, forgotten, can vanish. But it cannot be denied that something of it survives. For thinking has the element of the universal. What once was thought cogently must be thought elsewhere, by others: this confidence accompanies even the most solitary and powerless thought.[64]

> [Eigentlich ist Denken schon vor allem besonderen Inhalt die Kraft zum Widerstand und nur mühsam ihr entfremdet worden. Ein solcher emphatischer Begriff von Denken allerdings ist nicht gedeckt, weder von bestehenden Verhältnissen noch von zu erreichenden Zwecken, noch von irgendwelchen Bataillonen. Was einmal gedacht ward, kann unterdrückt, vergessen werden, verwehen. Aber es läßt sich nicht ausreden, daß etwas davon überlebt. Denn Denken hat das Moment des Allgemeinen. Was triftig gedacht wurde, muß woanders, von anderen gedacht werden: dies Vertrauen begleitet noch den einsamsten und ohnmächtigsten Gedanken.][65]

Among the many questions to which this remarkable passage gives rise, the following appear especially pertinent. If what has been thought emphatically can be repressed and forgotten, if it can vanish by "blowing away" (*verwehen* is Adorno's word) as if it were a mere autumn leaf in the wind, then how is it that part of it lives on? Even if a seemingly subjective thought has—to the extent that it was thought rigorously, convincingly, and compellingly (*triftig*)—an element of something general or universal in it, under what circumstances can it be said to survive or outlive itself ("etwas davon überlebt")? The answer to these questions appears to lie in the concept of an intellectual handing-down, a tradition of thinking that involves others who receive it and who are called upon to make this thought the object of their own singular acts of thinking. For Adorno, compelling or empathic thinking is nonidentical in that it does not come to rest in itself but must be rethought, thought again and onward, by others, in an as-yet-unnamed elsewhere ("muß woanders, von anderen gedacht werden"). It appears that a genuine thought comes into its own precisely when it is shared by the other, when it is no longer the property merely of this or that thinking self but rather travels toward and through the other, who is called upon to think it, with and against the self from which it traveled. But, one might ask, is the thought that comes to be rethought by others in an elsewhere—the compelling thought that will not rest in and with itself as a form of ipseity—then still the same thought? To what extent does it remain what it is when it is thought by the other in an unnamed elsewhere—by an unknown other perhaps hundreds of years and many thousands of miles separated from the local scene in which the thought to be handed down first came to pass? And in what sense must genuine thought be inscribed in some sort of iterability, the ability to be cited and repeated with a difference elsewhere, in the first place? Why is such thought the object of an elsewhere, a thinking to come, something that is to be understood as a form of (actual or anticipated) survival? And, finally, how can we begin to understand the trust or confidence ("Vertrauen") that Adorno claims attends to this perspective, a trust or confidence that harbors a certain amount of strength even for the most exposed, vulnerable, and desperate act of thinking? Is there a hidden community of thinking even for the lonely thought that is "most solitary," the "einsamsten Gedanken"?

Although Adorno does not elaborate on his apodictic remarks in the text in which they occur, leaving them provocatively open to interpretation and debate, I wish to suggest here that Adorno's complex concept of tradition sheds light on these questions. Indeed, one might even say that tradition becomes a privileged test case for the practice of the uncoercive gaze. After all, what is the movement by which a compelling and genuine thought becomes the object of thinking of and by others, in an unnamed elsewhere, if not the thinking of tradition, through which a thought is handed down? For, what Adorno has in mind here is presumably not merely a technical repetition or quasi-scientific mode of repeatability through which achieved results can be verified by others in another space and time. Rather, the transmissibility of what has been thought in a compelling and rigorous manner implies that others will open themselves to the challenge that this thought poses, submitting it to an ever-renewed labor of interpretation and active reflection.

When Adorno, while completing *Negative Dialectics*, dedicates a separate essay to the topic of tradition, he takes up a number of the concerns that occupied him with regard to tradition in *Negative Dialectics* while illuminating key facets of this problem in a new light. In "On Tradition," he works to develop an emphatic concept of tradition that is tied neither to the traditionalism of an outmoded, nostalgic, or reactionary consciousness nor to the shortsighted and antihistorical impulse to relinquish all tradition to whatever announces itself as the newest and the latest. The question that imposes itself is one that precisely concerns the hands that hand something down, the manual gesture that delivers something from one hand to another, from the hand of a self to the hand of the other: "Tradition comes from *tradere*; to hand down [*weitergeben*]. It recalls the continuity of generations, what is handed down by one member to another [*was von Glied zu Glied sich vererbt*], even the heritage of handicraft [*handwerkliche Überlieferung*]. The image of handing down [*Bild des Weitergebens*] expresses physical proximity, immediacy—one hand should receive from another [*eine Hand soll es von der anderen empfangen*]."[66] If Adorno, for the remainder of section I of the essay, continues to employ rhetorical figures of the hand (such as "das Von-Hand-zu-Hand," from one hand to another; "die Technik [hat] die Hand vergessen lassen," a form of technology that has made us forget the hand; the *Handwerk*, handicraft; and the "Begriff der handwerklichen Lehre," the concept of an apprenticeship in a manual craft," which once ensured tradition and now is but a remnant of a time that is no more), he does so in order to invite the reader to consider more carefully what it is that is now handed down from hand to hand, and to reflect on the ways in which the hand relates to all the other hands that stand to receive this or that handicraft, tradition, way of thinking, or mode of acting.[67] How and what does the *Über-lieferung* of the hand deliver, which to say, deliver over and across?

Setting the stage for his own negatively dialectical thinking of tradition, Adorno considers various historical moments of the contested concept of tradition. Whereas for Arendt these historical moments are marked by the tradition of political philosophy that stretches from Plato's *Republic* to Marx's transformative critique of political economy, Adorno's historical reference points include the tradition's tense relation with feudal economies, rationalism, bourgeois society, reactionary forms of consciousness, puritanism, and modes of ideology that mobilize a false notion of tradition in order to advance their particular political and economic aims. On the one hand, it may appear that the concept of tradition, in light of all the manifold abuses that have befallen it in the course of its long history—which is to say, in the tradition of tradition—should be cast aside or at least held in strict conceptual abeyance. Yet, on the other hand, it would be just as fateful to abandon the concept of tradition altogether, as performing such a gesture would be to advance an uncritical or merely self-serving version of it. Adorno's strategy, like Arendt's, is thus to argue that the difficult relation between the concept of tradition and tradition-less modes of thought and being must be thought. But he inflects his demand differently:

> To insist on the absolute absence of tradition is as naïve as the obstinate insistence on it. Both are ignorant of the past that persists in their allegedly pure relation to objects; both are unaware of the dust and debris which cloud their allegedly clear vision. But it is inhuman to forget because accumulated suffering will be forgotten and the historical trace on things, words, colors, and sounds is always of past suffering. Thus tradition today poses an insoluble contradiction. No tradition is present and none can be conjured, yet when every tradition is extinguished the march into inhumanity begins.[68]
>
> [Wie die in sich verbissene Tradition ist das absolut Traditionslose naiv; ohne Ahnung von dem, was an Vergangenem in der vermeintlich reinen, vom Staub des Zerfallenen ungetrübten Beziehung zu den Sachen steckt. Inhuman aber ist das Vergessen, weil das akkumulierte Leiden vergessen wird; denn die geschichtliche Spur an den Dingen, Worten, Farben und Tönen ist immer die vergangenen Leidens. Darum stellt Tradition vor einen unauflöslichen Widerspruch. Keine ist gegenwärtig und zu beschwören; ist aber eine jegliche ausgelöscht, so beginnt der Einmarsch in die Unmenschlichkeit.][69]

That which is without tradition—"das Traditionslose"—is just as problematic as that which clings obstinately to tradition, believing itself to live in a pure, nonmediated relationship to what is at hand. That which is without tradition relates to its objects as if this relationship were not affected by the invisible dust left behind by that which in the past has fallen into ruin and become an object of decay. But every genuine relation to an object, every "snuggling up to an object," and every "uncoercive gaze" upon that object, to recall Adorno's language in "Notes on Philosophical Thinking," also must be mindful of the ways in which a relation always is mediated by the "Staub des Zerfallenen," by the dust of decay, in other words, by the historical and genealogical inscriptions, the traditions that come to affect, consciously or not, every act of thinking and relating. To attempt to repress the mediatedness caused by tradition is not simply to commit an epistemological transgression against the precepts of historically aware thinking; it is also to turn a blind eye to the sedimented layers of accumulated suffering that are faintly recognizable to the careful reader of words, objects, colors, and sounds. There is no responsible way of engaging with the history and continued relevance, the perpetual memory and commemoration, of previous suffering without becoming a careful reader of the traces ("Spuren") of this suffering, even in a contemporary and transformed world that may believe itself to have outlived or simply overcome such concerns. Therefore, to erase the traces of tradition in the words, objects, colors, and sounds with which we engage means, tacitly or deliberately, to erase the traces of those who have suffered. Yet there is no obvious remedy for this predicament. The dialectical difficulty resides in the fact that both an obstinate, self-interested insistence on tradition and the strategic abandonment of tradition may lead to a form of barbarism and inhumanity, the "Unmenschlichkeit" that is evoked at the end of the passage. The question that Adorno's reflections thus help us to formulate is, to refunctionalize Lenin's words, what is to be done?

Whereas for Arendt the project of Marx (and, to a lesser extent, those of Kierkegaard and Nietzsche) are the key resources for understanding the fate of tradition, for Adorno's thinking of tradition, it is Kantian and post-Kantian critique that most deserves our attention. Here, in order to begin to think what the problem of tradition requires of us, it is necessary to see in Kant's insistence on the "critical path" ("*der kritische Weg*"), as it is called in the *Critique of Pure Reason*, not only a designation of philosophy's way forward through Kantian critique but also, more broadly, a call for critical reflection on the relationship between consciousness and (its) tradition. According to Adorno's understanding of Kant's insistence on the path of critique, it becomes crucial to locate in the Kantian turn not only a break with the tradition of Rationalism that preceded it but also, by the same token, a critical engagement with the very idea of a thinking and a consciousness that relates to a tradition, whether the tradition is rejected or affirmed, or, at times, both at once. As so often in Adorno's singular gestures of thinking, we are enjoined to consider the possible *relation* between critical consciousness and the tradition in which such a consciousness finds itself situated. His strategy is thus to argue as follows: "Not to forget tradition and yet not to conform to it means to confront it with the most advanced stage of consciousness and to pose the question of what carries and what does not [*was trägt und was nicht*]." To which Adorno adds: "But there is a relation to the past [*Beziehung zur Vergangenheit*] which, though it does not conserve, facilitates the survival of so many things through its incorruptibility [*doch manchem durch Unbestechlichkeit zum Überleben verhilft*]." If it is writers such as Rudolf Borchardt, Hugo von Hofmannsthal, Rudolf Alexander Schröder, as well as those affiliated with the George Circle who may be said to grasp in their work something of a negatively dialectical relation to the writing of tradition, this is because they "registered the transition [*Übergang*] of tradition into the inconspicuous [*das Unscheinbare*], into a position which no longer posits itself [*nicht sich selbst Setzende*], preferring those formations in which the truth content is deeply embedded in the material content to those in which it hovers over them like an ideology and thus is none at all."[70] Whereas Arendt regards the tradition—at least the tradition of political philosophy—to have come to an end with Marxian critique, Adorno focuses on these writers in order to make visible certain challenges of a post-traditional thinking of tradition. The challenge of a future critical relation to tradition here would be predicated upon the capacity for maintaining felt contact with elements of the tradition without becoming conservative and for enabling the survival of something not through its transfiguration or glorification as legacy but rather through a subtle and almost imperceptible affirmation of what remains incorruptible and nonidentical within it. Such a critical relation to tradition is enabled not by an ideological imposition, mobilized by this or that will to power of a conserving and conservative enforcement of a previous status quo, but rather by an opening up to what remains relevant, indispensible, and refractory within that which has been handed down. In the case of literary texts or works of art, for instance, no conservative literary history or history of art could prescribe the open relation that a future consciousness will have with a particular work, even as certain literary and artistic traditions are preserved by being included in the archives of a given tradition and therefore also rescued from oblivion.

To Adorno's uncoercive gaze, the tradition that is housed in an intellectual, textual, and cultural archive cannot be thought in isolation from the gesture of rescuing. Those parts of a tradition that are admitted into an archive are potentially rescued, while others, excluded from the archive through selection or chance, conscious decision or happenstance, are not. Yet even in the case of those works of tradition that are admitted into an archive and thus become the objects of a certain rescue operation, they suffer from the threat of being destroyed by thoughtlessness, an overly facile appropriation, or even manipulation and conscious misappropriation. It is therefore no surprise that Adorno not only warns of "ostensibly innocent gestures incorporated in the general manipulation of sanctioned cultural products" but also points to the mechanism by which "even significant older works or formations were destroyed through their rescue [*auch bedeutende ältere Gebilde wurden durch Rettung zerstört*]" because they "refused to be restored to what they once were," instead "shedding various layers according to their own dynamics."[71] In other words, attempting to rescue elements of a tradition, such as certain texts or aesthetic objects, by inserting them into a form in which they no longer feel at home—which may include even their own previous situatedness or shape—also can be a way of unwittingly erasing them from the tradition.[72] It is the way in which these elements of a tradition "shed layers" in idiosyncratic and hardly predictable ways that a critical relation to a tradition must work to confront. But this shedding of layers, which implies a dynamic flux and transformability, is not merely a threat to the tradition or a critical menace to guard against. On the contrary, it is precisely this malleability of the traditional element that is worth affirming in its nonidentity—both its nonidentity with itself and its nonidentity with any single prescribed understanding of the tradition in which it is embedded. Indeed, for Adorno, "this process alone inaugurates a tradition worth pursuing [*stiftet eine Tradition, der allein noch zu folgen wäre*]."[73] Whereas, in Arendt's view, tradition has come to an end, there appears to be a thinking of tradition in Adorno that is as yet unsaturated. Such a tradition is at odds with itself, resistant to ideological appropriations and self-serving manipulations, and always demanding to be kept alive in unexpected ways through renewed interpretation and creative reinscription.

But what, one might ask, would such a tradition that is at odds with itself mean for one's critical relation to the past and the present? How would the concept and practice of a nonidentical tradition allow for a critical illumination of the past or the present? How does a nonidentical tradition relate to the uncoercive gaze? Adorno's own answer can be found in a striking image, that of correspondence through distance. He writes of such a tradition that its

> criterion is *correspondance*. It throws, as something that steps forward in a new way [*als neu Hervortretendes*], light on the present [*Licht aufs Gegenwärtige*] and receives its illumination from the present [*und empfängt vom Gegenwärtigen ihr Licht*]. Such *correspondance* is not one of empathy and immediate affinity but requires distance [*bedarf der Distanz*]. Bad traditionalism is distinguished from tradition's element of truth in that it reduces distance and reaches for the irretrievable, which begins to speak

only in the consciousness of irretrievability. Beckett's admiration for *Effie Briest* is a model of genuine affinity through distance. It teaches how little tradition conceived in terms of *correspondance* tolerates what is traditional as a model.[74]

To begin with, it is instructive to note that the translators of the published English version provide, in the first line of this quotation, "and receives its illumination from the *past*," as if Adorno had written "und empfängt vom *Vergangenen* ihr Licht," when, it fact, he writes "and receives its illumination from the *present*," "und empfängt vom *Gegenwärtigen* ihr Licht." Perhaps they assumed that Adorno merely made a mistake that they could "fix" in the translation by substituting a word of his for one of its opposites or antonyms, "past" for "present." After all, they might well have thought, how could it be that Adorno's concept of *correspondance* can be said to cast light on the present but also to receive its light from that very present? Do we not have to choose one of the other directionality? But, we must insist, this is precisely the point of Adorno's singular reading of tradition here: *Correspondance* is the name of that which emerges or steps forward ("hervortreten" is the German verb at the root of Adorno's substantivized noun) in an unexpected manner in order to describe a dialectical relation in which it works to illuminate the present through what it brings to this present while in turn being illuminated—which is to say, read and interpreted—by the same present. Another way to put this is to say that, through the relational dimension named *correspondance*, tradition potentially allows for an active and critical penetration of the present, from which it differs, while simultaneously allowing itself to be constructed and made the object of exegetical debate by the present, without whose interpretive labors of reading no tradition could come into view in the first place.

One could now assume that, in light of the simultaneity with which the present is illuminated by tradition and which in turn illuminates tradition, a certain proximity is required. Adorno's strategy, however, is to argue the opposite. He thus asserts that it is precisely distance, rather than proximity, that allows for a truly critical engagement with the object. If a consequential reading of tradition requires distance rather than proximity, it is because it cannot be sustained by a false empathy and sense of relatedness. For Arendt and her account of tradition, the specific question of proximity and distance does not arise, but for Adorno, it is crucial. The rigorous reading of tradition that develops under Adorno's uncoercive gaze is distinguished from the conventions of mere traditionalism in that the former does not attempt to bridge a distance in order to retrieve something that is irretrievable but rather lets the distance stand, allowing it to remain infinitely distant and other without attempting to co-opt it into the discourse of the familiar and the merely available. It is as if Adorno's argument wished to guard against the danger of erasing the radical otherness of tradition by forcing it to conform to what is already a form of supposed sameness within the merely available that already surrounds us. In order to preserve the "consciousness of irretrievability [*Bewußtsein der Unwiederbringlichkeit*]," a critical relation to tradition thus would find its particular way of confronting certain ideas, objects, and ways of being handed down by a tradition precisely in their irreducible otherness, their dignified refusal merely to play along with the leading maxims and dominant assumptions of the age in which they are received.

The brief example that Adorno provides to make this point vivid stems from the literary tradition, Samuel Beckett's unexpected admiration for Theodor Fontane's *Effie Briest*. It is unknown whether or not Adorno discussed this topic with Beckett during one of the five personal meetings they are known to have had between 1958 and 1968 in Paris, Berlin, and Frankfurt.[75] Likewise, it is not obvious how Adorno's reference to Beckett here relates to his far-reaching essay on Beckett's *Endgame*, where he places the writer's work not in the wake of Fontane but primarily in that of Kafka and Joyce. There, Adorno suggests, if "Beckett's play is heir to [*beerbt*] Kafka's novels," it is because Beckett's "relationship to Kafka is analogous to that of the serial composers to Schönberg: he provides Kafka with a further self-reflection and turns him upside down by totalizing his principle."[76] But in the essay on tradition, Adorno inflects Beckett's relation to literary tradition in different terms, emphasizing the function of distance rather than that of proximity in the workings of a legacy. At first sight, Fontane's 1896 novel of German Realism, which came to be regarded in the German literary tradition as the canonical form for the modern societal novel, could hardly appear further removed from Beckett's own literary and theoretical concerns. Yet Beckett's great distance from Fontane's realist novel and his simultaneous admiration for it situates him as something of an ideal recipient of what it hands down through the tradition. Beckett takes on the tradition not by grasping for the irretrievable and thereby creating a false sense of its retrievability, which is to say, its availability as just another element of what already is operative and thinkable in the present, but rather by letting the irretrievable speak precisely as the irretrievable. By letting go of the concept of tradition as something merely at hand, by allowing it to remain distant and removed, one sets the stage for a genuine confrontation with it, which only happens when, within the proximity that also is implied by any engaged confrontation, an infinite distance is respected. One may say that this gesture amounts to thinking a tradition without traditionalism.

The distance that connects such divergent writers as Beckett and Fontane through an understanding of tradition without traditionalism is not limited to their particular formation of literary genealogy. On the contrary, what a thinking of tradition without traditionalism implies is the attempt to fashion modes of relating to the legacies of a tradition that "touch upon the true theme of rethinking tradition—that which was left along the way, neglected or overpowered, that which congeals under the name of the 'out of date' [*unter dem Namen des Veraltens sich zusammenfaßt*]. What is alive in tradition seeks refuge there rather than in the permanence of works which are said to have stood the test of time. All this escapes the sovereign perspective of historicism." Therefore, Adorno continues, the "vitality of a work is lodged deep within, under layers concealed in earlier phases which manifest themselves only when others have withered and fallen away [*absterben und abfallen*]."[77] A tradition without traditionalism thus would not limit its purview to putatively canonical or dominant works, ideas, or ways of being in the world. Rather, such a confrontation of tradition would also look in the margins of officially sanctioned discourses of cultural or intellectual transmission precisely in order to find forgotten or discarded elements, works, and ideas—elements of something that is felt by the current critical situation to be too late or too early, at odds with both the present and the past—that deserve to be engaged and rethought with an eye toward their future potentialities. In a gesture of remobilization from the margins that is not wholly unlike those practiced in the Weimar cultural criticism of his friends Benjamin and Kracauer, Adorno thus argues for a thinking and practice of tradition in which the untimeliness and internal self-differentiation of its contents come to play a central role in developing a counter-model to the workings of self-satisfied modes of traditionalism. In such a model of tradition, the "affirmative character of tradition collapses [*affirmative Wesen des Tradition bricht zusammen*]" to reveal the cracks and fissures that need to be rediscovered in order critically to take on the tradition anew.[78]

The emphasis on distance and marginality that the thinking of tradition thus requires—if it is not to be conflated with the historical and ideological appropriations associated with traditionalism—a markedly double relation to the legacies handed down through it. Adorno attempts to formulate this double relation in terms of a gesture of thinking that both preserves and shucks off its attunement to tradition. Taking the example of literary tradition—though, to the extent that a more general model of thought is at stake, other traditions would also have served him here—he specifies the critical comportment toward tradition that is thinkable only through a kind of paradox. Adorno renders this paradox operative in the uncoercive gaze as follows:

> Literary writing redeems its truth content only when it repels tradition at the closest point of contact with it. Whoever seeks to avoid betraying the bliss which tradition still promises in some of its images and the possibility buried beneath its ruins must abandon the tradition which abuses possibility and meaning in order to lie. Tradition may return only in that which unyieldingly denies itself to it.[79]

> [Dichtung errettet ihren Wahrheitsgehalt nur, wo sie in engstem Kontakt mit der Tradition diese von sich abstößt. Wer die Seligkeit, die sie in manchen ihrer Bilder stets noch verheißt, nicht verraten will, die verschüttete Möglichkeit, die unter ihren Trümmern sich birgt, der muß von der Tradition sich abkehren, welche Möglichkeit und Sinn zur Lüge mißbraucht. Wiederzukehren vermag Tradition einzig in dem, was unerbittlich ihr sich versagt.][80]

What Adorno says of tradition with regard to literary writing could be extended to a thinking of tradition more generally, and here it would enter an orbit of reflection that is not entirely alien to Arendt's understanding. The truth content within the work emerges at the point at which both a closely experienced contact with tradition and a simultaneous departure from that very tradition make themselves felt in the critical act. Whatever is valuable and irreducible in a work is not simply put there through an act of spontaneous inspiration, by a more or less original "idea" that is supposed to enable a relation with tradition in the first place. On the contrary, any idea in the moment of its articulation already finds itself inscribed in a tradition, even when it believes itself to be innovative. But the recognition of this inscription in a tradition by itself, as a form of emergent historical awareness, is not enough to activate the hidden possibility within the legacies of the traditional. Rather, only when the awareness of one's saturation with tradition is thought together with a break from that same tradition can the potentiality of a tradition emerge—as a sort of determined negation. What this determined negation unearths is not this or that recipe or program for bliss or salvation, but merely the images that promise, and thereby also affirm, a certain "Seligkeit" in the moment of its disappearance.

If Adorno speaks of this critical tradition in terms of a "verschüttete Möglichkeit," he points to a buried possibility, still to be excavated from among the ruins that surround it. But we would do well also to be mindful of another meaning of "verschüttet": "spilled." Whereas the first meaning of "verschüttet" designates something buried or hidden (yet in principle accessible), this other meaning of "verschüttet" brings to the fore the image of an accident, even a catastrophe in which something is forever spoiled or lost. Like milk that has been spilled, *verschüttete Milch*, the spilled possibility, "verschüttete Möglichkeit," can never be rescued—it remains the marker of a disaster whose aftermath any thinking of tradition also must confront. Hovering between possible excavation and absolute irretrievability, the concept of possibility here demands to be thought without any assumed guarantees, without safety net, and without any established precepts for recovery or redemption. If there is possibility lodged in the thinking of tradition, it remains tied to pure exposedness and vulnerability. By the same token, this is the point at which a genuine thinking of tradition first comes into focus—that is, becomes a category of critical reflection in the first place. In other words, it becomes a proper object of analysis for the uncoercive gaze.

If Adorno and Arendt, each in their own distinctive way, can teach us anything about tradition, it is that no thinking of tradition can claim to be a genuine thinking of tradition if it merely affirms the structure and content of a tradition that is handed down as legible and transparently appropriable. To allow the forces of this insight to be operative in one's critical practice is an eminently political moment—even and especially if it requires us to rethink the tradition of critique and, by extension, the realm of the political itself. Thinking tradition implies a thinking directed both against thinking and against tradition; only when it does not hand itself over to tradition, when it does not play along with the received wisdoms of a tradition, can tradition reassume a truly critical position in our intellectual horizon. To be attuned to tradition in a vigilant mode, to invite it in, and to be hospitable to it, one must also break with it. The further one moves away from tradition, the more closely one may follow it—but even then only under the aegis of a doubly *verschüttete* possibility.

CHAPTER THREE

The Inheritance of the Constellation
Adorno and Hegel

Adorno's singular ways of inhabiting a tradition and of being simultaneously at odds with that same tradition are inextricably intertwined with his complex inheritance of Hegelian thought.[1] In fact, his ways of casting an uncoercive gaze upon the objects of his critical inquiry cannot be thought in separation from his abiding engagement with the movements of thought that he encounters in the Hegelian tradition. For Adorno, as for other members of the early Frankfurt School, the challenge presented by Hegel's legacy is second to none in the way it has left its mark on the thinking of modernity as such. Indeed, Hegel's remarkable example in particular allows a number of the foundational difficulties of an intellectual inheritance, difficulties that also are crucial to Adorno's own singularity of thinking, to emerge in vivid relief. Yet our considerations of Adorno's uneasy inheritance of Hegelian modes of thought will not revolve primarily around the manifold consequences of Hegelian thought, nor will they involve a study of his reception that would retrace the determinate influences that Hegel exercised upon subsequent thinking. Nor is it a question here of inquiring into Hegel's legacy from a point of view that would discern, to speak with the Italian interpreter of Hegel Benedetto Croce, what still "lives" and what is "dead" in Hegel's philosophy. Not even the most consequential mainstream currents of the Hegelian heritage will be foregrounded—that is, neither right-leaning conservative Hegelians of the nineteenth century such as Eduard Gans and, later, Kuno Fischer, nor left-wing Hegelians such as Bruno Bauer, Ludwig Feuerbach, and David Friedrich Strauß; neither Hegel's materialist legacy through Marx, nor the critical delimitations of Schopenhauer and Nietzsche, nor the influential later adoption of Hegel in France through Alexandre Kojève; neither Ernst Bloch's utopia-oriented inheritance of Hegel, nor the latest onset of approaches to reading Hegel that began to make their mark in the second half of the twentieth century and that today—in the age of globally operating neoliberalism and capital-oriented pragmatism—are often associated, rightly or not, with names such as Charles Taylor. Even three of the most provocative and circumspect reassessments of Hegel of recent years will be bracketed, namely, those of Catherine Malabou, Rebecca Comay, and Slavoj Žižek, whose inheritances of Hegel would each deserve reflections and responses in their own right.[2] Nor will further additions be made to the existing interpretations of Hegel, which span over two centuries and, in the meantime, fill whole reading rooms—even if, at one point or another, an unexpected perspective on Hegel may happen to open up in the course of our reflections. After all, in following Hegel we in a certain sense constantly interpret him anew, whether or not he is expressly thematized, whether or not we intend to do so, indeed, whether or not we know it.

Instead, consciously narrowing in on the concept of inheritance as it is mediated for Adorno through Hegel should make a paradigmatic attempt at inheriting graspable, one that attempts in an idiomatic way to render, through a radical interpretation, Hegel's legacy generative for an uncoercive thinking, which in turn left its decisive mark on the canon of modern theoretical formation: Adorno's negatively dialectical modes of reflection. In the center of interest stands Hegel's early masterpiece, the *Phenomenology of Spirit* (1807), which shaped modern engagements with dialectical thinking as well as modern philosophical thought as such. The following reading of Adorno's attempt to "inherit" Hegel advances the thesis that every inheriting—which also is to say, every inheritance of an uncoercive gaze—takes place in and as language, and that a responsible appropriation of an intellectual legacy must develop a theory of reading that not only interprets the text to be inherited but also *at the same time questions its proper assumptions and unspoken presuppositions*. It therefore always (and thus, by extension, already in a Hegelian sense) must be a theory of the proper and the other—and thus a theory of the proper as the other and the other as the proper—just as much as it must make an attempt to delineate sharply the relation between the proper and the other, the one who inherits and that which is to be inherited, interpretation and legacy.

Before we turn to Adorno's particular inheritance of Hegel, however, we need to fasten more closely on the principal notion of inheriting Hegel in modern thinking. Here, several thoughts of Heidegger's former student Hans-Georg Gadamer provide some preliminary help. In his 1979 Stuttgart lecture, "The Heritage of Hegel," which he held upon receiving the Hegel Prize, Gadamer writes in answer to the question he poses himself, namely, how the legacy of Hegel is at work in his own thinking:

> No one should take upon himself the task of measuring all that has come down to us in the great heritage of Hegelian thought. It should be enough for each person to be the heritage oneself and to give account of what one has received from this inheritance. . . . Moreover, no one should imagine himself able to reap the harvest of an entire epoch, or indeed even merely to assess it. . . . Hegel knew better when he—ultimately to be sure in regard to himself as well—cited the following: "See, the feet of those who are going to take you away are already standing in front of the door."³

Here, Gadamer cites a passage from Hegel's *Lectures on the History of Philosophy* that itself adapts a citation from the fifth chapter of the Acts of the Apostles, which concerns, according to Hegel, the "indication of the nullity of philosophical knowledge through the history of philosophy itself."⁴ If one follows this line of thinking, it becomes clear that Hegel cannot be inherited as such, as a final authoritative instance that is simply at our disposal and that allows the tradition from which he stems and which he decisively influenced to appear as a storehouse from which one might arbitrarily draw in the service of undergirding one's prefabricated views. To the contrary, inheriting Hegel means to *give an account*—not before a court of law, but before the reading and thinking "I." To hold oneself accountable in this way also means, however, to assess one's debts to Hegel's legacy and, interpreting on the basis of this assessment, to think a relation to Hegelian language itself, without which his movements of thinking—both their disclosures and their immensities—could hardly be captured. If Gadamer cites Hegel's citation from the Acts of the Apostles, then this gesture should, especially in the context of the question of interpretative inheritance, be associated with the quasi-dialectical tenet that the feet of the heirs who stand before the door can inherit responsibly as well as irresponsibly, that they may be unable to wait to proceed with what is left behind in an already predetermined way or that they may be willing to learn to inherit by reading and thinking.

This process of inheriting and learning always bears on the simultaneous experience of the inevitability and inadequacy of linguistically mediated thinking. If, as Gadamer reminds us in his Hegel Prize speech, "Marx,

Nietzsche, and Freud" have "exposed limits to the self-certitude of thought thinking itself," then "it is not a matter of becoming Hegel's successor, but rather of interiorizing the exactions that he presents,"[5] and thereby, too, a matter of the "use that language finds in us whenever we think," a language that does not represent a mere instrument for understanding but that "pervades our whole experience of the world."[6] To inherit Hegel's legacy would demand of us, then, that we pose ever anew the question of the linguistic or textual character of this inheritance, each time from the perspective of changing points of view. "In the linguistic character of our access to the world," as Gadamer puts it,

> we find ourselves placed in the process of tradition that marks us as historical in essence. Language is not . . . a tool that we apply, but the element in which we live and that we can never so objectify that it ceases to surround us. . . . The element of language is not merely an empty medium in which one thing or another might be encountered. No, it is the quintessence of everything that can encounter us at all. . . . But since it surrounds us as what is spoken and not as a threatening field of otherness in relation to which there can only be self-affirmation, victory, or submission, language shapes the space of our freedom.[7]

What Gadamer associates with the heritage of Hegel is its irreducibly linguistic character, its mediation in and as language, which is considered here in the broadest sense as the relational nexus that both promises and postpones meaning, which not only unconceals world but *is* world. The question of whether and to what extent there can be a concept of freedom in this world, this questionable possibility and the associated notions and experiences of what can be tenable as freedom and therefore, too, as unfreedom, is what the legacy of language passes down to us.

If "Hegel's heritage will not set us free,"[8] we will not be able, for all our critique of metaphysics, to sever ourselves from the truth claims of his metaphysics—which critique would itself have to rest unconsciously on metaphysical assumptions. Instead, the claim holds true that Hegel's quasi-orphaned legacies would have to be interpreted anew, for the legacies he left behind will always appear orphaned when they are not subjected to a new rereading that radically places all that has been said in question and when they thereby threaten to perish as allegedly known matters, as dogma, as supposedly stable meaning and hermeneutic routine. Gadamer, for his part, expresses this state of affairs as follows:

> Precisely therein does it make sense to see oneself an heir of Hegel—not by thinking his anticipation of the absolute as a knowledge that we entrust to philosophy; still less by expecting philosophy to serve the demands of the

day and to legitimate any authority that pretends to know what the moment requires. It suffices to acknowledge with Hegel the dialectic of the universal and concrete as the summation of the whole of metaphysics until now, and along with this to realize that this has to be summed up ever anew.[9]

But if this is the case, then the concept of the absolute, of what has ab- or dissolved (*absolvere*) itself from all that is contingent, is not absolute in the sense that knowledge would have come to a limit or to a resolved closure. On the contrary, it could be affirmed: The absolute that the young Hegel's *Phenomenology* so systematically works to make thinkable is no telos, no end goal of static knowledge that could be reached; rather, the Hegelian absolute catalyzes in its own right the thinking inception of something wholly other, which would need to be understood and inherited, in turn. Hegel's absolute knowledge would then be one name among others for absolute inheriting.

To speak about Hegel's inheritance and the heirs of Hegel also means to read this heritage and these heirs in tension with a Hegelian utterance found in a text that was written, like the *Phenomenology*, during his time in Jena. In *The Difference between Fichte's and Schelling's System of Philosophy* (1801), Hegel attempts to delimit his yet-to-be-developed thinking of absolute idealism from the critical idealism of Kant, the subjective idealism of Fichte, and the objective idealism of Schelling in order to take the next step toward thinking beyond not only Kant's Copernican turn but also Fichte's absolute "I" and intellectual intuition, as well as Schelling's philosophy of nature, in which nature appears as solidified spirit. In the center stands the cautiously forward-thinking, slowly unfolding history of the dialectical movement of experience through which spirit can appear as absolute spirit. In the introductory section, "Various Forms Occurring in Contemporary Philosophy," Hegel writes: "Because in philosophy reason comes to know itself and deals only with itself, its whole work and activity are grounded in itself, and with respect to the inner essence of philosophy there are neither predecessors nor successors."[10] Hegel's way of seeing what is at issue here lies grounded in an understanding of thinking that, insofar as the concept of reason itself unfolds at its center, revolves first of all around itself and in so doing arrives at the knowledge that philosophical thinking names the place where reason has no business occupying itself primarily with this or that object, but rather with itself—its proper presuppositions, determinations, and limits. In this self-reflection of reason, philosophical thinking comes to itself, recognizing that it is its own proper object and that it can rigorously and dialectically go after its wishes to turn to other, external objects solely to the extent that it is prepared to turn toward itself. However greatly the so-called content of a philosophical thought process may differ—with its ever-changing objects and ever differently determined material conditions—at its kernel, thinking always revolves around a sort of critical self-dialogue of reason, which must give an account of its proper presuppositions and, as need be, its proper flaws, so that it can do justice in equal measure to that what is to be thought and to thinking itself. If, as Hegel maintains, the "whole work" of reason, as well as "its activity," lies in this self-reflection, if it always essentially remains equal to itself, regardless of all the differences among its so-called applications, and if it therefore constantly remains itself each time as another, then reason may be reckoned as the proper essence of philosophical thinking for the version of absolute idealism that is being prepared here. Under these conditions and from this particular outlook, Hegel can affirm that there are, properly speaking, neither predecessors nor successors in philosophy. As opposed to the notions of pre-decessors and successors, what is at stake here is a thinking that cedes itself in the procedure of philosophy itself. For the process of thinking constantly leads back to itself, even if it can only ever be treated in its own way, each time in its properly deviant way, as it were. Thus, it would be just as inappropriate to designate the thinking of the Pre-Socratics the predecessor to classical Greek philosophy as it would be to call historical materialism the successor of Idealism.

Now, however, the question imposes itself as to how a Hegelian system of knowledge, which has ultimately contributed more to the modern historical sense and to the idea of historical argumentation than any other attempt at thinking them, interprets the historical association between philosophical notions and postulates. If, on the basis of reason's abiding self-reflection—which itself pervades Western philosophical thinking—there are no philosophical predecessors and successors, as Hegel apodictically affirms, the following problem nevertheless remains to be confronted: the extent to which thinkers, especially when they expressly refer to one another in their writings, enter into a particular relation to one another that cannot be reduced to the biographical-historical model of influence, or that of preceding and succeeding. Even in bracketing succession, there is no way around the irreducible question of a legacy, of an inheritance, without which a thinking existence would hardly be imaginable.

From the points of view that occupy us here, it is therefore particularly provocative to bring back into focus the inheriting "successor" of a philosophical "predecessor" who maintains that there can be no predecessors and successors. For Adorno, the particular and heretical "heir" of Hegel around whom the following reflections will revolve in an exemplary fashion, attempts—partially successfully, partially in vain—to take on the orphaned legacy of this predecessor. And he seeks to do so in an idiomatic way, without becoming a mere follower or pursuing his proper course of thinking under the overarching concept of an after-phenomenon.

In surveying the ways that Adorno proceeds in order to appropriate the heritage of Hegel, the most direct way is, as is so often the case in thinking, the detour. Yet the detour to be taken here on the way to inheritance leads at first, surprisingly, to notions of the animal and animality. Of course, the pervasiveness of zoological motifs and animal names throughout Adorno's experiential world has been recognized at least since the publication of his letters to his parents, in which pet names drawn from the animal realm arise frequently enough, such as hippopotamus, giraffe, gazelle, horse, or even "horsy." Even on the postcard motifs selected by Adorno, giraffes and hippopotamuses resurface, while a group of toy giraffes sat enthroned upon his work desk during his Californian exile.[11] Decisively less foregrounded in the consciousness of his readers, however, is the fact that zoological figures and images assume strategic positions in his philosophical production as well.[12] Among the motifs of the section entitled "Improvisations" from *Quasi una fantasia: Essays on Modern Music* is a zoological garden that Adorno had visited as a child, which appears in a passage drafted in 1951. It is not only the animals that remain in Adorno's memory of this zoo but also a certain musical pavilion, in which, at times, the members of so-called exotic tribes delivered presentations. "Whether it be the memory of this," Adorno writes, "or simply the condensation of what has long been forgotten—even today, when I hear the kettledrum it brings back the memory of Tamasese, the tribal chief. And at the same time I recall that the heads of Tamasese's prisoners were used as drums, or perhaps they were the cauldrons in which the savages cooked human flesh."[13] Adorno continues: "Is the drum the successor of human sacrifice, or does it still sound the command to kill? In our music it resounds as an archaic survival. It is the legacy of violence in art, the violence which lies at the base of all art's order."[14] Wholly as if he were drawing subterranean parallels to Benjamin's testimony that there is no document of culture that is not, at the same time, a document of barbarism, wholly as if he wanted to conjure associations, at the same time, with the connection Freud draws between foregone forms of civilization and the psychic apparatus of modern neurotics, and wholly as if he intended one more time—this time in an autobiographically mediated way—to integrate the leading motif of the *Dialectic of Enlightenment* that he had composed a few years earlier with Max Horkheimer into a more seemingly literary thought-image—the motif, namely of the imbrication of rational-progressive demystification and unwanted regress—Adorno here lends the problematic of inheritance a strategic expression. The particular inheritance that turns out to be pivotal here is the secret survival of inhuman domination in the guise of purported human freedom, the retreat of violence into the spiritualized realm of an art that nonetheless continues to exercise that very violence just below the threshold of consciousness. Over and above the particular spiritualizing and aestheticizing operations of art, however, Adorno's language raises the *foundational* thematics of inheritance. And for both the particular inheritance of violence in art and the universal problem of inheritance as such, it would hold true that a responsible relation to them "keeps the consciousness of terror awake, the consciousness of all that can never be made good towards that which can no longer be made good."[15]

If the gateways to the zoological garden that is represented here open onto Adorno's entire writerly production, then the many-layered work of this thinker can be taken up as a series of attempts to give an account of his inheritance of the diverse representational and experiential worlds that preceded him at the conceptual, methodological, and political level. To this absolutely unrelenting engagement with the inheritance that conditions Adorno's uncoercive gaze—a legacy that was constantly to be transgressed and undermined anew—belong, among others: the inheritance of the Enlightenment, German Idealism, historical materialism, modern art and aesthetics, psychoanalysis, the experience of anti-Semitism, the history of German music, the second Vienna School surrounding Schönberg, modern literature from Kafka to Beckett and Celan, the dialectic of culture and barbarism, as well as—fundamentally—life "after Auschwitz." Readers of Adorno's texts inevitably become witnesses to an ever-renewed attempt to do justice to an inheritance in all its complexity, even when this means radically placing it in question or even breaking with it. For Adorno, thinking means, precisely, to inherit. And learning to philosophize means learning to inherit, for the particular mode of inheriting that each new object renders incumbent upon conceptual and experiential thinking cannot be prescribed once and for all, as if it were an instance for the application of Cartesian method; rather, it requires that it be, with each new act of inheriting, questioned, and interpreted anew, in a word, that it be invented (and thus found and found out, *er-funden*).

When Adorno's texts address the concept of inheritance explicitly, however, it is often associated with that which is not thought through, with the retrograde, the irritating, and even, at times, with the fascistic. In the most diverse contexts, he will write of inheritance as a "pre-critical substratum" or evoke the failed inheritance of Husserl, an inheritance of violence, the inheritance of a "planless monadological condition," a problematic occidental inheritance of positivism, a false inheritance of tonality, the inheritance of unfreedom, the inheritance of totality as the legacy of ideology, the inheritance of fascist ideology, or an "inheritance of barbarically primitive tribal conceptions,"[16] to name only a few examples. To put it more pointedly, a hard suspicion often arises for Adorno that inheritance is a particularly precarious way of thinking and relating: "in one Wild West show, for instance, a character says: when a large inheritance is at stake, villainy is not far behind."[17] Yet Adorno is thoroughly aware of the serious and constantly ambiguous demands of inheriting, as when he speaks of Alban Berg as an admired musician who "until the very end drew upon that inheritance and at the same time carried its burden, one that bowed his tall frame."[18] Precisely in the realm of aesthetics, the question of inheritance and inheriting poses itself for Adorno, for it is art, and especially music, that takes up a certain unanticipatable stance towards the scene of inheriting, which is conditioned by new possibilities and unspoken premises each time it presents itself. Accordingly, in a passage from the introduction to the *Philosophy of New Music* he solicits consideration for the way "the general social tendency—which has scorched from man's consciousness and unconsciousness the humanity that once underlay the now-available musical resources—today only tolerates the arbitrary reiteration of the idea of humanity in the vacuous ceremonial of the concert hall, while the philosophical legacy of great music has devolved exclusively upon what scorns that heritage."[19] What is to be considered is the question of what an inheritance takes up and scorns, what it constantly seeks to hold at bay, and what nonetheless remains inscribed in it as a haunting, orphaned legacy.[20]

Before the background of this general framework of inheritance, it is appropriate to recall that the irreducible question of how, precisely, Hegel's thinking is to be inherited pervades the entire work of Adorno, second to none.[21] The most elucidating recent literature on the relation of Adorno and Hegel reminds us that Adorno, even should one wish to call him a downright unorthodox Hegelian, practices a form of thinking that represents a Hegelianism *after* Hegel, a survival mode of dialectical thinking that thematizes the form which Hegelian concepts and representations assume when they are thought further, not only with Hegel, but also in the historical, epistemo-critical, and political successors that follow in his wake. And that always also means thinking through those concepts and representations after the disappointed revolutionary hopes of the Young Hegelians such as Marx, after the conceptual-critical interventions of Nietzsche, and, above all, after the Shoah.[22] Over and beyond this, however, the question of Hegel's inheritance always also requires consideration of the particular historical embeddedness of Hegelian thought. As Bloch remarks in his Jena speech, "Debate over Hegel," "Only a genuine comrade of his time is there, too, for the time to come,"[23] so that solely the radical respect of a work for its particular contemporaneity could allow it to live on in the context of a wholly other contemporaneity. But when Adorno himself reflects upon his inheriting relation to Hegel, he is most concerned neither with retracing the determinate influences of Hegelian thinking upon his own polymorphous traces of thought, nor with gliding off into an all-too-pedantic account of himself with respect to the powerful foundational assumptions of the concepts Hegel shaped, such as system, spirit, or dialectic. To the contrary, in the spirit of the nonidentical thought-figures that Adorno draws in his negative dialectics, what stands in the foreground is how Hegel in particular is to be inherited, and how to inherit at an intellectual-creative level *per se*.[24]

In his *Three Studies* on Hegel from 1963, three essays orbit around Hegel, "Aspects," "Experiential Content," and "Skoteinos, or How to Read," forming a constellation in which Adorno charts the foundational difficulties that are inseparably intertwined with his purpose to inherit Hegel in a way that is neither imitatively proximating nor overbearingly distancing, neither mimetically repetitive nor chronically historicizing in terms of a history of ideas. For Adorno, this "arrogance echoes in the loathsome question of what in Kant, and now Hegel as well, has any meaning for the present—and already the so-called Hegel renaissance began half a century ago with a book by Benedetto Croce that undertook to distinguish between what was living and what was dead in Hegel."[25] Thought should rather move, as it were, in the "opposite" direction: "The converse question is not even raised: what the present means in the face of Hegel; whether perhaps the reason one imagines one has attained since Hegel's absolute reason has not in fact long since regressed behind the latter and accommodated to what merely exists, when Hegelian reason tried to set existence in motion through the reason that obtains even in what exists."[26] If, in the realm of thinking opened by Hegel's orphaned legacy, it is in no way a question of the extent to which it stands up against the supposedly more advanced thought-patterns of the day, as when a successor—donning the presumptuous judicial robe of his later birth—believes himself to be superior, and in a position to assign different grades to the different points of view he sees in Hegelian thought; if it is just as little a question of letting the proper particularity of Hegelian thinking disappear, like a grain of sand on the shore, through a logic of sweeping comparisons—then it would instead be a question of asking how our scene of inheriting would look before the gaze of Hegel, how we stand before the testator as his heirs with our questions, assumptions, and societal situations.

This strategic inversion of sightlines, however, can in no way turn into a simple appreciation on the basis of a more or less covert belief in authority, which would amount to confirming what is already established in any case, or bustling to conserve a precious spiritual-cultural heritage. To the contrary, all "appreciations are subject to the judgment passed in Hegel's preface to the *Phenomenology of Spirit* on those are above something only because they are not in it. Appreciations fail from the start to capture the seriousness and cogency of Hegel's philosophy by practicing on him what he called, with appropriate disdain, a philosophy of perspectives."[27] From these circumstances it follows, in Adorno's sense, that Hegel's inheritance always demands a sort of surrender: "If one does not want to miss Hegel with one's very first words, one must confront, however inadequately, the claim his philosophy makes to truth, rather than merely discussing his philosophy from above, and thereby from below."[28] And it is no accident that Adorno draws on the imagery of language here ("with the first word"), and therefore on a rhetoric of language on language. For in Adorno's sense, coming to terms with the Hegelian heritage is not merely conceptual labor but also always a radically linguistic work, which means that Hegel's inheritance can be responsibly approached only when it is also constantly thought in and as language. Hegel's inheritance appears questionable and worthy of question (*frag-würdig*)—in other words, as a linguistic phenomenon. This way of thinking inheritance adheres to one of Adorno's observations from his *Philosophical Terminology*: "Essential to philosophy is its language, philosophical problems are largely problems of its language, and the disengagement of language from concerns that one finds in the so-called sciences, is not valid in the same way for philosophy."[29]

What is particular to Adorno's way of linguistically and conceptually inheriting Hegel's thinking is, as we will see in the following, the notion that the first question to be considered on the scene of inheriting is that of the manifold factors involved in determining the *relation* to an object. For only in clarifying a relation to things and concepts—the primary preoccupation of the uncoercive gaze itself—is it possible to determine more closely the relation that a subsequent instance of thinking is at all in the position to assume toward one that came before it.[30] This question does not revolve around the models of "influence" that so often appear foregrounded in procedures of philosophical, literary, and art-historical derivation. Rather, it turns upon the possibility of an unsaturated, hitherto undetermined, and perpetually displaced relational nexus. One possible name for this reflection upon the relation to an object (and that of objects to one another) is the *constellation*, which Adorno was partially spurred to adopt, as is well-known, by Benjamin's book on the *Origin of the German Mourning Play*.[31] On the one hand, the concept of the constellation is to be thought fundamentally as a *spatial* category, arising as it does with the study of astronomical phenomenology, which aims to track the positioning of heavenly bodies relative to one another and the corresponding system of relations on the part of the observer. On the other hand, it is nevertheless at the same time to be thought as standing in time; the constellation designates a spatial phenomenon that cannot be conceived apart from its temporality. The particular German concept of "space-time" (*Zeitraum*) gives testimony to this entanglement. Inheritance, for its part, can similarly be grasped as a thoroughly temporal phenomenon, even if it cannot be limited to thinking in terms of sheer seriality or succession—whereby Adorno's model of the constellation decisively contributes to the elucidation of this concept.[32]

If the constellation describes the possibilities and the interpretive reading of a space-time and if it is therefore, at the same time, spatially and temporally determined, it renders precisely the thought-figure that Adorno wishes to place in the service of a radical inheritance of Hegel, one that strategically reads Hegel "against the grain."[33] The constellation presents, after all, both movement and standstill, a resistant conjunction, which is in the position to set the inheritance of Hegelian texts into a particular dimension of self-reflection. "To make an anachronistic comparison," Adorno remarks, "Hegel's publications are more like films of thought than texts. The untutored eye can never capture the details of a film in the way it can those of a still image, and so it is with Hegel's writings."[34] It is therefore incumbent upon the reading heir of Hegel to receive this film both in its full length and developmental dynamics and, at the same time, to interrupt it, to cut in when it comes to a certain word or image, and, by means of the constellation, to inscribe it into what Benjamin would call a dialectic at a standstill. The constellation—which at the same time proceeds and interrupts, stands within time and pauses in its temporality—designates for Adorno the most commensurate form for circumspectly approaching an inheritance in general as well as the particular inheritance of Hegel, via the categories of the ever-displaced referential relations among its singular elements.

In this sense, *Negative Dialectics* brings the thinking of the nonidentical and the form of the constellation into close conjunction. Admittedly, no philosophical thinking, not even the one practiced by Adorno, can presume to be in a position to absolve itself from the conceptual. For precisely the insight that Hegel formulated in the preface to the *Phenomenology of*

Spirit—"true thoughts and scholarly insights" are "only to be won in the labor of the concept"[35]—binds as much as ever the forms of self-conscious reason to the universality of a thinking that labors away at the concept. In order to set his understanding of the conceptual dialectic apart from that of Hegel, however, Adorno explains in *Negative Dialectics*, which was written shortly after the *Three Studies of Hegel*:

> The unifying moment survives without a negation of negation, but also without delivering itself to abstraction as a supreme principle. It survives because there is no step-by-step progression from the concepts to a more general over-arching concept. Instead, the concepts enter into a constellation. The constellation illuminates the specificity of the object, the aspect that is indifferent or burdensome to a classifying procedure. The model for this is the way language relates. Language offers no mere system of signs for cognitive functions. Where it enters the scene essentially as a language, where it becomes presentation, it will not define its concepts. It lends objectivity to them by the relation into which it places the concepts, centered about a concern. Language thus serves the intention of the concept to express completely what it means. Constellations alone represent from without what the concept has cut away within: the "more" which the concept wants so much to be as it cannot be. By gathering around the object of cognition, the concepts potentially determine the object's interior and reach, in thinking, what was necessarily excised from thinking.[36]

Like Hegel, in looking to what is to be thought and rendered experienceable—and in looking precisely to the problem of double negation—Adorno is convinced of the need to labor on and in the concept.[37] However, inheriting the Hegelian model would, for him, have to take shape in such a way that the concepts relate differently to themselves and to the concerns they are mobilized to address. Whereas in his labor on the concept, Hegel steps out through it in order to step it up to a new, higher or more universal conceptual level (and thus to let the singular concepts ultimately vanish as purely preliminary stages—that is, to *sublate* [*aufheben*] them in the manifold sense of "lifting up" and "canceling out"), Adorno's efforts do not revolve around aiming to sublate concepts in a way that would leave them behind and delegate them to the status of mere predecessors or preliminary stages. Instead, they orbit around the relation of concepts to the concept of the conceptual itself and translate it into newly thinkable forms. Only through the experimental clustering of singular concepts in relation to one another and to the object is the particularity of the object respected as such, rather than serving merely as indifferent material to be consumed along the way to another: to the next overarching concept, to knowledge *per se*, to absolute spirit itself. The conceptual fixed stars of the constellation enter into a sort of elective affinity with one another, an affinity that is in the position to illuminate the singular and irreducibly idiomatic aspects of the matter of concern and its related circumstances. The relation of concepts to one another as the well as their relation—both individually and as a constellation—to the object around which they cluster is thus to be conceived as a thoroughly open one that must always be thought through anew, and that is therefore principally inconclusive. The ever-shifting relations that make the constellation thinkable in the first place are inalienably bound up with a reading that is always about to begin anew, and thus with the demands and exactions of a permanently shifting interpretation whose adeptness has, at every point, to prove itself yet one more time, and thus to prove itself true.

Yet what the constellated, variable clusters of concepts surrounding a concern cannot circumvent is the mediated conjunction of language and object that first establishes meaning. At this point, the false impression could arise that Adorno's uncoercive gaze means to develop a conceptual model that, on the one hand, refuses the hermeneutically oriented negation of negation—from which Hegel derives the positive positing of a further, sense-laden set of circumstances—but that he nonetheless wishes to introduce through the back door a similarly disposed thought-figure, in that he suppresses the irreducible difference among sign, signifier, and signified as they are charted in, for example, Saussure's foundational studies on the structure of language. But the opposite is the case. In Adorno's model of the constellation, language is always also the name for that precarious realm where, besides the meaning that is supposedly imparted within a commonly shared system of signs, the acute danger remains to be considered at the same time that meaning may dissolve and what was intended may disintegrate utterly. Already in the early "Theses on the Language of the Philosopher," Adorno therefore writes: "Objects, however, are not at all adequately given through language, but rather adhere to language and stand in historical unity with it."[38] Language stands in "historical" unity with objects because a thinking mode of speaking that is not itself dependent on the conditioned character and unreliability of language is an illusion. Thinking (and therefore, too, the thinking of inheritance) thus never comports itself neutrally with respect to its linguistic composition. Here, the moment of the nonidentical, upon which so much pivots, especially for the late Adorno, finds its authentic deposition in language. Language here is not to be thought as an expression of the identity between signs and things, but rather as the engagement with the ever nonidentical, incommensurate, treacherous character of irreducibly linguistic structures *per se.* Differing from the position represented by Hegel that the identical and the nonidentical are ultimately inscribed in the identical, the identical and the nonidentical remain, in Adorno, nonidentical.[39]

If Adorno's thought revolves around the thinking of constellations—a concept that he often and with good reason evokes in the plural—in order to raise to consciousness what refuses the concept (or "what the concept has cut away within"), then this thinking of an excess, of a "more" through which the concept wants to come to what it cannot be itself, embodies an ongoing commentary on what thinking as such cuts off as incommensurate with itself, on what thinking "excises," as Adorno affirms in a consciously drastic vocabulary. Using a different formulation, one could say that the discourse of constellations in Adorno allows the element that resists the concept from within the concept to come into its own right, in that the constellation makes it possible to think language as a relation of language to itself and to consider concepts as a clustering relation to an object.

Consequently, the constellation would also have to be understood as a sort of labor on what lacks concept within the concept, and thus as Adorno's proper labor on the heritage of idealism. In his circumspect essay on Adorno's understanding of conceptual lack, Mirko Wischke rightly reminds us of this conceptual-theoretical heritage: "Proceeding from the assumption that every cognition is a 'cognition through concepts,' Kant, as is well known, made the experience that concepts never refer immediately to an object; no 'images' of objects lay the foundation for concepts; thinking is nothing other than cognition through concepts: the pure concepts of understanding deliver 'no cognition of things.'" He continues:

> Hegel agrees with Kant not only in thinking that concepts constitute their own reality; in the *Phenomenology of Spirit* he radicalizes this insight with the assumption that immediate being cannot be brought to linguistic expression. On the basis of this irreducible limit of language, it is ultimately "impossible ever to say a sensual being that we mean," since the concept exists in something other than sensual reality.[40]

In short, he holds that "Kant's view that concepts, in ordering different views into a universal representation, are knowledge of things through universal representations, shapes the theoretical foundation for Hegel's testimony that what we say of sensual being is different from sensual reality."[41] And this differentiation, as we can now affirm, was made experienceable for Adorno in the thought-figure of the constellation. There, it is to be brought to consciousness, which was always already determined by this very differentiation in a more or less unspoken, even spectral way. If, when it comes to the differentiation of concept, language, and object, Adorno feels himself to be the heir, too, of Hegel's reading of Kant, he also extends this heritage decisively when he inserts it into a constellation relating the questions of conceptuality and the possibility of linguistic presentation to their concrete objects.

By employing the figure of the constellation in order to engage himself with inheriting Hegel inheriting Kant, Adorno at the same time implicitly relates his thinking to Nietzsche's critique of concepts. At the center of Nietzsche's critique stands the instance of violence that is inscribed in every conceptual operation. In the early theoretical text on language, "On Truth and Lie in the Extra-Moral Sense," he writes:

> Let us think in particular of the formation of concepts. Every word becomes a concept as soon as it is supposed to serve not merely as a reminder of the unique, absolutely individualized original experience, to which it owes its origin, but at the same time to fit countless, more or less similar cases, which, strictly speaking, are never identical, and hence absolutely dissimilar. Every concept originates by the equation of the dissimilar. Just as no leaf is ever exactly the same as any other, certainly the concept "leaf" is formed by arbitrarily dropping those individual differences, by forgetting the distinguishing factors, and this gives rise to the idea that besides leaves there is in nature such a thing as the "leaf," i.e. an original form according to which all leaves are supposedly woven, sketched, circled off, colored, curled, painted, but by awkward hands, so that not a single specimen turns out correctly and reliably as a true copy of the original form.... Overlooking the individual and the real gives us the concept, just as it also gives us the form, whereas nature knows no forms and concepts, hence also no species, but only an *x* that is inaccessible and indefinable for us. For even our distinction between individual and species is anthropomorphic and does not stem from the essence of things although we also do not dare to say that it does *not* correspond to it. For that would be a dogmatic assertion, and as such as just as unprovable as its opposite.[42]

There is no concept without the equation of what is, in itself, dissimilar and unequal, no concept that does not, on the way to the next, more general overarching concept, threaten to veil or even to extinguish the singularity and dignity of what it subsumes. To be sure, it is one of the classical tasks of philosophical thinking to seek the more encompassing generality of the conceptual order behind or above the manifestations of the particular and concrete. But in so doing, it pays a high price: insight into the individual, and thus the real. The concept therefore works in both an illusory and a dis-illusioning way, betraying a costly trade-off—it brings to light the universal aspect of the particular, contingent, and accidental, and it proves insight into the sheer illusory nature or immediacy of the particular, but it also falls short of its proper claim to knowledge on the basis of its self-delusion, which traces back to the way that the concept fails to relate to the differentiality of what it is brought to bear upon and grasp. The thinking of the constellation that Adorno promotes, however, sets out to account for the particular and unprovable aspects of the individual in such a way that does not occlude the conceptual completely (for otherwise it would not be accessible to philosophical or theoretical thinking at all), but that, at the same time, sets the particular object of thought in a position to gather about itself, in clustering formations, those possible concepts that are drawn to grasp it. These concepts, in turn, are determined by neither dogmatic principles nor arbitrary will, but are shaped by the primacy of openness and inconclusiveness. They thereby thematize ever and again the relation into which they enter with one another and with the particular object. In this way, concepts enter into a potentially "free" relation to their objects and to the task of thinking itself. And in the domain of free relations—for which the constellation has stepped in as an advocate and as the condition of its possibility—the objects have, for their part, begun their arrangements to extricate themselves from the patronizing hold of the concept that structurally equalizes the dissimilar, and to wrest themselves from the iron grip that would subordinate the particular to a superior order.

Which foundational questions does the inheriting reading of the *Phenomenology of Spirit*—in many respects Hegel's most consequential text, which, for its part, inherits German Idealism in order, at the same time, to end it—have to pose? Adorno is well aware that the *Phenomenology* is dedicated to the presentation of the appearance of knowing, as it sets itself apart from the critical idealism of Kant, the subjective idealism of Fichte, and the objective idealism of Schelling, in order to develop the notion of an absolute idealism. The slowly progressing self-transformation of spirit into absolute spirit is the theme of Hegel's movement of thought, which pursues the question of how spirit becomes what it is. The subject, in its proper, irreducible temporality, forms itself through experience and action by opening in a dialectically mediated way to the other, and so through the transactions of mutual recognition processes, it becomes what it is itself: a form of historically conditioned self-positing spirit.[43] Of primary interest is the experience of consciousness as self-consciousness, an experience that consciousness is in the position to make from its spiritual formation and to account for in speculative discourse. This account issues onto the absolute concept of itself. In the determinate negation—that is, in the negation which strategically enters into the particular aspects of what it negates, and through the negation of negation formulates the movement of the dialectic itself—spirit becomes conscious of itself through its progressive motion, and thereby comes to itself.[44] This cleaving apart of the concept and its experience becomes, in turn, itself a theme for spirit and advances to become the central problem of philosophical thinking *per se*.[45]

Through this cleaving of concept and experience, Hegel also introduces an alternative notion of philosophical doubt, which demarcates itself from the doubting-thinking *cogito* of Cartesianism. The concept of knowing that is at stake for Hegel "can therefore be viewed as the way of doubt," as the *Phenomenology* avers, "or more properly as the way of despair; for what takes place along the way, is not what tends to be understood as doubt, namely a shaking of this or that supposed truth," but rather "the conscious insight into the untruth of what appears to be knowing, where what seems to be most real is, in truth, the unrealized concept."[46] The truth-content of any concept of knowing, which can always manifest itself as doubt and despair in the experience of a thinking, developing consciousness, is only to be had in such a way that the concept takes up an unobvious interpretation of the phenomenon as its yet outstanding conceptual consolidation. For the concrete realization of the concept still stands to be carried out; it remains to be achieved through the labor of thinking and experience.

The attempt to inherit Hegel's texts therefore has to orient itself toward a perspective that both recognizes what is thought in them as truth-content solidified in historical form, and that thematizes their contemporary legacies with each subsequent reading. "Even ideas that were at one time firmly established," as Adorno argues, "have a history of their truth and not a mere afterlife; they do not remain inherently indifferent to what befalls them. At the present time Hegelian philosophy, and all dialectical thought, is subject to the paradox that it has been rendered outdated by science and scholarship while being at the same time more timely than ever in its opposition to them."[47] For, Adorno remarks further, "if one wishes to avoid halfheartedly preserving . . . while at the same time watering down his [Hegel's] philosophy, then one has no choice but to set the very moments in him that cause consternation into relation to the experiences his philosophy incorporates, even if those experiences are encoded within it and their truth is concealed."[48] It is no accident that Adorno employs the expression *"set into relation"* here. For the legacy of Hegelian philosophy, understood dialectically, relates to the commentary of any given present that would inherit it in a way that is at the same time outdated and most timely, and thus enters into a constellative relation, showing itself as an element of the very constellation that construes it. Hegel's heritage first posits itself in the process of inheriting.

This Hegelian self-positing of the constellative cannot, however, prescribe the orientation of each respective constellation or presuppose it as though it were simply a given. The warning therefore needs to be taken into account that a constellation and the mode of thinking from which it stems refuse to be recognized and evaluated from a point of view shaped by personal convictions. For this reason, Adorno emphasizes:

> According to Hegel's distinction between abstract and real possibility, only something that has become real is actually possible. This kind of philosophy sides with the big guns. It adopts the judgment of a reality that always destroys what could be different. Even here, however, one should not judge Hegel solely on the basis of one's convictions. Persistent involvement with Hegel teaches one—and this is probably true of every great philosophy—that one cannot select what suits oneself from his philosophy and reject what one finds consternating. It is this somber necessity and not an ideal of completeness that engenders the seriousness and substantiality of Hegel's systematic claims. The truth of those claims lies in the *skandalon*, not in its plausibility. Hence rescuing Hegel—and only rescue, not renewal, is appropriate for him—means placing oneself before his philosophy where it is most painful and wresting truth from it where its untruth is obvious.[49]

The *that* and not the *what* would therefore stand first of all in the center of the Hegelian heritage. The fact that thinking presents itself in *this* way is already in itself the provocation, the truth to be rescued. To rescue Hegel by inheriting him—and thus to rescue Hegel's legacy—does not demand that we explain away what seems questionable but that we confirm the interruption, the caesura with which we must engage before all pretensions to understanding any of its content.

Insofar as Adorno approaches the Hegelian inheritance by way of the constellation, he is no doubt aware of a major difficulty within the *Phenomenology*, namely, that many of its individual parts do not seem connected in a compulsory-logical way, while its architectonics does not always follow the systematic construction principles that the concept developed in the text of a compulsorily developing system seems outright to demand. In the scholarship on Hegel, this problematic of a textual structure that cannot be wholly reconstructed is often pointed out—a problem that cannot be explained away by pointing to the haste with which the last part of the *Phenomenology* was written or by regarding the text as a work of youth.[50] However, Adorno's work toward a constellative interpretation of the structure of the *Phenomenology* could be taken up as a particular form of rescue ("and only rescue . . . is appropriate for him"). For the figure of the constellation allows the implicit structures of relation among the individual textual elements to be brought to light in the belatedness of an interpreting inheritance without proceeding arbitrarily or brushing over the real breaches and vertiginous caesurae in Hegel's text.

But to what extent, we may now ask, does Hegel's thinking, both as it unfolds in the *Phenomenology* and in the texts that follow it, demand a particular hermeneutic commitment when it comes to the inheritance of this thinking and its postulates? This question poses itself all the more urgently if what scholars so often maintain is true, as when Robert B. Pippin writes, "Hegel's *Phenomenology of Spirit* is a book that had no predecessors and that, with the possible exception of works such as Nietzsche's *Genealogy of Morals*, Proust's *Remembrance of Things Past*, Lukács's *History and Class-Consciousness* or Pound's *Cantos* (and perhaps Wittgenstein's *Investigations*), no true successors."[51] Adorno presents the difficulty of an interpreting mode of inheriting by showing how the Hegelian system of thought relates to its possible interpretation and thereby enters into a *relation* with this interpreting approach:

> Like other closed systems of thought, Hegel's philosophy avails itself of the dubious advantage of not having to allow any criticism whatsoever. All criticism of the details, according to Hegel, remains partial and misses the whole, which in any case takes this criticism into account. Conversely, criticizing the whole as a whole is abstract, "unmediated," and ignores the fundamental motif of Hegelian philosophy: that it cannot be distilled into any "maxim" or general principle and proves its worth only as a totality, in the concrete interconnections of all its moments. Accordingly, the only way to honor Hegel is to refuse to allow oneself to be intimidated by the virtually mythological complexity of his critical method, which makes criticism seem false no matter what, and instead of graciously or ungraciously listing or denying his merits, got after the whole, which is what Hegel himself was after.[52]

The thinking that a productive inheritance of Hegel would have to enter into, even if it were oriented toward its critique or toward placing it in question, cannot limit itself to an act of censorship that praises certain elements of Hegelian thought while criticizing others. Inheriting Hegel means neither speaking for its putative indisputability, which would permit only an immanent self-comparison among the contents of Hegel's texts, nor does it mean performing an instrumental division of the useful from the useless. Any procedure oriented according to such maxims would give the "honors" neither to Hegel nor to his inheriting commentator. This is the case not only because, in Hegelian philosophy "[e]ven the marks of its miscarriage were struck by truth itself"⁵³—which means that, in the dialectical sense, its failings can also always be read as a success, as a successfully carried-off failure—but also because Hegel's entire movement of thought demands a commensurate form of inheriting, which Adorno would see to anchoring primarily in constellative thinking.

The more an inheriting reading is committed to the logic of the constellation and enters into the foundational question of its interpretation and engagement with the linguistically mediated concept, the less it can limit itself to the interpretation of individual moments, even if it must, at the same time, forgo "the lecherous urge for the 'grand total' (Benjamin)."⁵⁴ Thus, Adorno emphasizes that his inheriting mode of reading "does not claim to accomplish of itself the illumination of Hegel's main works, something that is long-outstanding. It merely formulates considerations of principle bearing on this task; at best it hazards guesses about how one would arrive at an understanding, without dispensing anyone from the efforts involved in concretizing those considerations with regard to the texts."⁵⁵ After and according to Adorno, reading to inherit Hegel means to enter into fundamental reflections on the scene of inheritance, where something wishes to be given over and understood, and therefore provides covert hints as to how it might be read—thus inventing its ideal reader—while placing in question the conditions of possibility for a correct interpretation of those hints. "The issue is not to make the reading of Hegel easier," Adorno thus confirms, "but to prevent the extraordinary exertions that Hegel requires, now as then, from being wasted."⁵⁶

The productive movement of constellative thinking in Adorno's reading of Hegel therefore often owes itself to the unsettled meaning of the text to be inherited. For this reason, in the third part of *Three Studies on Hegel*, "Skoteinos, or, How to Read"—which refers not only to the reading of Hegel but also, at the same time, to Adorno's reading and to the inheriting reading of difficult texts *per se*—Adorno remarks: "In the realm of great philosophy Hegel is no doubt the only one with whom at times one literally does not know and cannot conclusively decide what is being talked about, and with whom there is no guarantee that such a decision is even possible."⁵⁷ The condition of possibility for a responsible inheritance cannot be found in the supposedly stable meaning of a text—as if what remained to be understood were already understood and appropriated—but is indebted to a certain deferral of meaning. Reading does not relate to the Hegelian text as though an already existing meaning that happens to be misrepresented by external circumstances (such as its presentation) were to be recovered through corresponding efforts. Rather, the condition for a radically interpretive inheritance rests upon the irreducible possibility of its impossibility, upon an undecidability that does not persist because one does not know how to decide among already existing interpretive possibilities, but because the Hegelian text *fundamentally* places the notion of such a decision in question. What could otherwise appear as a sheer risk or lack is, in reality, the precondition for a concentrated interpretive inheriting, which must proceed all the more rigorously precisely because it can, at no point in time, be sure of its immediate possibility or even take itself for granted.

It is not the case that the individual moments of the constellation open themselves to interpretation while, for the interpreting heir, their constellated collective shape remains in the dark. To the contrary, only an engagement with the constellation as it escapes immediate hermeneutic grasp makes clear what was always already covertly the case with regard to its individual moments: namely, that they, too, are in motion and in no case yield themselves lightly to the prying of interpretive disclosure. For Adorno, this element of inheriting Hegel's texts stands in an exemplary fashion for philosophical-speculative thinking as such. He therefore states:

> The specificity of philosophy as a configuration of moments is qualitatively different from a lack of ambiguity in every particular moment, even within the configuration, because the configuration itself is more, and other, than the quintessence of its moments. Constellation is not system. Everything does not become resolved, everything does not come out even; rather, one moment sheds light on the other, and the figures that the individual moments form together are specific signs and a legible script. This is not yet articulated in Hegel, whose mode of presentation is characterized by a sovereignly indifferent attitude toward language: at any rate it has not penetrated into the chemism of his own linguistic form.[58]

The linguistic appropriation of the inheritance left behind in his texts would therefore have to depart from a concept of the constellation in which the individual moments present themselves as *already* highly constellated *in themselves*. And it would have to open to a language, a script, and a presentational style in which the linguistic character of the constellative is thematized as (its) linguistic character *per se*. This critical gesture and point of departure would also mean, however, parting ways with the texts of Hegel in order to go over and beyond them, as their most radical insights light upon the situation of each proper attempt at inheriting and interpreting. To remain true to Hegel's inheritance would likewise mean, however, to break with it strategically, to confront it with itself, in order to place thinking in the position to be thought with, against, and through itself. If the constellation is not and could never be a system—not even a Hegelian one—then it may also, in this truly treasonous self-thematization, allow a late revival of an Early Romantic gesture to shine through Adorno's prose as well, one which Friedrich Schlegel's dictum expresses: "It is equally fatal for the mind to have a system and not have a system. One will simply have to decide to combine the two."[59]

Just as the singular conceptual elements of a constellation do not stand still once and for all, but are always disposed to reconsideration according to their varying preponderance, so too does the relation of the moments of thought in Hegel still remain hovering, "interpretable" solely "in light of knowledge of the general train of Hegel's thought, and especially the conceptual structure" that properly belongs to every single Hegelian text.[60] Yet this very moment of hovering, which installs the concepts that in each passage emerge to enter into a constellation, calls for emphatic recognition in the act of an interpretive inheriting: "One cannot simply gloss over those passages in which it remains up in the air what is being dealt with; their structure must be inferred from the substance of Hegel's philosophy. Its hovering character is in accordance with the doctrine that the truth cannot be grasped in any individual thesis or any delimited positive statement. Hegel's form is commensurate with this intention."[61] One could say that Adorno relates the hovering character that forms Hegel's writing and thinking syntactically to the truth-content of the constellative cluster, where likewise no single concept, no single grasp on the object, may be incorporated with an absolute claim to validity. Rather, the constellation names the site where the true—if the latter allows itself to be fleetingly glimpsed at all—comes to light as a nontotalizing conjunction of singularities, which in turn remain "up in the air," and which, in this hovering condition, test each time their freedom relative to one another and to their object.

Adorno, with Hegel, sets himself apart from the geometrically and mathematically oriented ideal of clarity, which has determined the discourse of metaphysical thinking since Descartes and which proceeds without regard for the aporia that "the demand for clarity gets tangled up linguistically because language does not actually permit the words themselves clarity."[62] In so doing, he enters into a constellative concept of the speaking subject, which is never fully master of its language and which therefore cannot reduce language to the instrumental dimension of communication. For this reason, Adorno can appeal to a concept of the subject that departs from the notion "that the subject too is not static like a camera on a tripod; rather, the subject itself also moves, by virtue of its relationship to the object that is inherently in motion—one of the central tenets of Hegel's *Phenomenology*."⁶³ The camera image that Adorno's rhetoric employs here is no accident. For if the subject is not static like a camera on a tripod, it also is no pure recording device for capturing an independently existing world of things that capitulates and subjects itself to its primacy on the basis of certain laws. Instead, the subject makes its entrance as a constellative element inscribed in the scene of recording, and itself adapts according to its proper presentational techniques and its objects, in that it constantly adopts a new standpoint. There is no inheriting and speaking subject without a constellation, and no constellation without an ongoing process of shifting, displacing, and reconfiguring. The subject that is at stake here cannot, therefore, "capture" in the photographic sense the inheritance that comes down to it; it can picture no image of the inheritance; it *is not in the picture*. It inherits rather, in that it removes itself and keeps its objects up in the air, without ever being able to depict them completely or to fasten them in the spell of an endlessly reproducible recording.

This elusive aspect of the constellation, which constantly installs itself anew, marks the process of the constellation as one which finds itself in the midst of becoming. In his "Remarks on Philosophical Thinking," Adorno therefore notes, as we recall from our discussion at the beginning of this book: "Truth is a constellation in the midst of becoming, not something running continuously and automatically."⁶⁴ If truth thus becomes constellation, however—and here the emphasis should be placed, throughout, on the progressively unfolding dimension of *becoming*—it now stands to reason that Hegel's *inheritance* would likewise be an evolving constellation. "The fact that," in Adorno's sense, "no philosophical thinking of quality allows of concise summary, that it does not accept the usual scientific distinction between process and result—Hegel, as is known, conceived truth as process and result in one—renders this experience palpably clear."⁶⁵ The palpable, which the inheriting consciousness grips in the concept's concrete work of making something graspable, cannot therefore separate process and result in the figure of the constellation, because the constellation takes place in and as what cannot be held fast. From the lyrical perspective of Hegel's school friend and lifelong conversation partner Hölderlin, to whom Adorno dedicates his important study of parataxis, one could say of the constellation: "yet it takes place, the true [*Es ereignet sich aber / Das Wahre*]."⁶⁶ It takes place, in other words, in the self-reflexive, self-positing gestures of those shifting relations and relays that displace it.

The legacies Hegel leaves behind, for which Adorno feels himself responsible and for which he employs the constellation, are constantly to be encountered on at least two levels. They demand to be read and interpreted, for without reading and without interpretation, they could not be disclosed and worked through. At the same time, however, the very conceptual force and productive momentum that characterize these legacies as such remain inherent in the foundational experience of *skoteinos*—that is, in the darkness and obscurity that cannot be sublated or canceled by any dialectic. It is no coincidence that Adorno forms the question of how to read and inherit Hegel through the concept of *skoteinos*. For each inheriting turn towards Hegel's legacy would have to take on anew the consternating constellation that opens between the necessity to read and to disclose what is left behind—a necessity that will not leave off—and the irreducible experiential content of *skoteinos*. In the abyssal opacity of *skoteinos*, inheriting, reading, and interpreting enter into a lucidly recalcitrant constellation in order to elicit a seminal version of the uncoercive gaze.

CHAPTER FOUR

Judging by Refraining from Judgment
Adorno's Artwork and Its Einordnung

In a passage from his 1951 essay "Cultural Criticism and Society," Adorno evokes a kind of dialectical thought that focuses on an immanent critique of its object by attending to the ideological principles that are at work within that very object. Such thinking "takes seriously the principle that it is not ideology itself which is untrue but rather its pretension to correspond to reality."[1] According to this logic, it is not simply the value-positing content of this or that ideology that deserves our critical attention—in the manner prescribed by conventional forms of *Ideologiekritik*—but rather the very relation between that content and the world in which it is first conceptualized. Any ideological operation that proceeds by way of positing a more or less narrowly defined set of correspondences forecloses in advance any inquiry regarding the contingent, and therefore—in principle— changeable relation of the ideological content to the world in which it is formed and from which it also departs. That is to say, the kind of thinking that would break open the fossilized structures of an ideological formation must first center on an investigation of the ways in which the presupposition of a stable correspondence in actuality works to displace and even dissimulate its own contingency. What kind of judgment, then, would be required to approach this set of concerns? What type of judgment would thinking have to elicit when it wishes to posit such norms or to evaluate such ideas, phenomena, and behaviors? And what is it, in

Adorno's uncoercive gaze, that locates the core of such acts of judgment in works of art and, more generally, in the realm of the aesthetic?

Given Adorno's refractory modes of argumentation and paratactical development of concepts, there is nothing self-evident about the idea that his version of critical theory as negative dialectics—to say nothing of the uncoercive gaze itself—should speak to the vexed constellation of ideology, judgment, and the aesthetic at all. His thinking of a negative dialectics remains a provocation, even a scandal, to readers who yearn for a more concrete, future-oriented propositional model of critique. Already Thomas Mann, who had enlisted Adorno for consultation regarding the musicological dimensions of his novel *Doktor Faustus*, writes to him in the course of their twelve-year-long correspondence: "If there were only ever a single positive word from you, my revered one, that would permit as much as a glimpse of the true society to be postulated! . . . What is, what would be, the right thing?"[2] Mann's general disquiet continues to echo in various forms and iterations today. For instance, the philosopher Rüdiger Bubner complains that Adorno at bottom wishes for something that, in Bubner's view, is inadmissible—namely, to aestheticize philosophy itself.[3] In a similar vein, the well-known German philosopher and media theorist Norbert Bolz, who began his career by devoting his doctoral dissertation to Adorno's aesthetics, in a recent conversation goes so far as to state in a polemical spirit: "Is Adorno part of our theory eclecticism at all anymore? I have my doubts. I am no longer able to learn anything from Adorno and Benjamin. Adorno, perhaps more than other authors, has to be seen as a historical phenomenon."[4] And when the Italian philosopher Giorgio Agamben sets out to reconstruct the messianic commitments of Adorno's older friend and erstwhile mentor Walter Benjamin by forging links to the Judeo-Christian tradition of the Pauline Epistles, he finds it expedient to cast Adorno as an Other to any messianic, liberatory, or transformative tradition.[5] Unlike the scholar of Judaism and philosophy of religion Jacob Taubes, who espies in Adorno's thinking an unwarranted aestheticization of the messianic, Agamben asserts that the "whole of Adorno's philosophy is written according to impotential meaning that the *as if* can only be taken as a warning signal at the heart of this intimate modality of his thought." In Agamben's view, "Adorno could never even conceive of restoring possibility to the fallen, unlike Paul, for whom 'power [*potenza*] is actualized in weakness' (2 Cor. 12:9). Despite appearances, negative dialectics is an absolutely nonmessianic form of thought, closer to the emotional tonality of Jean Améry than that of Benjamin."[6] According to this reading, even the subtitle of Adorno's book of thought-images, *Minima*

Moralia: Reflections from Damaged Life, merely betrays "something akin to resentment" so that, ultimately, "all gestures that could claim to lift the spell are absent."[7] On this view, any judgment as postulated by a negatively dialectical thought only would confirm its own lack of potency, emerging exclusively as an "impotential" that itself harbors no potential for intervention or dialectical reversal.

But, one might ask, would such a rush to judgment about a certain impotence or inconsequentiality of judgment not itself fall prey to the threat of the impotential? What if the forms of judgment that traverse the work of art kept alive not merely the demands of an immanent critique but also—even when they come to pass on the far side of any messianism—opened up unanticipatable possibilities of disclosure that exceed mere impotentiality? Can an artwork produce forms of judgment that extend beyond the particular experience of a singular aesthetic appearance? What does judgment—especially value-positing, ideological, or political judgment—entail when it is mediated by the idiomatic forms of an aesthetic object or event—that is, by forms without which there would be no art?

The significance of the general status of judgment in Adorno's thinking has not escaped some of his most-attentive readers. For instance, as Alexander García Düttmann suggests in his meditation on the formal question of judgment, Adorno's strictly hypotactically organized sentences, which are themselves inscribed in mostly paratactically organized paragraphs or sections, relentlessly call into question the possibility of any form of synthetic judgment, the kind of judgment that, at least since Kant, has related the act of judging to the practice of critique.[8] And Christoph Menke draws our attention to the ways in which aesthetic judgment can be understood as an act of critical judgment as well as, at the same time, a calling into question of that very judgment, especially in relation to the very "judgeability" of a phenomenon such as an aesthetic object.[9] Yet what concerns us here is something distinct. At stake is a specific case of aesthetic judgment, namely, the particular form of aesthetic judgment that, paradoxically, judges precisely by withholding judgment. This judgment without judgment is inseparable from Adorno's uncoercive gaze.

In an often-overlooked passage from the section "Enigmaticalness, Truth Content, and Metaphysics" of his unfinished and posthumously published *Aesthetic Theory*, Adorno reads the poem "Mausfallen-Sprüchlein" ("Mousetrap Rhyme") by the nineteenth-century German Biedermeier poet Eduard Mörike in a manner that is meant to show, in exemplary fashion, the ways in which the artwork judges precisely by refusing to judge. Adorno cites Mörike's poem as follows:

Mausfallen-Sprüchlein
Das Kind geht dreimal um die Falle und spricht:
Kleine Gäste, kleines Haus.
Liebe Mäusin, liebe Maus,
Stell dich nur kecklich ein,
Heut nacht bei Mondenschein!
Mach aber die Tür fein hinter Dir zu,
Hörst Du?
Dabei hüte Dein Schwänzchen!
Nach Tische singen wir
Nach Tische springen wir
Und machen ein Tänzchen:
Witt witt!
Meine alte Katze tanzt wahrscheinlich mit.[10]

[***Mousetrap Rhyme***
The child circles the mousetrap three times and chants:
Little guest, little house.
Dearest tiny or grown-up mouse
boldly pay us a visit tonight
when the moon shines bright!
But close the door back of you tight,
you hear?
And careful for your little tail!
After dinner we will sing
After dinner we will spring
And make a little dance:
Swish, swish!
My old cat will probably be dancing with.][11]

Adorno then proceeds to provide a brief and, one might say, surprisingly apodictic commentary on Mörike's poem:

> The child's taunt, "My old cat will probably be dancing with"—if it really is a taunt and not the involuntarily friendly image of child, cat, and mouse dancing, the two animals on their hind legs—once appropriated by the poem, no longer has the last word. To reduce the poem to a taunt is to ignore its social content [*Inhalt*] along with its poetic content. The poem is the nonjudgmental reflex of language on a miserable, socially conditioned ritual, and as such it transcends it by subordinating itself. The poem's gesture, which points to this ritual as if nothing else were possible, holds court over the gapless immanence of the ritual by turning the force of self-evidence into an indictment of that ritual. Art judges exclusively by abstaining from judgment.[12]

Why Mörike? If Adorno here chooses a rather unlikely poem by a rather unlikely poet to develop his politically inflected argument about art—after all, literary history considers Mörike and the German Biedermeier period hardly as revolutionary or politically transformative—he returns to him as a subtly subversive poet. Mörike also figures prominently in Adorno's earlier essay "Lyric Poetry and Society" and as an author with whom other major thinkers also have grappled, including, famously, Benjamin in his frequently used image of the "*bucklicht Männlein*," or little hunchback, from Mörike's literary world, and Heidegger in his exchange with the literary scholar Emil Staiger on Mörike's poem "Auf eine Lampe" ("Upon a Lamp").[13] Given his intense musical and musicological interests, Adorno also would have been familiar with Austrian composer Hugo Wolf's musical interpretation of the "Mausfallen-Sprüchlein" as it appears in his cycle of *Mörike-Lieder*.

To begin to comprehend Adorno's provocative claim that the work passes judgment precisely by refusing to judge, it is necessary to consider the most important sentence in this passage: "The poem is the nonjudgmental reflex of language on a miserable, socially conditioned ritual, and as such it transcends it by subordinating itself." In the original German, Adorno's sentence reads: "Urteilsloser Reflex der Sprache auf einen abscheulichen, sozial eingeübten Ritus, übersteigt es diesen, indem es ihm sich einordnet."[14] Whereas the English translation chooses "subordinates" to render "einordnet," it is important to note that subordination, which in German would be "unterordnen," is not quite what is at stake. Because *what* Adorno says can never be separated from *how* he says it, we would do well to be attuned to the difference here. A subordination or "Unterordnung" signifies a movement of subservience, relegation, and demotion, a placement under or below something else that is thereby acknowledged as superior or predominant. But "einordnen" is not "unterordnen," as the former evokes a movement not of subordination but rather of coordination, in which the language of the poem insinuates itself or installs itself into the very logic or even ideological formation from which it, as an artwork, had set out to depart. In other words, the epistemo-political gesture of the language of the poem consists neither in criticizing a status quo that is deemed to be in need of change nor in departing from that which is the case by rendering an external judgment on it, a judgment that would view the posited relation between ideological content and the world in which it occurs as problematic or even untenable. The language of Mörike's poem is not a form of *Ideologiekritik* in relation to a detestable social ritual that calls for replacement by other, purportedly more desirable social rituals or even the abolishment of the very idea of social ritual; rather, the poem transcends what it stages precisely by remaining within it. The movement of an aesthetic *Einordnen* propels thought into the very fibers of that with which it is at odds, without thereby collapsing the difference between the critical impulse of thought and its object or target.

Yet what kind of judgment can be said to be at work in this movement? Adorno speaks of an "urteilsloser Reflex der Sprache," which is not quite "nonjudgmental," as the published English translation has it, but more precisely a judgment-free or, most literally, judgment-less reflex of language. The judgmentless judgment of language points to a form of judging that turns upon itself. "Nur durch Enthaltung vom Urteil urteilt Kunst," Adorno suggests, "art judges exclusively by abstaining from judgment," in a gesture that paradoxically becomes ever more potent the more it refuses to comply with its own conventional demands—that is, the more it abstains from its own actualization. Adorno is fully aware that *Enthaltung* and its reflexive verb form, *sich enthalten*, also have a technical meaning in German legal discourse, where they are employed to designate a formal abstention from voting, a refusal to cast one's vote in the context of a decision to be made. If this logic leads us to a precinct of thought that is no longer fully governed by a more recognizably Kantian logic of judgment—and particularly by the *Urteilskraft* of a specifically aesthetic judgment—then where does art's way of judging through a certain self-recusal or abstention from judgment leave us?

It is as if this form of judgment, which proceeds not by departing from its object but rather by insinuating itself within it, had taken up and extended a Hölderlinian inflection of the concept of judgment. In his early reflection "Seyn, Urtheil, Modalität" ("Being, Judgment, Modality"), Hölderlin argues that "*judgment*, in the highest and strictest sense, is the original separation of object and subject which are most deeply united in intellectual intuition, that separation through which alone object and subject become possible, the arche-separation [Urtheil *ist im höchsten und strengsten Sinne die ursprüngliche Trennung des in der intellektuellen Anschauung innigst vereinigten Objects und Subjects, diejenige Trennung, wodurch erst Object und Subject möglich wird, die Ur-Theilung*]." And he continues: "In the concept of separation, there lies already the concept of the reciprocity of object and subject and the necessary presupposition of a whole of which object and subject form the parts [*Im Begriffe der Theilung liegt schon der Begriff der gegenseitigen Beziehung des Objects und Subjects aufeinander, und die nothwendige Vorausezung eines Ganzen wovon Object und Subject die Theile sind*]." Hölderlin concludes by writing: "'I am I' is the most fitting example for this concept of arche-separation as theoretical separation, for in the practical arche-separation it [the 'I'] opposes the non-I, not itself

[*'Ich bin Ich' ist das passendste Beispiel zu diesem Begriffe der Ur-theilung, als Theoretischer Urtheilung, denn in der praktischen Urtheilung sezt es sich dem Nichtich, nicht sich selbst entgegen*]."[15] By focusing on the primordial separation or, more precisely, partition ["*Theilung*," in Hölderlin's older spelling], at work in judgment, its *Ur-Teil*, we see that what distinguishes judgment from intellectual intuition, *Anschauung*, is the way in which judgment separates what is unified in the *Anschauung*—namely, subject and object—so that it is only in the act of judgment that the two are made visible as distinguishable entities of reflection. What is more, only after subject and object have been separated by judgment into—at least in principle—distinguishable entities of reflection can the thinking of their relation commence. The question of the ever-shifting relation between subject and object is therefore predicated upon the act of judgment itself. The proposition "Ich bin Ich" is a prime instantiation of the relation-producing effects of a primordially partitioning judgment to the extent that, in theoretical judgment, a certain nonself-identity obtains even within identity. In other words, whereas in practical judgment a self is opposed to a nonself, in the kind of primordial partitioning performed by theoretical judgment the self is opposed, among other things, to itself—it becomes visible as being traversed by an other that is, precisely, itself.

Is there, in the form of judgment that Adorno wishes to think toward—that is, the form of judgment that judges by refraining from judgment—not also something of the Hölderlinian primordial partitioning at work? If the judgment that comes to pass in the language of Mörike's poem judges by *einordnen* itself, by finding its place in the order of things that it also wishes to disrupt, then the judgment can be understood as dividing itself as a form of nonidentity. It inscribes itself into its object through its judgmentless ordering or ordinating procedure while at the same time resisting the very object into which it installs itself. That is to say, the partitioning judgment of the *Ur-teil* is both itself and its own other—an other which is also the self—in that it mobilizes a critical impulse that both leaves the object intact and departs from it, affirming it, as it were, by merging with it, while at the same time remaining fundamentally at odds with it. The tension of this double situatedness is lodged in the primordial partitioning effected by the judgmentless judgment itself and vies for recognition in the artwork.

The way in which this recognition of the effects of the judgmentless judgment in the artwork is to be conceptualized requires some clarification. It does not come to pass on any literal level of an artwork—for instance, on the semantic level of a poem. In artworks, Adorno insists, "nothing is literal, least of all their words [*am letzten ihre Worte*]."[16] On the contrary, the nonliterality of works of art requires the constant labor of rigorous interpretation and reinterpretation, not to decode and eventually arrest a final, stable meaning—after all, "their meaning appears as if it were blocked [als ob ihre Bedeutung blockiert wäre]"—but rather to engage in what Adorno calls *deutende Vernunft* or "interpretive reason."[17] Harkening back to the concept of interpretive reason that he had first developed in his 1931 Frankfurt inaugural lecture "Die Aktualität der Philosophie," Adorno mobilizes the concept here in order to emphasize the radically interpretive nature of a theoretical engagement with the aesthetic, in which meaning remains an open question mark, not a merely factual or metrical piece of information to be accessed by instrumental reason. For interpretive reason, even authorial intention, or an author's wish to refuse interpretation altogether, cannot suffice. "That great artists," Adorno writes, "the Goethe who wrote fairy tales no less than Beckett, want nothing to do with interpretations only underscores the difference of the truth content from the consciousness and the intention of the author. . . . Artworks, especially those of the highest dignity, await their interpretation."[18] Interpretation is not something that is added to reason when it engages with the aesthetic; rather, when it engages seriously with the aesthetic, reason comes to the realization that it was always already imbricated with interpretive activity—that interpretation is its constitutive, irreducible category of reflection.

In the case of the judgmentless judgment, which insinuates itself into its object as a primordial partitioning, the judgment's force, too, is inseparable from the extent to which—and the intensity with which—it engages the faculty of *deutende Vernunft*. The particular poetico-political judgment that Adorno locates in Mörike's poem does not unfold on its semantic, literal, or disclosive level. For instance, it is not to be found in the aesthetic immediacy of the constellation of dancing child, mouse, and cat. Rather, it unfolds on the level of what Adorno names a work's "truth content." For him, the "truth content of artworks is the objective solution of the enigma posed by each and every one. By demanding its solution, the enigma points to its truth content. It can only be achieved by philosophical reflection. This alone is the justification of aesthetics."[19] Adorno here takes up, without explicitly mentioning his source, Benjamin's evocation of "Wahrheitsgehalt" in the 1924 essay on Goethe's *Elective Affinities*.[20] For both Adorno and Benjamin, the truth content of an artwork does not attach to its propositional structure; it cannot be extracted, with appropriate effort and labor, as the kernel or essence of a work; nor does it reveal in any conventional sense this or that meaning of an artwork, even as it refuses to resign itself to mere meaninglessness.

But what is meant by truth content? The linguistic particularity of the German term "Wahrheitsgehalt" may provide a clue. In German there are two words that translate into English as "content," for English does not normally distinguish between the two: *der Gehalt* and *der Inhalt*.²¹ One could think of *Inhalt* as the garden-variety content of a work, its aboutness—say, the way in which the content of Balzac's *Comédie Humaine* may be understood to be the singular lifeworld of post-Napoleonic nineteenth-century France, or an Edith Wharton novel may be perceived to have as its content the social norms and cultural politics of the late-nineteenth-century and early-twentieth-century American East Coast upper class, or a Gerhard Richter painting may be viewed as being about German left-wing terrorism of the 1970s. But the kind of content signified by *Gehalt* would better be thought of as import, substance, significance, or weight. Thus, when the English translation of *Aesthetic Theory* renders "Wahrheitsgehalt" throughout as "truth content," the import of Adorno's *Gehalt* on the far side of content—of "mere" content, as it were—threatens to be effaced.²² *Wahrheitsgehalt*, as substance or import, is also what is excessive to a work of art, an uncontainable surplus that reaches beyond both itself and the work in which it sets itself into motion.

With respect to the question of judgment, then, *Gehalt* and *Inhalt* as distinct modes of content relate differently to the artwork. If *Inhalt* can render or provoke judgment, it is an overt judgment, a stated or disclosed judgment, one that comes to pass on the level of the work's manifest content. Although such judgment is not coextensive with the Kantian precept that would demand the shared or communal form of aesthetic judgment encoded in the statement "This is beautiful," it does depend on the shared apperception of a judgment's grounds and validity. For instance, Dave Eggers's recent dystopian novel *The Circle* will be read primarily as passing strong judgment on the tyrannical, enslaving aspects of the Internet and its evolving ideology, along with the powerful companies that rule over it—and, ultimately, over us. But *Gehalt*, as something strangely excessive to the work yet lodged in its very fibers, refrains from such overt judgment. This restraint is neither a mere ruse nor does it happen on the level of authorial or artistic intention. On the far side of intentionality, the elusive surplus of *Gehalt* betrays an import that judges by refraining from judgment, by holding back. It is to this excessiveness of *Gehalt*, rather than to the circumscribed precincts and precepts of *Inhalt*, that Adorno's insistence upon *Enthaltung* ("Nur durch Enthaltung vom Urteil urteilt Kunst") refers us. The critical abstention performed by Adorno's *Ent-haltung* calls upon us to become mindful of what comes to pass, respectively, as *In-halt* and as *Ge-halt* within the work of art. We might say that *Ent-haltung*, mediated by the tension between *In-halt* and *Ge-halt*, demands a particular critical *Haltung* (attitude or stance), but one that can only be thought and practiced without a firm *Halt* (hold). This form of *Haltung* without secure *Halt* is a kind of de-stancing, an *Ent-haltung*.

The "holding" that *Gehalt* performs, as an *Ent-haltung*, is simultaneously a disclosive gesture—in the sense that a glimpse of something is offered in and as aesthetic semblance—and a certain kind of withholding or retreat. To relate to this double gesture, it is important to be attuned to the sense of *Zurückhalten*, the holding back or restraint, that an *Enthaltung* also occasions with respect to the work of art. The *Ent-haltung* of *Ge-halt*, then, is operative not only on the level of a movement of containing something (as in "etwas enthalten") or refraining from something (as in "sich einer Sache enthalten"), but always also on the level of a withholding, holding back, or retreat of the very content that is being held into the world by aesthetic semblance. This content of the holding (*Halten*) is held back even as it is offered, and its own *Gehalt* consists, to a significant extent, in providing an implicit commentary, within aesthetic semblance, on its own withholding—that is, on the singular ways in which a particular work of art withholds precisely in its holding forth. We might say that, through *Enthaltung*, the *Gehalt* of an artwork emerges as an each-time idiomatic and self-reflexive commentary on its singular double movement of revealing and withholding. Learning to relate to the *Gehalt* of a work of art would entail learning to relate—*freely* (so as to respect the work's unsaturated future possibilities) yet *rigorously* (so as to do justice to the stringent demands that are placed upon us by the incommensurable logic, rhythm, and tonality of a particular work)—to how the work teaches us, in turn, to relate to the relation between the holding forth and withholding that it performs.

If one wishes to think the *Gehalt* of the artwork along the lines of *Enthaltung* articulated so far, one will soon discover how difficult this concept or semi-concept of *Gehalt* is to cast into sharp relief in relation to individual works. First, there is the problem of how one knows when one encounters a genuine work of art that inquires into the modalities of its own *Gehalt* through *Enthaltung*, and how one knows when one deals with a merely affirmative, commercial, or predigested product of what Adorno denounces as the culture industry. To risk an epigrammatically condensed answer, we might say that, for him, genuine works of art (such as those of Schönberg, Celan, Beethoven, Mahler, Beckett, and others that he so often evokes) open up the possibility of forging a free and unregimented relation to the world in which they were created and to the worlds which they in turn create. The genuine artwork proceeds by "crystallizing in itself as something unique to itself, rather than complying with existing social norms and qualifying as 'socially useful.'" In short, the genuine artwork "criticizes society by merely existing [*durch ihr bloßes Dasein*], for which puritans of all stripes condemn it."[23] If, for Adorno, the genuine work criticizes, and even disrupts, the world in which it was created by merely existing (and prior to the claims and demands made by any *Inhalt*), then one of the criteria that may be used to ascertain if a product is a genuine work of art is to inquire into whether and how its sheer existence provokes resistance and disruption in the world from which it stems. The artwork's provocation of the world by merely being in the world is inseparable from its *Wahrheitsgehalt*, for the genuine work of art embodies Adorno's conviction that "only what does not fit into this world is true."[24]

A further problem relating to our understanding of *Gehalt* is brought into focus by the question as to what, precisely, comes to pass when one engages with any particular artwork on its own terms. A work will always follow its own idiomatic laws and autonomous formal singularities, as Adorno was well aware in his own studies, later collected under the heading *Notes to Literature*, of literary artworks by such writers as Goethe, Hölderlin, Balzac, Heine, Proust, Valéry, Kafka, George, and Beckett, among many others. As Adorno suggests in his "Short Commentaries on Proust," initially broadcast as a radio address to mark the completion of the German translation of Proust's *Recherche* and first published in the literary journal *Akzente* in 1958, the critic's task is not "to advance an interpretation of the whole that would at best simply repeat the statements of intention which the author himself inserted into his work" but rather "through immersion in fragments to illuminate something of the work's *Gehalt [durch Versenkung ins Bruchstück etwas von seinem Gehalt aufleuchten zu lassen]*, which derives its unforgettable quality solely from the coloring of the here and now."[25] The remarkable proximity to Adorno's concept of the uncoercive gaze is striking here. Perhaps it is possible, then, to make vivid some of the potential ways in which the *Gehalt* of the judgmentless judgment makes itself felt in a work by briefly considering a constellation of specific moments in three remarkably self-reflexive contemporary novels: one German, Martin Walser's *Ein springender Brunnen* (*A Gushing Fountain*); one American, Philip Roth's *The Dying Animal*; and one British, Julian Barnes's *The Sense of an Ending*.

Walser's autobiographically inflected coming-of-age novel, originally published in German in 1998, chronicles both a boy's German childhood and the haunting ways in which his small town on Lake Constance, for all its apparent quotidian mundanity, slowly but steadily sinks into a new and rather different kind of normalcy, German National Socialism. From what kind of an aesthetic and epistemological perspective could such a work of memory and engagement with the past be fashioned in the first place? The novel commences with the following sentences, which will have left none of the many sentences that follow it untouched: "As long as something is, it isn't what it will have been. When something is past, you are no longer the person it happened to, but you're closer to him than to others. Although the past did not exist when it was present, it now obtrudes as if it had been as it now presents itself. But as long as something is, it isn't what it will have been." And the text continues: "When something is past, you are no longer the person it happened to. When things were that we now say used to be, we didn't know they were. Now we say it used to be thus and so, although back when it was, we knew nothing about what we say now."[26] What kind of position can the literary work of art assume in relation both to the mnemonic labor that flows into its evocation and interpretation of a past as well as to the political transformations that suffuse its narrative? The language of the novel finds itself unfolding in a certain ruptured temporality, a time that is "out of joint" as Hamlet might put it, because it is required by its historical inscription to impute a consciousness to the time that it narrates when in fact at the time in which the narration takes place no such consciousness could have existed, and no attendant interpretation could have been predicated upon a constellation of knowledge and experience that came into being only in the long history of its aftermath. In the literary artwork, the remembered voice and the remembering voice are not coextensive but rather at odds with each other, even if the remembering voice mobilized by the text believes to feel a certain elective affinity toward the remembered voice. If, under the sign of these genealogical imbrications, the narrative perspective of Walser's novel must remain indeterminate, it is precisely this indeterminacy that it takes as the very center of its reflections—rather than seeking to resolve it. To the extent that, as Adorno writes, "the purpose of the artwork is the determination of the indeterminate," the precision and rigor with which the indeterminate is determined work not to resolve, and thereby undo, the indeterminacy of aesthetic semblance, but rather to engage with the implications and consequences of this indeterminacy for any thinking of the artwork as such.[27] A text's work of determining the indeterminate consists in specifying the idiomatic and each-time singular ways in which the text resists determination. Recognizing that the artwork engages in the work of determining the indeterminate without erasing or undoing it also means arriving at the realization that the artwork lives in and as its own lack. In Adorno's terms, "All artworks are writing [*Schrift*], not just those that are obviously such;

they are hieroglyphs for which the code has been lost, a loss that plays into their *Gehalt*. Artworks are language only as writing."[28] We might say that *A Gushing Fountain* renders something like a judgmentless judgment not only on its constellation of the personal and the political under the sign of an irreconcilable temporality of narration, but also engages in a judgmentless judgment of its own status as a lack or loss that comes to pass in writing. Its *Gehalt*, it could be argued, is inseparable from this mobilization of an aesthetically mediated judgment that takes place precisely as a refusal to judge—that is, as a way of confronting, without seeking to efface, the tension at the heart of its literary gestures of memory, mourning, and archiving what cannot ultimately be retrieved or redeemed.

A judgmentless judgment of a different kind is at stake in *The Dying Animal*. The novel's first-person narrator is David Kepesh, an aged college professor, also active as a public intellectual and cultural critic, whom Roth had introduced as a protagonist in his earlier novels *The Breast* and *The Professor of Desire*. Kepesh becomes erotically attached to a twenty-four-year-old student of his, Consuela Castillo, the voluptuous daughter of an affluent Cuban émigré family living in New York City. *The Dying Animal* is composed as a self-reflexive chronicle of their tumultuous relationship, for the most part from the perspective of several years after its ending, and thus also under the sign of the indeterminacy upon which Walser's narrator remarks, namely, that "when things were that we now say used to be, we didn't know they were." Yet here it is the special imbrication of eros and death that structures the novel's way of determining the determinate as indeterminate. Throughout the novel, Roth's narrator is especially attracted to Consuela's voluptuous breasts, commemorated by a postcard she sends him toward the middle of the work, a reproduction of a 1919 oil painting by Amedeo Modigliani, *La Grand nu,* housed in the Museum of Modern Art. Kepesh remarks upon the "trademark Modigliani nude, the accessible, elongated dream girl he ritualistically painted and that Consuela had chosen to send, so immodestly, through the U.S. mail." He notes the painted figure's "cylindrical stalk of a waist, the wide pelvic span, and the gently curving thighs" as well as "the patch of flame that is the hair that marks the spot where she is forked," adding, "A nude whose breasts, full and canting and a bit to the side, might well have been modeled on her own. . . . A golden-skinned nude inexplicably asleep over a velvety black abyss that, in my mood, I associated with the grave. One long, undulating line, she lies there awaiting you, still as death."[29] This foreshadowing of finitude anticipates a crucial turn later in the novel: the cancer that drives Consuela to the brink of death and that requires a mastectomy. Contemplating not only his abiding obsession with her and her decision to leave him years ago, but also, at this point in the novel still implicitly, the relation of eros and death in a conversation with his friend George, the narrator is told: "'You tasted it. Isn't that enough? Of what do you ever get more than a taste? That's all we're given in life, that's all we're given *of* life. A taste. There is no more.' George was right, of course, and only repeating to me what I know."[30] The ephemerality of experience, the relation to radical finitude that structures all being-in-the-world, comes to pass in this novel not merely as one theme or motif among others. It judges this experience by ultimately refusing to pass judgment on it, by letting the mere "taste" linger as writing, knowing that this short-lived taste is all that humans are ever allowed: "A taste. There is no more." The novel does not judge by suggesting, for example, either that this taste-structure of Being is merely a lamentable state of affairs, nor does it triumphantly transfigure this taste-structure by identifying it as the condition of possibility for human experience as such, thereby tacitly redeeming it as a form of ontology or as a quasi-dialectical sublation. Rather, the work lets its judgment-less judgment stand—paratactically, unredeemed, unfinished—among the ruins that are its characters' lives and remains.

The unredeemed, unfinished, and apodictically posited qualities of a life as it emerges in the aesthetic semblance of the literary work of art also traverses, albeit in different modulations, Barnes's *The Sense of an Ending*. Like *A Gushing Fountain* and *The Dying Animal*, *The Sense of an Ending* pivots on a narrator's attempt to forge a thinking relation, in and through writing, to a past whose interpretation and judgment refuse to yield itself fully to him, a judging interpretation that is both absolutely necessary and foreclosed at the same time, potentially readable and effectively unreadable. Tony Webster, the novel's retired, late-middle-aged first-person narrator, is haunted by a past when close friends from his childhood reemerge in his world, a lifeworld that he had thought he understood but that now unravels ever more quickly because of an uncanny legacy involving his former girlfriend, Veronica, and his former friend, the philosophically astute Adrian, who has committed suicide. As Webster, in part two of the novel, must gradually reconfigure the entire interpretation of his life as narrated in part one, he reflects: "Sometimes I think the purpose of life is to reconcile us to its eventual loss by wearing us down, by proving, however long it takes, that life isn't all it's cracked up to be."[31] The narrator's potentially self-erasing gesture of reconciliation with finitude implicitly alludes to the trope, taken up by numerous thinkers in the Western tradition, including Plato, Cicero, Montaigne, and Derrida, that to philosophize is to learn how to die. But, as Derrida confesses in his final interview only months before his own impending death, this learning how to die is not fully attainable: "That's been the old philosophical injunction since Plato: to philosophize is to learn how to die. I believe in this truth without being able to resign myself to it." He explains: "We are all survivors who have been granted a temporary reprieve [*en sursis*]. . . . But I remain uneducable when it comes to any kind of wisdom about knowing-how-to-die or, if you prefer, knowing how to live."[32] In order to bring into view the inextricably imbricated ideas of learning-how-to-die and learning-how-to-live from the perspective of the artwork, it would need to be considered if, and under what conditions, a character may change over time and, if so, to what kind of a change, beyond the aleatory contingency of this or that assumed character trait, such development might lead. Thus Barnes has Webster wonder: "Does character develop over time? In novels, of course it does: otherwise there wouldn't be much of a story. But in life? I sometimes wonder. Our attitudes and opinions change, we develop new habits and eccentricities; but that's something different, more like decoration." And he continues: "Perhaps character resembles intelligence, except that character peaks a little later: between twenty and thirty, say. And after that, we're just stuck with what we've got. We're on our own. If so, that would explain a lot of lives, wouldn't it? And also—if this isn't too grand a word—our tragedy."[33] Beyond engaging the irreducible and unjudgeable difference between an empirical reality and an aesthetically produced reality, between life and text, Webster here touches upon a certain tragic element in the relative stasis of a character, the basic features of which Freud tells us are more or less firmly in place, with only minor future variations, as early as age five. The tragedy does not lie in the idea that fundamental change in character is foreclosed from relatively early on; it rather lies in the ultimately unbridgeable discrepancy between, on the one hand, a life's claim to malleability, its supple plasticity—through which it can even become, *pace* Nietzsche and Foucault, a work of art in its own right—and its inscription in a narrative and a trajectory that are forever at odds with that supple plasticity, even if only on a subterranean, unacknowledged, perhaps even ghostly level. *The Sense of an Ending*, as a work of art that confronts these tensions in the space of the literary without resolving them, abstains from passing any judgment on them. Its judgment lies in its refusal to judge as the novel concludes with the lapidary statement: "You get towards the end of life—no, not of life itself, but of something else: the end of any likelihood of change in that life. . . . There is accumulation. There is responsibility. And beyond these, there is unrest. There is great unrest."[34]

Having turned to the variegated forms of judgmentless judgment that traverse these three heterogeneous novels, is it not possible now to suspect that the judgmentless judgment informing the movement of *Einordnung* also sheds light on Adorno's conviction that the explosiveness of a work is all the more forceful the more deeply it is buried within the material itself? In a letter to Benjamin from November 6, 1934, Adorno avers: "No one is more aware than I am that every single sentence here is and must be laden with political dynamite; but the further down such dynamite is buried, the greater its explosive force when detonated."[35] It is as though that which can make itself felt within a work as the most powerful and transformative form of *Gehalt* first needed to remove itself from the surface, take itself out of the realm of the more obvious forms of critique in order ultimately to leave no part of its object untouched. The gesture of *Einordnung* hides its secret dynamite in the most subterranean and cavernous precincts of aesthetic form.

There is a dimension of aesthetic *Gehalt* and its relation to judgmentless judgment that has not been explicated thus far: the relationship of an artwork's *Gehalt* to its historical situatedness. Is the *Gehalt* of the work of art, beyond its material content, a function of its historical situation? That is, does what it allows to emerge as its import stand in a relation of contingency to the time in which it was produced? If so, how can this relation begin to be thought? Is a work's *Gehalt* a mere expression or illustration of what was already the case in the historical contexts in which it was created, or does it provide a genuinely autonomous perspective that is irreducible to the precepts of this or that historical contingency? Like Nietzsche, for whom, when it comes to our most important concepts, it is only possible to provide histories, but not definitions, Adorno views the concept of the artwork as thoroughly genealogical in the sense that the "concept of art is located in a historically changing constellation of elements; it refuses definition."[36] In other words, there can be no rigorous thinking of the work of art or its concept that ignores its status as having-become. This having-become of the artwork conditions not only its temporal embeddedness but also, by extension, its relation to what it contains or, more precisely, to what it does not contain. "Because art," he argues, "is what it has become, its concept refers to what it does not contain [*Das Gewordensein von Kunst verweist ihren Begriff auf das, was sie nicht enthält*]."[37] Adorno here employs the word *enthalten*, which, as we saw, he also chose in the context of his discussion of Mörike's poem in the form of the noun *Enthaltung* ("abstention") in one of its other senses, namely "to contain." We might say that he employs *enthalten* here (rather than the equally common German verb for containing, *beinhalten*) because he wishes to keep alive the question of how *Inhalt* and *Gehalt* relate to various issues pertaining to judgment and the abstention from judgment. For Adorno's uncoercive gaze, as this particular passage suggests, it would be a mistake to assume that the having-become-ness of art as such and of a particular artwork renders them merely historically contingent phenomena that reflect or stage their own historical moment. Rather, the *Gehalt* of an artwork takes into account the ways in which it is called upon to negotiate its shifting relations to its own status as having-become, its *Gewordensein*.

To specify the movement by which artworks negotiate their respective having-become-ness, it is necessary to consider a certain historical doubling of their situatedness. To appreciate this doubling, it is helpful to learn to read a striking image that Adorno offers in *Aesthetic Theory*: "Kunstwerke begeben sich hinaus aus der empirischen Welt und bringen eine dieser entgegengesetzte eigenen Wesens hervor, so als ob auch diese ein Seiendes wäre."[38] In the published English translation, this crucial sentence reads: "Artworks detach themselves from the empirical world and bring forth another world, one opposed to the empirical world as if the other world too were an autonomous entity."[39] The richly textured expression that the translation renders in a somewhat impoverished manner as "detach themselves" (as if Adorno had merely written, in a decidedly more pedestrian tone, "sich ablösen") is "sich hinausbegeben." Adorno's elevated diction here evokes a stepping out, a process of going out of something or leaving something behind—to let oneself, or even to give oneself, out. What the image suggests is an artwork's gradual stepping out of the empirical world (in which it nevertheless will always have originated and with which it therefore remains irrevocably imbricated) and into another world, one created by aesthetic semblance itself. This other world, the world of its aesthetically produced semblance, demands to be related to in an "as if" mode, as if it, like the world from which it originated, were a form of being. (Adorno for good reason speaks simply of "ein Seiendes," a being or a form of being, not of an "autonomous entity," as the published translation has it. To the extent that it remains primordially related, even if in a negative dialectic, to the empirical world from which it perpetually departs, autonomy cannot be its own category of being, and Adorno therefore does not mobilize the language of supposedly autonomous entities here.)

It is crucial to develop a feeling for this in-between character of the stepping-out as it emerges in "sich hinausbegeben." The artwork is neither fully on one side of the border nor the other, neither all on the side of the empirical world in which it originated nor exclusively in the aesthetic world that it itself creates. If the *Gehalt* of the artwork cannot be thought outside of its historical situatedness, Adorno's image suggests a certain shuttling between two worlds, a mediation between two forms of genealogical inscription, each with its own legacy and its own potentialities for future transformation. The artwork passes judgment on the empirical world in which it was created only by refraining from judging it—a judgment, for instance, that would merely find fault with this or that aspect of its empirical world. Rather, it judges its world by *einordnen* itself within it yet stepping away from it at the same time; its withholding of judgment is enacted by a stepping across without arriving and a stepping back without returning. Rather than merely judging, the artwork is continually in the process of taking a step between and across its two worlds; one could even say that the artwork is another name for this "betweenness" itself. As a between, the artwork ceaselessly crosses over from one world to the other, its stepping describing the movement of (its) history.

The stepping across that the artwork performs is not predicated upon the premise that the world in which it originates, and from which it departs, is already fully known and accessible to those who inhabit it. On the contrary, the interpretation of the world in which the work originates is an abiding question mark. It is precisely through the stepping-across performed by the artwork that the world from which the artwork stems is rendered worthy of questioning. The stepping between and across worlds that comes to pass in the work of art exposes the very concept of world to its radical contingency. The world in which it was created is denaturalized, exhibited as something other than self-evident and merely given. Just like the semblance of another possible world that is intimated by the stepping-across broaches questions as to the content and logic of this other world, so too the very world—or, more precisely, what was previously taken to be the world—in which the work was created is retroactively opened up to questioning. Although the thinking of the other world of semblance that Adorno has in mind is not coextensive with a Blochian notion of *Vorschein*, in which the artwork provides intimations or glimpses of a utopian world to come, the unknown world opened by the work shines a light not only on the transformative possibilities that the new world harbors but also advances the possibility that the world from which it is in the process of departing has hitherto remained largely unthought and therefore deserves to be queried as if for the first time. The stepping between and across worlds that the artwork occasions gives rise to an intense vigilance with regard to these worlds that did not exist in this particular way before.

To suggest, as Adorno does, that the artwork embodies a certain movement between worlds is to focus on a perpetually transitional aesthetic sphere that makes the work what it is even while never allowing it to rest simply in and as itself. Adorno's conception differs markedly, for instance, from that offered recently by the philosopher Alexander Nehamas in *Only a Promise of Happiness: The Place of Beauty in a World of Art*. Nehamas is concerned with reinstating our understanding of beauty and its semblance or appearance as a key category that connects art and desire with the world in which these occur. Although he concedes that traditional categories of the aesthetic and its theory have become problematic, these problems, for him, "leave beauty untouched, for beauty ... is part of the everyday world of purpose and desire, history and contingency, subjectivity and incompleteness." And he adds: "That is the only world there is, and nothing, not even the highest of the high arts, can move beyond it."[40] To be sure, Nehamas's specific concern lies with the category of beauty rather than with the artwork or with aesthetic form as such. Yet it is striking to note the contrast of his discourse—which wishes to retain the wordily groundedness of beautiful semblance or appearance without even any gesture of transcendence, its permanent and intransigent inscription in the here and now of its world—to the artwork's stepping between more than one world, as Adorno conceives of it. Whereas for Nehamas an artwork's beautiful semblance forever connects it with a world that cannot be transcended, Adorno emphasizes precisely the world-making properties that an artwork generates when it allows for a consideration of the ways in which it is both inscribed in the world in which it was created and simultaneously capitalizes on the specific and each time idiomatic ways in which it refuses to be fully coextensive—which also is to say complicitous—with that very world.

In one of his aphorisms, the Austrian writer Karl Kraus, whose work was well-known to Adorno, Benjamin, and their early Frankfurt School circle, notes: "Kunst ist das, was Welt wird, nicht was Welt ist" ("Art is what becomes world, not what is world").[41] The artwork's stepping between and across the world in which it was produced and the world to which it itself gives rise can be seen as an instantiation of this process of *werden*, or becoming. But it is a becoming that cannot ever fully come into its own in that it cannot simply arrive in a new state of being or a newly fashioned world, as much as it defines itself in terms of its departure from its old world. Its stepping forth, which is always also a *leave-taking*, a saying good-bye to a world that merely is, does not imply any *arrival* in the other world, as much as the creation of the semblance of that other world is necessary for the artwork to be a genuine artwork and not simply a form of mimetic plagiary—whether with an affirmative or critical aim matters little—from an already existing world. If art is that which becomes world without being that which already is—or claims to be—world, it does so only by refraining from the sort of judgment that already has decided upon a stable interpretation of a set of relations: the relations between the two worlds to each other; the relation of the artwork to each of these two worlds; and the relation of the artwork to the relation between the two worlds. Whenever the thinking of, or uncoercive gaze upon, these heterogeneous relations is allowed to remain free and open—for instance, when an arresting and final judgment on these relations is permitted to open onto the unpredictable consequences of its deferral—then the particular and singular form of judgment that an artwork may sponsor outlives itself by one more day.

CHAPTER FIVE

The Literary Artwork between Word and Concept
Adorno and Agamben Reading Kafka

The poet W. H. Auden once memorably averred that if one had "to name the artist who comes nearest to bearing the same kind of relation to our age that Dante, Shakespeare, and Goethe bore to theirs, Kafka is the first one would think of."[1] If this assessment still rings true today, it is because Kafka's relation to our age is one not only of a certain spirit of the times, a cultural episteme, a given political configuration, or a certain *Lebensgefühl*, a feeling of life, in the experiential orbit of an alienated modernity. It also pertains with particular force to the ways in which Kafka's writing incessantly takes as one of its main categories of reflection the very question of the philosophical interpretability of what we call literature. What is one to make, on the level of the concept, of a text that begins with a protagonist named Gregor Samsa who awakens one morning to the realization that he has been inexplicably transformed into a monstrous vermin, even an unthing ("*Ungeziefer*"), as in Kafka's *The Metamorphosis*? And what kinds of philosophically interpretive thoughts are elicited by a related scene of awakening, in which the character Josef K., a high-ranking bank official, finds himself unexpectedly detained by two officers waiting in his apartment? "Someone must have slandered Josef K.," Kafka famously begins *The Trial*, "for one morning, without having done anything wrong, he was arrested."[2] It is as if such scenes figuratively staged the experience of a baffled reader who awakens to a refractory text that he or she is now called upon to interpret—without a reliable key or a hermeneutically stable frame of reference. The reader, like Josef K. himself, comes to inhabit a certain narrative disruption. As the German writer Martin Walser rightly reminds us with regard to *The Trial*, the "event begins only at the moment when the disruption occurs."[3] In this state of disorientation and hesitation, the drawn-out trial of reading, as well as the exigent process of reading itself, commence—a double meaning that is encoded in the German title of Kafka's novel, *Der Process*, which means both "trial" and "process." But to whom or what does one awaken when reading a literary text from a philosophical perspective? And is this form of awakening not also a way of dreaming—that is, of learning to follow the singular dream-logic of an artwork?

In a reflection dating from the eight intensely creative months (September 1917 through April 1918) that Kafka spent at his sister Ottla's house in the Bohemian town of Zürau, he writes:

> Art flies around truth, but with the definite intention of not getting burnt. Its capacity lies in finding in the dark void a place where the beam of light can be intensely caught, without this having been perceptible before.[4]

> [Die Kunst fliegt um die Wahrheit, aber mit der entschiedenen Absicht, sich nicht zu verbrennen. Ihre Fähigkeit besteht darin, in der dunklen Leere einen Ort zu finden, wo der Strahl des Lichts, ohne daß dieser vorher zu erkennen gewesen wäre, kräftig aufgefangen werden kann.][5]

If art swirls and circles around truth like a moth around the light of a flame, profoundly attracted by it yet always requiring a certain distance from it in order not to be destroyed altogether, it marks a site upon which the relationship between the aesthetic object and its possible illuminations, its *Schein* or appearance, first becomes a discrete matter of inquiry. One of the central questions that here impose themselves concerns the ways in which the elusively idiomatic artwork relates to the kind of rigorous conceptual labor that it, in addition to the pleasure that it typically affords, also elicits. If we can accept the premise that, as Gayatri Spivak puts it in a different context, "reading literature, we learn to learn from the singular and unverifiable," then the relation between, on the one hand, the singularity and unverifiability of the artwork and, on the other hand, the concept that seeks general validity, is itself one of the main axes around which aesthetic production and its interpretation circle.[6] The intricate question about the nature and potentialities of this complex relation inflects the way in which we may begin to understand Kafka's image of art as it playfully yet purposefully swirls around the flame of truth without being consumed by it entirely.

There can hardly be a conceptually subtle understanding of the work of art without the aid of philosophy. Yet if the philosophical interpretation of the work of art were entirely successful—that is, if it did not leave a remainder within the artwork that also resisted the translation of aesthetic form into this or that meaning—the artwork would, in a sense, become superfluous. What it achieves conceptually could have been achieved in another way, through discursive logic. Therefore, a seminal concern that permeates Kafka's writings, including his unfinished, fragmentary novel *The Trial*, is the very way in which a literary artwork both calls for philosophical interpretation and resists such interpretation at the same time. One way of registering this aporia is to appreciate how, as Kafka puts it in another observation from the Zürau period, for "everything outside the phenomenal world, language can be used only allusively [*nur andeutungsweise*], but never even approximately in a comparative [or analogous] way [*niemals auch nur annähernd vergleichsweise*], since, corresponding as it does to the phenomenal world, it is concerned only with property and its relations."[7] If the literary work of art unfolds precisely on the far side of the phenomenal world in which language can be said to operate in a comparative, analogous, and therefore principally other-directed way, the language of the literary text inhabits an orbit of signification in which it can only ever allude, but never actually fully name, what it may be "about" on the conceptual level. Another way of putting this is to say that the language of the literary artwork requires a certain philological, theoretical, and philosophical interpretation in order to address both its allusive character as such and that unspoken or hidden sphere of signification to which its allusiveness seems to point, but to which it cannot ever refer in any unmediated way.

Kafka himself exhibits a keen awareness of this difficult-to-fulfill requirement throughout the entire trajectory of what he calls his *Schriftstellersein*, or constitutive "being-as-a-writer." When, for instance, he writes to his two-time fiancé Felice Bauer—whose initials, F. B., are also those of the character Fräulein Bürstner in *The Trial*, one of protagonist Josef K.'s erotic interests—to inquire about the possibility of finding any meaning in the story he wrote concurrently with *The Trial*, "The Judgment," he betrays his uneasy sense that a conceptual interpretation is both necessary and impossible: "Can you discover any meaning in the 'Judgment'—I mean some straightforward, coherent meaning that one could follow? I can't find any, nor can I explain anything in it [*Findest Du im "Urteil" irgendeinen Sinn, ich meine irgendeinen geraden, zusammenhängenden, verfolgbaren Sinn? Ich finde ihn nicht und kann auch nichts darin erklären*]."[8] As the first reader of his own text—and thus as something akin to a primordial type of reader in relation to the constellation of challenges posed by the Kafkan text to the very category of understanding—Kafka finds himself pushed by language to the limits of what can be translated into a form of recognizable meaning or sense ("Sinn"), especially if by meaning or sense is meant a hermeneutic disclosure, an effect of meaning derived from linearity, coherence, and followability. Yet Kafka the reader is unable simply to content himself with the enigma that Kafka the writer has created for him—and, by proxy, for all readers. His text refuses to be explicated according to any conventional notions of conceptual unfolding, yet it continues to provoke, in its own singular idiom and perhaps against all better judgment, ceaseless attempts to explicate.

There are few philosophical readers of Kafka more attuned to the tension between the artwork and its conceptual exposition than Adorno.[9] Indeed, his practice of the uncoercive gaze can hardly be understood without attending to this tension. In his *Aesthetic Theory*, Adorno puts the matter in an epigrammatically condensed way when he argues that "art stands in need of philosophy that interprets it in order to say that which it cannot say, whereas art only is able to say what it says by not saying it."[10] Adorno here puts his finger on the predicament at the core of the relation between philosophical commentary and aesthetic production. On the one hand, the artwork—especially the self-consciously self-reflexive, high-modernist variety of Schönberg, Alban Berg, Samuel Beckett, and, precisely, Kafka, that Adorno so often would explore—requires philosophical discourse to bring to the fore as a graspable, cognitive, and propositional structure the *Wahrheitsgehalt*—the speculative truth content, import, or substance—that, in the absence of critical commentary and conceptual elucidation, lies latent. On the other hand, the very thing that philosophy claims the artwork says, that on behalf of which philosophy acts as a kind of conceptual translator, can be said by the artwork only when it remains silent about it. If the artwork actually said what it says in a transparent cognitive proposition, shorn of the mediations and aberrations of its imaginative flourishes and its singular expression of beauty and form, then it would cease to be an artwork. It would simply be a philosophical treatise concerning a conceptual content that now no longer could claim membership in the domain of art. Yet if the artwork can be itself only by not saying what philosophy claims it says—that is, if the cognitive propositional content on which philosophy focuses cannot be verified in the articulations and inscriptions of the artwork itself, lest it abdicate its status as a work of art—then how can one clarify and verify philosophy's claims about the content and meaning of artworks? Why does art continue to stand in need of philosophy's translational services? And if Adorno's uncoercive gaze is so acutely aware of this tension, what is it that makes him retain his conviction, even his "model," the supposition of which is "that artworks unfold in their philosophical interpretation"?[11]

Any philosophical interpretation of an artwork must confront the following paradox: if the meaning of an artwork were to remain sealed off from all logical comprehension, then no philosophy could ever truly speak to this meaning. But if the meaning of an artwork were to reveal itself readily, then no artwork would be needed—since its "content" could have been stated more easily in prosaic, discursive language that would require no philosophy to expound upon it. One lesson to be derived from this state of affairs is that what is required in engaging with a literary text such as Kafka's *The Trial* is a certain guardedness in relation to "the illusion that what is said is immediately what is meant [*die Illusion, es wäre, was geredet wird, unmittelbar das Gemeinte*]." Instead, the character of language as an elusive token (*Spielmarke*) reveals "the way that all words behave: that language imprisons its speakers one more time; that language, as the proper medium of its speakers, is a failure."[12] What a philosophical approach to a literary text would have to consider, then, is the relationship between, one the one hand, the tension obtaining between an aesthetic object and its conceptual content, and, on the other hand, the ways in which the aesthetic object breaks with what it appears to be saying at first sight.

The push and pull of calling forth and resisting philosophical interpretation, though shared in principle by all great literary works, is staged by a particular work in specific ways that are idiomatic and singular to the individual text. In others words, the heterogeneous ways in which literary works by Hölderlin, Goethe, Eichendorff, or Proust confront the tension between their apparent content and the philosophical interpretation of their import or substance are quite different from the variegated ways in which texts by Mann, Dickens, Wedekind, Beckett, or Heine approach the same tension—to cite the names of some of the authors to whom Adorno chooses to devote substantial essays, later collected in *Notes to Literature*. One central problem that arises out of this constellation of aesthetic form and the philosophical interpretation of its import is that of the nature of the relationship between the literal and the figurative nature of a text's rhetorical operations. Adorno's richly layered essay "Notes on Kafka" ("Aufzeichnungen zu Kafka") was begun in 1942 and first published in *Die Neue Rundschau* in 1953, and it represents—next to the many occasional references to Kafka throughout his work—his most sustained engagement with Kafka. There, he suggests that Kafka's "two great novels, *The Castle* and *The Trial*, seem to bear the mark of philosophical theorems."[13] These theorems can be approached only through an interrogation of the ways in which literality and figurality interact with each other in a hermeneutically unpredictable manner.[14] The "principle of literalness," in which Adorno espies "a reminiscence of the Torah exegesis of the Jewish tradition," is both upheld and undermined by Kafka's writing.[15] If Adorno is right that, from the perspective of the uncoercive gaze, "Kafka's authority is textual," it is a textuality that does not reside in any mere mastery of understanding or in an ability to spawn philosophical ideas with a palatable literary packaging but, rather, in the singular ways in which "Kafka's works protected themselves against the deadly aesthetic error of equating the philosophy that an author pumps into a work with its metaphysical substance."[16] After all, if Kafka's texts were to operate in this way, "the work of art would be stillborn; it would exhaust itself in what it says and would not unfold itself in time."[17] In order to guard against a premature hermeneutic desire that "jumps directly to the significance intended by the work," two basic rules are to be followed: "take everything literally" and "cover up nothing with concepts invoked from above." To follow this double precept, a certain "fidelity to the letter" is required. Yet, at the same time, absolute fidelity to the letter, which also entails a reticence, even a refusal, to say what an artwork cannot say on its own, poses the danger that the reader will "lose all ground on which to stand."[18] A critical reading therefore "must cling to the fact that at the beginning of *The Trial*, it is said that someone must have been spreading rumors about Josef K., 'for without having done anything wrong, he was arrested one fine morning,'" a clinging that presumably is motivated by the suspicion that the literalness of the novel's sentences is also perpetually self-undermining.[19] In other words, the demand for literalness is from the outset vexed by the very fact that the tacit content of that literalness speaks of phenomena of nonliteralness, such as rumor, possible slander, or conjecture, all of which are matters precisely of interpretation rather than transparent literalness.

Kafka's own keen awareness of this tension is encoded, for instance, in the self-reflexive ways in which he introduces subtle hermeneutic doubt into the apparent matter-of-fact literalness of *The Trial*'s opening sentence. Although Adorno does not comment on this aspect of the text, it is germane to his discussion. In German, the sentence reads: "Jemand mußte Josef K. verleumdet haben, denn ohne daß er etwas Böses getan hätte, wurde er eines Morgens verhaftet."[20] Kafka's deceptively literal declarative sentence, which appears merely to report on an objective state of affairs, in fact stages an implicit call for nonliteral interpretation on an almost subterranean level. The "mußte" ("must have") not only sets the stage for a novel that, despite being told for the most part through third-person narration, will unfold from the more limited personal perspective of its central character, Josef K. Its introduction of a decidedly interrogative and interpretive mood also serves to open the trial of reading and understanding: Josef K. "must have" been slandered, but he and we cannot be sure. Along similar lines, Kafka's ambiguous reference to "etwas Böses" far exceeds the referential confines of the English "anything wrong," for the German locution raises the interpretive stakes with respect to Josef K.'s possible guilt, alluding both to something naughty (as when a German child is scolded for having been "böse"—that is, for having been badly behaved) or, by contrast, something truly evil, *das Böse*. In addition, as has often been remarked in Kafka scholarship, the subjunctive form presented by the phrase "etwas Böses getan hätte"—which is impossible to reproduce in the English translation to the extent that it renders Josef K. as having done "nothing wrong" and thereby allows the character to appear simply as having been wrongly accused—introduces a subtle moment of interpretive doubt. This doubt is expressed merely by the umlauts that Kafka places over the "a" in "hätte"—he easily could have written "hatte," thus "ohne das er etwas Böses getan hatte," a straightforward past-perfect form indicating that Josef K. had not done anything wrong. Kafka's seemingly innocent shift from "hatte" to "hätte," from past perfect to subjunctive, works to open the proceedings of at least three interrelated trials: the novel *The Trial* as such, the perpetually deferred trial(s) of Josef K., and the textual trial of reading itself.[21] It is no coincidence, one might add, that Kafka bore within himself a concern with the precarious aesthetics of the umlaut, the fate of "ä"; as he writes in a 1910 diary entry, "The ä, detached from its sentence, flew away like a ball on the meadow [*Das ä, losgelöst vom Satz, flog dahin wie ein Ball auf der Wiese*]."[22]

The movement of dispersal that characterizes Kafka's recalcitrant writing even when it insists on keeping the category of literalness alive cannot be contained by the logic of symbolism and the symbol. The symbol works to gather what has been disseminated, collecting the fragments and shards of meaning into an allegedly stable relation. As Adorno emphasizes in his reading of Kafka, if "the notion of the symbol has any meaning whatsoever in aesthetics . . . it can only be that the individual moments of the work of art point beyond themselves by virtue of their interrelations, that their totality coalesces into meaning." But, he adds, whereas even some of Goethe's supposedly allegorical texts in the end work toward a movement of unification within the wholeness or totality promised by the symbol and symbolism, "nothing could be less true of Kafka."[23] On the contrary, in Kafka's work, "which shoots toward" the reader "like a locomotive,"²⁴

> each sentence is literal [*steht buchstäblich*] and each signifies [*bedeutet*]. The two moments are not merged, as the symbol would have it, but yawn apart and out of the abyss between them blinds the glaring ray of fascination. Here too, in its striving not for symbol but for allegory, Kafka's prose sides with the outcasts. . . . It expresses itself not through expression but by its repudiation, by breaking off. It is a parabolic system the key to which has been stolen: yet any effort to make this fact itself the key is bound to go astray by confounding the abstract thesis of Kafka's work, the obscurity of the existent, with its substance. Each sentence says "interpret me," and none will permit it [*Jeder Satz spricht: deute mich, und keiner will es dulden*].²⁵

If Kafka's text does not belong to the order of the symbolic, it is because, at odds with the correspondence-based operation of the symbol, it does not reconcile the literal and the figurative. In classical rhetorical understanding, the gathering force of the symbol is seen as superior to other modes of figuration such as allegory precisely because it unites within itself a certain literality and a figurative dimension. For instance, the crown acts as a symbol of monarchy because it depicts something that is literally part of the object for which it stands (the crown on the monarch's head) in addition to signifying its object of reference in a more abstract or indirect manner. But in Kafka's sentences, no such unification is to be found. On the contrary, the task that they impose on their interpreters is inseparable from the task of coming to terms with the multiply refracted ways in which their literal signification is at odds with anything that they may evoke on an allusive, figurative level. Indeed, the insurmountable abyss that opens up between the literal and the figurative level of Kafka's sentences is precisely what calls for philosophical intervention and interpretive exegesis in the first place.²⁶ It embodies, we might say, the tacit provocation of reflective engagement that Nietzsche, with whose thinking Kafka's texts are in constant spectral conversation, conjures in aphorism 146 of *Beyond Good and Evil*: "And when you look long enough into the abyss, the abyss also looks into you."²⁷

If the reader's task, then, consists in looking into the abyss while also being looked at by the abyss, this task cannot be thought in isolation from the idea that a philosophically informed understanding of a literary text such as *The Trial* must remain perpetually mindful of how the literal and the figurative dimensions of the text unfold in uneasy relation to each other. For Adorno, one way of thinking the effects of this constantly shifting relation in Kafka's writing—which makes itself felt, among many other ways, in the tension between his characters' words and their enigmatic gestures—is to acknowledge the writing's "ambiguity [*Vieldeutigkeit*], which, like a disease, has eaten into all signification in Kafka [*die wie eine Krankheit alles Bedeuten bei Kafka angefressen hat*]."[28] But even this radical ambiguity, this sickness that has befallen signification in Kafka's textual world, cannot be counted on to remain self-identical. As Adorno points out, even the ambiguity is ambiguous, even the *Krankheit* that has eaten into the text will not always retain the upper hand when it comes to the assignment of meaning, as it were. After all, what is the reader to make of the apparently literalist yet simultaneously dream-like depictions, in *The Trial*, of how "Leni's fingers are connected by a web, or that the executioners resemble tenors"?[29] How are we to tell when a passage or image in Kafka's novel is to be taken literally and when figuratively—and when, by extension, the two dimensions are inextricably intertwined with each other in a space of indeterminacy?

Adorno's insistence on confronting the elusive ways in which the literal and the figurative relate, or fail to relate, in Kafka's text raises the fundamental question as to the status of the rhetorical in any attempt at providing theoretical or philosophical readings of a literary text. Whereas Jacques Derrida's assessment, in "White Mythology: Metaphor in the Text of Philosophy," allows us to appreciate the ways in which a *philosophical* text is ultimately unable to control, even through an elaborated concept of figuration, its own metaphoric productions, Paul de Man's consideration of the divergence of figurative and literal language that can occur within one and the same utterance helps to cast the question of the rhetorical dimension of the specifically *literary* artwork into sharp relief.[30] When working (ultimately unsuccessfully) to decide whether, for instance, the final line of Yeats's poem "Among School Children" ("How can we know the dancer from the dance?") is to be understood figuratively or literally, the reader confronts the consequences of a precise insight: what is at stake is not the notion "that there are simply two meanings, one literal and the other figural, and that we have to decide which one of these meanings is the right one in this particular situation." Something else makes itself felt here. The properly rhetorical moment is reached "not when we have, on the one hand, a literal meaning and on the other hand a figural meaning, but when it is impossible to decide by grammatical or other linguistic devices which of the two meanings (that can be entirely incompatible) prevails." From the vantage point of such "vertiginous possibilities of referential aberration," de Man suggests that one should "not hesitate to equate the rhetorical, figurative potentiality of language with literature itself."[31] To the extent that literature acts as a site upon which the rhetoricity of language makes itself felt with an idiomatic and uncontainable force, the reading of a literary text is no longer directed at decoding this or that meaning. The critical task would then not be to adjudicate between the rhetorical prevalence of a literal meaning and that of a figurative meaning but rather to trace the specific and each-time-singular ways in which the very idea of being able to decide between the two levels is exposed as the more or less concealed trademark of the text.

Although, unlike Adorno, de Man does not take Kafka as his touchstone, it is apparent that a concern with the relation between the literal and the figurative dimensions of the text and its interpretation inflects Kafka's sentences at every turn. *The Trial*'s pivotal doorkeeper legend, which can be said epigrammatically to condense the novel as a whole, self-consciously speaks to the problem of how to relate to the vexed relation between the literal and the figurative. Kafka first included this short text as a freestanding story under the title "Before the Law" in his 1919 collection *A Country Doctor*, six years before Max Brod published a version of it in *The Trial* from Kafka's literary estate in 1925, the year after Kafka's death. Here, the man from the country who approaches the gate, guarded by a doorkeeper, behind which he believes the law to reside, presupposes a literalist understanding of the law, according to which it is in principle possible to enter that law. In the course of the episode, the man from the country misinterprets the doorkeeper's deferral of the permission to enter as its denial. If the doorkeeper episode, like *The Trial* as a whole, rigorously demands interpretation (on the part of the man from the country as well as from the reader) while also strenuously resisting it, the question of the text's own literalness is cast precisely into figurative terms. As Derrida points out in his reading of Kafka's parable, it "does not tell or describe anything but itself as text," which is to say that it "guards itself, maintains itself—like the law, speaking only to itself, that is to say, of its non-identity with itself. . . . It is the law, makes the law, and leaves the reader before the law."[32] In this sense, the man from the country fails to appreciate how "the singular crosses the universal, when the categorical engages the idiomatic, as a literature always must." As a result, the "man from the country had difficulty in grasping that an entrance was singular and unique when it should have been universal, as in truth it was. He had difficulty with literature."[33] This difficulty with literature, with the nature and implications of the specific interpretive demand issued by *The Trial* as well as with literature as such, is the difficulty whose traumatic wound Kafka's novel will never quite allow us to close, as if it were another textual instantiation—or iteration—of the horrific wound, infested with living worms, into which Kafka dares us to stare in the story "A Country Doctor."

Learning to learn from the singular and unverifiable form of writing we call literature, then, involves learning to read a text figuratively and literally *at the same time*. To appreciate its "law," we must not repeat the error that Kafka's man from the country makes when he mistakes the literal for the figurative, as well as the singular for the universal. Yet how such learning might be accomplished is itself a matter of dispute in the logic of Kafka's writing. It is no accident that in the "Cathedral" chapter, in which the doorkeeper parable is put into the mouth of the prison chaplain, Josef K. jumps to the apparently false interpretive conclusion that the doorkeeper must have deceived the man from the country by withholding from him access to the law. "'Don't be overly hasty,'" the chaplain reprimands Josef K., "'don't accept someone else's opinion unchecked [*übernimm nicht die fremde Meinung ungeprüft*]. I told you the story word for word according to the text [*im Wortlaut der Schrift*]. It says nothing about being deceived.'"[34] The category of deception is disqualified from the discourse of interpretation because the text's literal level, its *Wortlaut*, does not contain it. In light of Josef K.'s hasty efforts to assign figurative meaning to the literality of what the parable presents, the chaplain issues a categorical warning: "'You don't have enough respect for the text [or for writing, *Schrift*] and are changing the story [*'Du hast nicht genug Achtung vor der Schrift und veränderst die Geschichte'*].'"[35] What Josef K. fails to appreciate in the course of the novel is that although the literalness of the text cannot be maintained in interpretation, its translation into a figural meaning harbors just as much danger, which is to say, causes the text to change into something that it is not. Paradoxically, then, the philosopher's or critic's intervention through interpretive commentary is both necessary and superfluous, a sign of abiding faithfulness to the text and its simultaneous violation. It is also because of this aporia that the prison chaplain instructs K. that "the text [or what is written, writing, *Schrift*] is unchangeable, and opinions are often only an expression of despair over it [*die Schrift ist unveränderlich und die Meinungen sind oft nur ein Ausdruck der Verzweiflung darüber*]."[36] Writing remains identical (merely) with itself, withdraws into its own self-referentiality, yet simultaneously is exposed to its radical nonself-identity in the force field of critical attempts to provide philosophical commentary upon it.

By the same token, this special form of interpretive despair attaches to a related conclusion that Kafka's prison chaplain relays to K.: "Correct understanding of something and misunderstanding of the same thing are not entirely mutually exclusive [*Richtiges Auffassen einer Sache und Mißverstehen der gleichen Sache schließen einander nicht vollständig aus*]."37 Presumably, if the lesson of the chaplain's sentence is correct, then that lesson applies also to the sentence itself, in which case we cannot even be sure that we have begun to understand the sentence correctly in the first place and thus may have to renounce the apparent lesson that it has taught us and that forms the basis, presumably, upon which it itself is to be interpreted. The particular basis of this renunciation, however, in turn could have come into being only through our attempted interpretation of the sentence. Is this merely an aberrant thought on Kafka's part? Is it a manifestation of the "disease" that Adorno suspects has befallen all meaning in Kafka's literary world? Or is such perhaps the ultimate fate of all attempts at philosophical readings of literature?

A special test case for this particular constellation of questions may be found in Giorgio Agamben's recent interpretation of *The Trial* as Kafka's commentary on the relation between law and slander. For, as we shall see, Agamben's interpretation of Kafka's novel works tacitly to place under erasure the abiding undecidability that obtains between the literal and the figurative and that is irrevocably lodged at the heart of Kafka's text. Much of the critical commentary on the novel since its appearance has focused, often in an existentially oriented perspective, on motifs of guilt, accusation, and a denied proper trial. We might think here of influential early studies by such critics as Heinz Politzer, a collaborator of Brod's in the editing and dissemination of Kafka's texts. In Politzer's view, *The Trial* mobilizes K. primarily as a figure in whom the court can anchor its problematic, even illegitimate, claims and juridical manipulations so that the novel can be seen fundamentally as placing the court itself on trial.38 Implicitly breaking with this exegetical tradition, Agamben, by contrast, shifts our attention to the question of slander and, in particular, self-slander. Pointing out that in the tradition of Roman law with which Kafka, as a lawyer, was well familiar, a false accuser could be punished by having the designation of "kaluminator," Latin for slanderer, engraved upon his forehead in the form of the abbreviation "K," which also, of course, is the only initial by which the last name of the novel's main character is known and which also is the single initial-name of the protagonist in *The Castle*. Whereas critics in the wake of Brod have tended to reduce the K. by expanding it into "Kafka," here it becomes the mark of slander as such. Although Agamben does not mention this, it is worth noting that already Kafka himself problematizes—and thereby turns into a matter of debate and interpretation—his employment of the letter "K." when he writes in a diary entry on May 27, 1914, the year in which he commences work on *The Trial*, that "I find the letter *K* offensive, almost disgusting, and yet I write it down, it must be very characteristic of me."[39] For Agamben, reinterpreting the letter K. is a crucial step toward the recognition that "slander represents the key to the novel—and, perhaps, to the entire Kafkaesque universe, so potently marked by the forces of law."[40] And he goes even further when he suggests that if the letter *K* is not merely seen as referring to a false accusation, or *kalumnia*, but rather is thought to point to the false accuser, *kaluminator*, himself, then the protagonist of *The Trial* can be understood to conduct "a slanderous trial against himself. The someone (*jemand*) who, with his slander, has initiated the trial is Josef K. himself."[41] The novel as such can then be read as the record of a slanderous self-accusation in which the protagonist struggles to come to terms with the consequences of his illicit self-betrayal.

In order to substantiate this interpretation, Agamben reminds us that not only is Josef K. advised by a court official that he does not know whether or not he has been accused; he is also told that his having been detained is not to be construed as requiring a departure from his ordinary life. Indeed, "the judges do not seem to have any intention of initiating" a trial against K., and "the trial exists only to the extent that K. recognizes it as such," a state of affairs that "K. himself anxiously concedes to the examining magistrate during the initial inquiry."[42] As further evidence of his understanding of the text, Agamben adduces the words said to K. by the prison chaplain at the end of the "Cathedral" chapter: "The court does not want anything from you. It receives you when you come and dismisses you when you go."[43] From the perspective constructed here, the court is not the instigator of the trial but merely the site, imaginary or real, upon which the juridical and ethical negotiations between a subjective consciousness and its experience of the "lawness" of the law—the law *as* law—find a stage as well as an archive.

One of the conclusions that Agamben draws from this interpretation of *The Trial* is that Josef K.'s self-accusatory slander speaks to a certain condition within the relation between law and subject. Indeed, he argues,

> every man initiates a slanderous trial against himself. This is Kafka's point of departure. Hence his universe cannot be tragic but only comic: guilt does not exist—or rather, guilt is nothing other than self-slander, which consists in accusing oneself of a nonexistent guilt (that is, of one's very innocence, which is the comic gesture par excellence).[44]

But this comic gesture has a rather serious purposiveness. If, as Agamben argues, humans will slander themselves, it is the task of the law to distinguish, in the cases that come into its orbit, between groundless accusations and those that are potentially legitimate. From the perspective of such a distinguishing function of the law in relation to slanderous self-accusation, it becomes possible to read "the subtlety of self-slander as a strategy to deactivate and render inoperative the accusation, the indictment that the Law addresses toward Being" because the "only way to affirm one's innocence before the law (and the powers that represent the law: for example, the father, or marriage) is, in this sense, falsely to accuse oneself."[45] The paradoxical need for self-slander to protect one's innocence when faced with the law then becomes a way for Josef K. to attempt to avoid a trial, to defer the machinations of the legal system. Such a reading opens up the sense in which "K.'s strategy can be defined more precisely as the failed attempt to render the confession, but not the trial, impossible."[46]

What are we to make, at this point, of the lingering problem that is named by the tension between literal and figurative understandings of the artwork—between, on the one hand, letting the artwork, as it were, rest in and as itself and, on the other hand, helping the artwork say what it cannot say on its own, even at the risk of thereby making it superfluous as a work of art? Could it be that *The Trial* lends itself to legal-political (re) inscription in the history of the aftermath of a particular legal system— in this case, Roman law? It is as though Agamben's interpretive strategy, for all its perceptive meritoriousness, implicitly followed the dictates of a certain displacement. It works to displace the fundamental tension between the literal and the figurative dimension of the language of the artwork onto the question of how the thematic complex of the protagonist's guilt—and, by extension, his relation to the lawness of the law as such—engenders a certain perpetuation and simultaneous rupturing of certain elements inherited by our tradition from Roman law. In this sense, Agamben's reading privileges the figurative dimension of the artwork, rendering *The Trial* in principle as an allegory of the political implications of self-slander within the framework of a certain legal and moral-juridical inheritance. By translating the refractory and meaning-resistant language of the novel, through an admittedly bold new reading, into the conceptual discourse of the politics of self-accusation, Agamben believes to have found the hermeneutic key that Adorno tells us has been purloined. It is from this perspective, too, that Agamben feels emboldened to assert that the politicizing question of self-slander is lodged so deeply in the core of the artwork that this "is precisely what an attentive reading of the novel demonstrates beyond all doubt."[47] "Beyond all doubt"—as though as readers we were free to disregard the prison chaplain's warnings to Josef K. about the uncontainable aberrations and dangerous vicissitudes of interpretation itself.[48]

The wish to establish "beyond all doubt" the relations among slander, self-slander, and the law in *The Trial* presupposes the possibility of a remainderless translation between the literary text's literal and figurative dimensions, as well as their often aleatory interaction with each other. Yet this premise is complicated by the resistance of Kafka's literary language itself. When Maurice Blanchot writes that "Kafka's trial can be interpreted as a tangle of three different realms (the Law, laws, rules)," he is quick to add that this "interpretation, however, is inadequate, because to justify it one would have to assume a fourth realm not derived from the other three—the overarching realm of literature itself." "But," he reminds us, "literature rejects this dominant point of view, all the while refusing to be dependent upon, or symbolized by, any other order at all (such as pure intelligibility)."[49] If literature refuses to be derivable from other principles and realms of signification, and if it will not allow itself to be subsumed under external categories as their subspecies, its particular modes of signification also will not permit the construction of a close stretto between a text's literal and figurative levels. The reader, standing not just before the text of the law but also before the law of the text, will have to learn to do better than the man from the country. This learning, if it is to come to pass at all, would indeed have to be situated on the far side of pure intelligibility. It would have to register, along with any propaedeutic mission, something of the self-reflexive despair to which Kafka himself confesses in a diary entry from December 6, 1921, five years after he had abandoned the fragments that constitute *The Trial*: "Metaphors are one among many things which make me despair of writing [*Die Metaphern sind eines in dem Vielen, was mich am Schreiben verzweifeln läßt*]."[50]

To the extent that a "disease of all signification" makes itself uncannily felt in *The Trial*, it helps us register more precisely the contours and uncontainable effects of a certain aesthetic idiomaticity: the vicissitudes of symbolic and allegorical language that bestow upon the literary text a restless and searching experience of cognition and its deferral each time these linguistic vicissitudes come to pass in a new and singular way in a different literary artwork. A philosophically motivated reading of a literary text such as *The Trial* would have to take into account the destabilizing effects of this particular mode of deferral. In other words, a philosophically oriented interpretation would need to open itself up to the far-reaching implications of the fact that a rigorous confrontation with the text cannot occur in isolation from the experience of our abiding inability to differentiate between the literal and the figurative dimensions of the aesthetic object. If Kafka's German biographer Reiner Stach worries that "Kafka's *Trial* is a monster"—regardless of whether one considers the "genesis, manuscript, form, content, or interpretation of the novel"—and that "nothing here is normal, nothing is simple," with "obscurity wherever one looks," we might say that the burden of this obscurity is both perpetuated and illuminated by the irreducibly necessary yet rigorously unmeetable demand of conceptual interpretation that Kafka's novel issues with each sentence anew.[51] It is here that the artwork becomes recognizable not merely as the sensate appearance, or even embodiment, of an idea but rather as an aesthetic form that both elicits and resists its philosophical interpretation. And it is here, too, that the trial(s) of language will have commenced with no authoritative court and no hermeneutically stable basis for judgment in sight.[52] Before the philosophical imperative to know and to decide, the literary work of art remains an outlaw.

CHAPTER SIX

The Artwork without Cardinal Direction
Notes on Orientation in Adorno

The German systems theorist Niklas Luhmann once described the attitude and altitude of abstract thought as follows: "This theory design pushes the presentation [*Darstellung*] to unusually high levels of abstraction. Our flight must take place above the clouds, and we must reckon with a rather thick cloud cover. We must rely on our instruments. Occasionally, we may catch glimpses below of a land with roads, towns, rivers, and coastlines that remind us of something familiar." "But," he continues, "no one should fall victim to the illusion that these few points of reference are sufficient to guide our flight."[1] When thinking works to push beyond what already has been thought, not in the merely additive sense of annexing or occupying new territory but in the sense of engaging with what remains unthought and perpetually in withdrawal, it may no longer be possible to rely upon our usual organs of sense perception. Does not the thinking that wishes to transgress what is customary and admissible to think fly without the burden or benefit of received models of orientation? Would orientation itself not have to be rethought, pried, for example, out of the hands of what in the recently reformed German university system often is referred to, in a perhaps prematurely triumphant tone, as *Orientierungswissen,* or orientational knowledge? Would this thinking not also require a reinscribing of orientation into the very question—indeed, *as* the very question—of the relation between thinking and orientation? And what implications might such a reinscription have for our various discourses of thinking orientation, such as spatial orientation, sexual orientation, and mathematical orientation? In what ways might this reinscription problematize our understanding, for example, of architectural orientation and its reliance upon the sun and cardinal directions to denote the directionality of a building? After all, the etymology of "orient-ation" can be traced back to "the Orient" as that which lies in the East. And might not our insistence upon such a moment of nonself-identity inadvertently undermine our orientation to person, place, and time as measured by a psychiatric mental status exam that seeks to ascertain whether symptoms of psychotic disorder, dementia, dissociative amnesia, or other such breakdowns in orientation might have occurred? One also thinks of what in the United States and elsewhere is called "student orientation," an event that takes place before these same students go, in a hideous yet telling phrase, "shopping for classes."

Georg Lukács's well-known 1920 formulation of "transcendental homelessness,"[2] which recalls Novalis's early romanticist definition of philosophy as a perpetual homesickness, speaks to the question of orientation in modernity, as does Michel Foucault's epistemic intuition that our "present epoch will perhaps be above all the epoch of space. We are in the epoch of simultaneity: we are in the epoch of juxtaposition, the epoch of the near and far, of the side-by-side, of the dispersed." "We are at a moment," he continues, "when our experience of the world is less that of a long life developing through time than that of a network that connects points."[3] Although it might be argued that the category of the "far," in the oppositional pair of the near and the far, has been increasingly eviscerated, since Foucault's 1967 intuition, in favor of an (electronically mediated) experience of perpetual nearness, availability, and simulated presence—so that "farness" in the twenty-first century has, in a sense, ceased to exist—the question as to how to orient oneself in that reconfigured space of experience has hardly left us. On the contrary, what orientation may mean to the critical field today cannot but be thought in relation to the networks of a cultural and political paradigm sponsored by a relentless global technocapitalism, in which, as J. Hillis Miller reminds us, the orientational viability of critical thought today must measure itself against such heterogeneous threats as "global climate change . . . that may soon make the species *Homo sapiens* extinct," a "global financial meltdown brought about by the folly and greed of our politicians and financiers," "catastrophic unemployment," "endless and unwinnable war," "weakening local communities" undermined by the effects of "global telecommunication," a perpetual onslaught of electronic devices, video games, and so-called social networks that "are rapidly diminishing the role literature plays in most people's lives," not to mention "our universities," which, "like glaciers worldwide, are in meltdown mode, especially in the humanities."[4] Given this undeniable, and undeniably urgent, state of affairs, the temptation may seem great today for critical thinking to demand a strong orientational gesture, perhaps along the lines of what Fredric Jameson once called an "aesthetic of cognitive mapping" through which "we may again begin to grasp our positioning as individual and collective subjects and regain a capacity to act and struggle which is at present neutralized by our spatial as well as our social confusion."[5] Such cognitive mapping, intended to locate the self in a system of relations that otherwise seems impenetrable and unnavigable, implies an orientational activity that allows an individual consciousness to assess its position and fundamental situatedness in a network of differences and shifting forces of attraction and repulsion.[6]

If the practice of critical thought today frequently feels called upon to apply the rigor of its conceptual movements to the orientational promise of promoting a cognitive map, what is the significance of Adorno's work, which so often appears to complicate the project of orientation itself, especially in relation to the precinct of the aesthetic? Why is it that, when he casts his uncoercive gaze, he withholds any unequivocal affirmation of a stable cognitive map, resisting existing programs and available systems while, at the same time, locating this refusal precisely in, and as, the condition of possibility for the idea of a nonforeclosed futurity, an experience of life and cognition that is yet to come? We may find helpful hints by reflecting on an aspect of Adorno's uncoercive gaze that is not usually discussed or even noticed: his abiding engagement with the question of orientation as such. In so doing, we will allow the thinking of orientation to open onto a set of broader theoretical and aesthetic concerns that preoccupy, even haunt, his writings.

Although Adorno never composed a single, sustained text on the question of orientation, a rigorous engagement with this concept nevertheless punctuates his corpus at decisive moments. The problem of orientation may well belong to those heterogeneous figures that are meant to bestow, from ever-shifting vantage points and under the auspices of constantly revised modulations, different names on the concerns of Adorno's uncoercive gaze and his ways of thinking a philosophy concerned with the liberatory potential of the nonidentical. Orientation belongs, we might say, to what Adorno's former student, the philosopher Herbert Schnädelbach, considers one of the open secrets of his work: that "Adorno's philosophy in truth consists of one single thought that, however, cannot be expressed in one sentence."[7] It is as if Adorno's writing, underneath its far-reaching variety, tacitly enacted Heidegger's belief—although Adorno himself may well have resisted this conjunction—that a genuine thinker thinks but a single thought, mobilized in legions of different guises and particular engagements throughout an oeuvre.

We might also suggest that the question of the general contours of these mobilizations has been lodged, directly or in a more mediated fashion, at the heart of recent commentators' efforts to reorient our experience of Adorno's singularity in relation to its particular (and often dissimulated) conceptual truth-content. For instance, the German philosopher Martin Seel argues that this singularity emerges in the ways in which Adorno's thinking reinterprets a consciousness of contemplation that ultimately no longer is opposed to praxis but rather "keeps its distance from that with which it is concerned because it cares about that from which it gains its distance."[8] Adorno's editor Rolf Tiedemann reminds us that the specific philosophical content of Adorno's writing can "only rarely be grasped firmly with one's hands [*läßt . . . nur selten sich mit Händen greifen*]" because it requires of the reader a congenial sunkenness into the subject matter in which we "receive no formulas and recipes . . . but first of all the instruction to re-embark on the path of thinking and once more to take upon ourselves the labor and effort of the concept."[9] And although the American philosopher J. M. Bernstein orients our understanding of Adorno's often enigmatic thought by reconstructing from it a political and ethical theory that, after Auschwitz, revolves around the articulation of a new post-Kantian categorical imperative, the Belgian art historian and critic Thierry de Duve suggests that, paradoxically, we may learn how to relate to Adorno precisely by also learning to resist him—that is, by returning to a more nondialectical form of Kantianism.[10] But prior to orienting ourselves to what Adorno's multilayered and far-reaching oeuvre demands of us today, we would do well to orient ourselves to orientation itself. In fact, in Adorno's case, orienting ourselves to the ways in which orientation calls for understanding—that is, its perpetual need for reinterpretation and reinscription—demands an abiding openness to one of the hidden preoccupations that subtly inflects his corpus.

If orientation belongs to those temporary and variegated concerns that nevertheless relate in fundamental ways to the core of Adorno's uncoercive gaze as a whole, we should note from the outset that orientation itself assumes different shades of meaning throughout his texts. Often, the concept of an overly facile movement toward orientation is cast as the expression of a relentless instrumentality, even an inadmissible concession to—mobilizing a key phrase from the *Dialectic of Enlightenment*—instrumental reason itself. For instance, in his introduction to the controversy over positivism in German sociology, the so-called *Positivismusstreit*, Adorno argues that the view of science and scholarship (*Wissenschaft*) favored by positivism leads to an inhibition of radical thinking itself: "Its instrumental character, that is to say, its orientation according to the primacy of available methods [*Orientierung am Primat verfügbarer Methoden*] instead of the object and its interest, inhibits insights that concern scientific and scholarly method as well as its subject matter."[11] The process of orientation here is inextricably bound up with the affirmation of a ruling totality in which the experiential mode and the questioning mode of interpretive engagement are bracketed in favor of a scientific—or, more precisely, scientivistic—mimetic repetition that masquerades as proximity.

Along similar lines, Adorno, in his "Resumé Concerning the Culture Industry," equates the process of facile or faux orientation to the perpetuation of a certain delusional context: "The most sophisticated defense of the culture industry today celebrates its spirit, which one may well call ideology, as a factor of order [*Ordnungsfaktor*]. It provides human beings in a supposedly chaotic world with something like measuring sticks for orientation [*Maßstäbe zur Orientierung*], and that in itself is said to be laudable." Adorno adds: "But what they consider to be preserved by the culture industry is destroyed all the more thoroughly. The cozy old pub is demolished more by color film than bombs ever could. . . . No *Heimat* survives its adaptation by the films that celebrate it and that turn everything unique and distinctive, on which they feed, into something confusingly similar [*alles Unverwechselbare, wovon sie zehren, zum Verwechseln gleichmachen*]."[12] Orientation, in this sense, lives off the semblance of providing an order that it itself, however, in actuality undermines. By calling attention to itself as the measure of what appears immeasurable, this form of orientation erases singularity in the name of fortifying it, eliding interpretability precisely by pretending to serve as that interpretability's archive. What would be required to question orientation in a more deliberate fashion would also call upon us to enter a certain disorientation with respect to orientation, if what is meant by orientation is the setting into place of what can be thought, and experienced as thought, in the first place.

We find similar frameworks of analysis with regard to *Orientierung* in a variety of Adorno's texts, from his exposition of the false orientation provided by daily newspaper horoscopes to the pseudo-orientation offered by popular forms of music that are not actually popular—that is, of the people—but propagated and mobilized by boardrooms and their business interests. To what extent might it be possible, then, to read a long stretch, perhaps the entire distance, of Adorno's curvy path of thinking—from his Frankfurt dissertation on Husserl, completed at the tender age of 21, and his 1931 habilitation on Kierkegaard's aesthetics, via *Minima Moralia*, *The Philosophy of New Music*, and *Notes to Literature*, all the way to *Negative Dialectics* and his posthumous *Aesthetic Theory*—as an open and infinitely demanding series of engagements with, and meditations upon, the question, now explicit, now hidden, of orientation itself?

When engaging issues such as orientation in Adorno's thought, one would do well to remain faithful and vigilantly responsible to the perpetual difficulty posed by the fact that virtually all his writing issues from a seemingly concurrent and refractory attachment to both possibility and impossibility, affirmation and negation. As Derrida professes, "I admire and love in Adorno someone who never stopped hesitating between the philosopher's 'no' and the 'yes, perhaps, sometimes that does happen' of the poet, the writer or the essayist, the musician, the painter, the playwright, or scriptwriter, or even the psychoanalyst." He adds: "In hesitating between the 'no' and the 'yes, sometimes, perhaps,' Adorno was heir to both. He took account of what the concept, even the dialectic, could not conceptualize in the singular event, and he did everything he could to take on the responsibility of this double legacy."[13] In learning how to read the legacy of orientation, we too become heirs of the doubling of which Adorno himself is heir, a double inheritance in which possibility and impossibility can be neither conflated nor kept apart, a thinking that perpetually disavows its self-identificatory allegiances in order to become what it is or strives to be.

To orient ourselves, then, to the question of orientation in Adorno while also affirming the potentialities of disorientation in critical thought and aesthetics—still on the far side of Luhmann's cloud line of visibility—we may turn to Kant, a thinker who was first brought into the center of Adorno's intellectual orbit through Saturday afternoon readings of the *Critiques* with his older friend and later Frankfurt School colleague Siegfried Kracauer. Adorno would return to Kant again and again at decisive moments in his work. Though shunning the contemporary trends of German neo-Kantianism, Adorno maintained his abiding relationship to the other end of German Idealism embodied in the proper name Hegel. Adorno even devoted a series of lecture courses to Kant's critical thought. Kant's analytic conjunction of thinking and orientation occurs specifically in his 1786 essay, "Was heißt: sich im Denken orientieren?" (literally "What Is Called Orienting Oneself in Thinking?" and sometimes translated, a bit problematically, as "What Is Orientation in Thinking?"). Here, Kant not only intervenes in a quarrel between Moses Mendelsohn and Friedrich Heinrich Jacobi over Lessing and Spinoza; he also tacitly functions as a kind of orienting device for Western critical thought itself. Just as Adorno's thinking provides an orientational framework for the first generation of

Frankfurt School Critical Theory, both in its confrontation with, and in its problematization of, Kantian philosophy and facile mobilizations of orientation, Kant's critical philosophy establishes what he calls a "signpost or compass" with respect to all who write and think in the wake of Kantian critique. It is perhaps no accident that the poet Hölderlin, in a remarkable letter written on New Year's Day 1799 to his brother, ascribes a certain orientational function to the philosopher when he suggests that "Kant is the Moses of our nation, leading it out of its Egyptian exhaustion into the free, solitary desert of speculation."[14]

If the Kantian project establishes critical concepts that cannot be derived from a priori interpretations of experience, yet are said to enrich and deepen our cognition of the relation among understanding, reason, and experience, then the abstract thought that is mobilized in this endeavor cannot be articulated apart from the category of orientation. Kant writes: "To orient oneself, in the proper sense of the word, means to use a given direction—and we divide the horizon into four of these—in order to find the others, and in particular that of *sunrise*. If I see the sun in the sky and know that it is now midday, I know how to find the south, west, north, and east." "For this purpose, however, I must," Kant continues, "necessarily be able to feel the difference within my own *subject*, namely that between my right and my left hands. I call this a *feeling* because these two sides display no perceptible difference as far as external intuition [*Anschauung*] is concerned."[15] Acknowledging that the process of orientation unfolds in constant interaction with a set of a priori coordinates, the objective data in the sky, Kant emphasizes the ways in which orientation becomes a matter of a subjective consciousness entering into a particular constellation not only with external orientational data but also, significantly, with itself. Thus, he argues,

> in spite of all the objective data in the sky, I orient myself *geographically* purely by means of a *subjective* distinction; and if all the constellations, while in other respects retaining the same shape and the same position in relation to each other, were one day miraculously transposed so that their former easterly direction now became west, no human eye would notice the slightest change on the next clear night, and even the astronomer, if he heeded only what he saw and not at the same time what he felt, would inevitably become disoriented.[16]

Kant, extending his concept of orientation from space to thought—that is, from a mathematically defined entity to a logically defined one—locates the feeling of a need within reason itself, because "while ignorance is in itself the cause of the limits of our knowledge, it is not the cause of the errors within it."[17] Kant's thinking of orientation, then, is predicated upon the premise that "to orient oneself in thought means to be guided, in one's conviction of truth, by a subjective principle of reason where objective principles of reason are inadequate."[18]

Although for Kant reason does not feel, it does impose on consciousness the experience of a felt need in thinking that itself cannot be justified within the limits of reason alone. In other words, reason's mode of orientational thinking—along with the thought of freedom and the freedom of thought—imposes its own laws on itself, emphasizing the self-positing of *autonomia* (that which gives itself its own laws) over *heteronomia* (that which receives its laws from elsewhere). Therefore, "freedom of thought also signifies the subjection of reason to no laws other than those *which it imposes on itself*,"[19] while at the same time "freedom of thought, if it tries to act independently even of the laws of reason, eventually destroys itself."[20] The constellation of stars that makes orientation thinkable in the Kantian sense thus always illuminates by reflecting a light that is both necessary and insufficient, providing a frame of reference for a model of relational orientation at whose core is lodged a self-referential concept of reason that works to sponsor an intimation of the moment at which a thinking and feeling consciousness finds itself placed into its setting.

It is this question of a consciousness having been placed into an orientational setting that also concerns another careful reader of Kant's essay on orientation: Heidegger. In division one of *Being and Time*, on the spatiality of Being-in-the-World (paragraphs 22–24), Heidegger emphasizes that Kant's model of orientation—as it unfolds in "Was heißt: Sich im Denken orientieren?"—does not take the ontologically constitutive role of Being-in-the-World quite seriously enough. Although Kant's concern is with the subjective foundation of orientation as such, in Heidegger's account the subjectivity of objective orientation is to be thought in terms of the essential directedness of Being-in-the-World as such ("wesenhafte Ausrichtung des Daseins überhaupt") that is always already determined by the experience of finding oneself, and thinking about ways of finding oneself, in such and such a world.[21] The later Heidegger's poetically condensed statement, in *Aus der Erfahrung des Denkens* ("From the experience of thinking," translated as "The Thinker as Poet"), also implicitly casts the Kantian concern with orientation in thinking in terms of a movement of thinking toward one element in the celestial constellation, the star: "Auf einen Stern zugehen, nur dieses. Denken ist die Einschränkung auf einen Gedanken, der einst wie ein Stern am Himmel der Welt stehen bleibt" ("To head toward a star—this only. To think is to confine yourself to a single thought that one day stands still like a star in the world's sky").[22] In keeping with his conviction that a true thinker thinks, in the course of his variegated production, at bottom only a single thought, Heidegger's image depicts the movement whereby orientation in thinking also can mean a decisive *Einschränkung*, or confinement, to a single arrested thought that will illuminate an otherwise obscure and unthought mode of dwelling in the world. Orienting oneself in relation to this ever-more-rigorous self-confinement of thinking also necessitates a reconsideration of what calls for thinking and of what thinking itself may impose upon, and require from, us when our orientational efforts no longer can take the history and authority of metaphysics for granted.

For Adorno, the radical thinking of critique can have no guiding image and no image to guide it, even and especially when it assumes the complex inheritance of the Kantian self-critique of reason. In his conceptual preface to a collection of essays concerning questions of art, aesthetics, and ideology, *Ohne Leitbild. Parva Aesthetica*—written, with the exception of the Chaplin essay, between the late 1950s and the mid-1960s—Adorno unhinges the very idea and tenability of a *Leitbild* or image capable of serving as a unifying orientational model. Wishing to submit to scrutiny "what the call for guiding images suggests [*was es mit dem Ruf nach Leitbildern auf sich hat*]," he writes: "If one calls for them, they are already no longer possible; if one pronounces them out of a desperate wish, they are transformed by a spell [*verhext*] into blind and heteronomous powers that only increase powerlessness and as such conform to totalitarian attitudes." And Adorno continues: "In the norms and guiding images which, fixed and immovable, are said to aid human beings in achieving orientation in relation to intellectual production [*zur Orientierung einer geistigen Produktion*] whose innermost principle is, after all, freedom, what is reflected is only the weakness of the I over against circumstances which they believe themselves not to be able to control and the blind power of that which is."[23] Might not the premature call for orientation in thinking also function as the symptom of a foreclosure in whose name a normativity and affirmation of something that already exists anyway is given the tacit legitimacy of reflexive judgment? "Those who today oppose, in an incantatory manner, so-called chaos with a cosmos of values," Adorno argues, "only demonstrate the extent to which this very chaos already has become the law of their own actions and mental images." Instead, they might do well to realize that especially in the realm of the aesthetic, "artistic norms and criteria," to the extent that they exceed their status as emblems of an a priori dogma, cannot be "finished," cannot be complete, cannot provide guiding lessons and orientational norms that lie beyond their "own movement [*eigenen Bewegung*]."[24] The self-reflexive orientational question of this *eigene Bewegung*, particularly and above all in the sphere of the artwork, will never leave Adorno.[25]

Another way of posing the question of an artwork's movement or automovement in relation to issues of orientation is staged in the literary work of Kafka, an author to whom Adorno, like his early teacher and interlocutor Benjamin, devotes sustained reflection, as we saw in chapter 5. In a text from 1920 that Kafka's friend and literary executor Max Brod later assigned the title "Kleine Fabel," or "Little Fable," Kafka writes:

> "Ach", sagte die Maus, "die Welt wird enger mit jedem Tag. Zuerst war sie so breit, daß ich Angst hatte, ich lief weiter und war glücklich, daß ich endlich rechts und links in der Ferne Mauern sah, aber diese langen Mauern eilen so schnell aufeinander zu, daß ich schon im letzten Zimmer bin, und dort im Winkel steht die Falle, in die ich laufe."—"Du mußt nur die Laufrichtung ändern", sagte die Katze und fraß sie.
>
> ["Oh," said the mouse, "the world is becoming narrower with each day. First it was so wide that I was afraid; I kept running and was happy that I finally saw walls to the left and right in the distance, but these long walls are rushing so quickly toward one another that I am already in the last room, and there in the corner stands the trap into which I am running."— "You only need to change the direction of your running," said the cat and ate it.][26]

The three sentences that constitute Kafka's deceptively simple text are too rich, too deeply nuanced, and too far-reaching for a full discussion here. After all, it behooves us to recall once again Adorno's sentiment that Kafka's work "expresses itself not through expression but by its repudiation, by breaking off. It is a parabolic system the key to which has been stolen.... Each sentence says 'interpret me,' and none will permit it." Kafka's sentences are closer to allegory than to symbol in that each "is literal and each signifies," but, for Adorno, as we recall from our discussion of *The Trial* in chapter 5, these "two moments are never merged, as the symbol would have it, but yawn apart" in the perpetual deferral and noncoincidence that is the allegorical mode.[27] We therefore might narrow our perspective on this allegorical text—reenacting, as it were, the relentless movement of narrowing that the mouse itself perceives—to the question of directionality and the attendant problem of orientation that saturate it. What the mouse initially perceives as the lamentable unidirectionality of its uneasy forward trajectory, caused by an intense anxiety regarding the world's fundamental heterogeneity and potential unreadability ("First it was so wide that I was afraid [or anxious—"*daß ich Angst hatte*"]"), narrows into a vortex that propels the mouse along ever-more-quickly rushing walls straight into a trap. It is from the perspective of the cat, who perhaps has been observing the scenario all along, that the advice to change direction is uttered—but this very advice, only superficially intended to reverse the unidirectionality that leads the mouse into the trap, provides no viable alternative to the mouse. One might say that this figurative change of directionality unravels not only the meaning of the reorientation but also the meaning of meaning itself. Here, understanding is shown to be in perpetual need of understanding. At the precise moment when the cat interrupts the scene by violently devouring the mouse, both text and animal are terminated, leaving the hermeneutic determination of this termination both under- and overdetermined.

The figure of a change of direction that fails to provide any viable coordinates for orientation is made vivid from yet another perspective. The words that Kafka has the cat speak—"Du mußt nur die Laufrichtung ändern"—stage an intertextual allusion to the famous last line of Rilke's 1908 poem "Archaischer Torso Appolos," "Du mußt Dein Leben ändern" ("You must change your life.")[28] The laconic and apodictic declarative mode and mood of this statement, its tone, syntax, words, and style, conjure the image of a possibility. The promise of a new orientation appears to emerge in both Rilke's and Kafka's declarations, if a change of direction can be realized. "Du mußt nur die Laufrichtung ändern"—"Du mußt Dein Leben ändern." Whereas Rilke's line appears to provide no judgment as to the relative difficulty of this change of direction, Kafka's line, through the addition of the adverb "nur" ("only") seems to suggest that achieving this change of direction would be a relatively simple endeavor. But although the poetological vision of Rilke's line appears to hold out the promise of redemption as a reward for the successful change of course by a determined consciousness, in Kafka's version the evoked ease of the "nur" is negated by the consequences that follow upon its realization: the mouse's death. Kafka's "nur," then, ultimately reveals itself as the quasi-theatrical staging of a scene of bad faith (in which the cat never had any intention of offering the mouse life-sustaining advice but only wished to further its own self-interest) or as the radical undoing of the actual possibility of a change of direction as such. If Kafka's text is read as an allegory of its own unreadability, this interpretation engages with the double necessity of seeking reorientation and failing to achieve it, which is to say, failing at something for which there are no known conditions of success. We might say that Adorno's general diagnosis with regard to all of Kafka's sentences ("Each sentence says 'interpret me,' and none will permit it") is staged with particular force when Kafka's sentences engage the vexed problems of directionality, orientation and reorientation, and the elusive promise of redemption that his sentences both engender and foreclose.

Had work on his magnum opus, the *Aesthetic Theory*, not been terminated by his untimely death in the summer of 1969, Adorno might have appreciated the 1988 literary prose text *Zur Frage der Himmelsrichtungen* ("On the question of cardinal directions") by the German writer Reinhard Lettau, member of the famed Group 47 and close ally of Adorno's friend and Frankfurt School colleague Herbert Marcuse.[29] There, in the first scene of the text, the first-person narrator, standing on a roof overlooking the San Francisco Bay, finds his friend pointing westward to refer to the world of the East, causing the narrator to ponder whether east is always located in the East, west in the West, and so forth. The narrator spends the rest of the text wittily deconstructing the idea of orientation and the question of cardinal directions, but precisely with the objective still of orienting himself. Whereas the one who would set out to walk around the globe would see the East turn itself into the West with each step, the narrator whimsically, even grotesquely, ends up by locating the secret center of the world in a place where one would not have expected it: in the small German town of Erfurt, Lettau's hometown in Thuringia, which emerges as the one reliable spot in the world, within the logic of the linguistic artwork, from which any and all geographical directions actually make sense.

Whereas Lettau's narrator succeeds in identifying the secret center of the world and, by extension, the very practice of orientation itself—if only ironically—Adorno's writing allows no such moment of imagined relief. For those seeking orientation, Adorno will hardly serve as a guide. No intellectual gyroscope emerges from his writing, no instrument that would ensure orientation and its navigating measurements. Instead, readers are asked to follow his uncoercive gaze, moving toward formulations of concrete thought and charting the paths of reading and thinking as unregimented, nonpredigested forms of experience. The extreme conditions of this icy-desert require their own orientational strategies and adaptive gestures. As Adorno stated in an interview only weeks before his death, "In my writings, I have never offered a model for any kind of action or for some specific campaign. I am a theoretical human being who views theoretical thinking as lying extraordinarily close to his artistic intentions."[30] He elaborates on this perspective by emphasizing that "philosophy cannot in and of itself recommend immediate measures" but that it rather "effects change precisely by remaining theory." "I think," Adorno confesses, "that for once the question should be asked whether it is not also a form of resistance when a human being thinks and writes things the way I write them. Is theory not also a genuine form of praxis?"[31] To orient oneself properly with regard to orientation, then, also would mean not to allow the disappointment that attaches to disorientation to efface prematurely the transformative potential that suffuses both rigorous conceptual reflection and radical artistic experimentation.

Taking up and extending Adorno's concern with orientation in thinking, we might say that no thinking is possible without some kind of orientation, if only a minimal, residual, hesitant attachment, a fleeting commitment, to the possibility of ordering space and locating sense within it. Yet what thinking, rigorously understood, demands always exceeds thinking itself, its orientation and localization, its justification and delimitation, its stable cognitive map. Within orientation, disorientation also lingers. Under Adorno's uncoercive gaze, the artwork orients us precisely to disorientation.

Allowing oneself to be oriented toward disorientation also means orienting oneself toward a nonsaturated thinking to come. This orientation toward disorientation ultimately requires something of the double logic with which the artist, in another essay from 1967's *Ohne Leitbild*, "Die Kunst und die Künste" ("Art and the Arts"), is obliged to approach his craft—that is, the double gesture that remains faithful to its treacherousness. The artist must, in a sense, know what he does and at the same time not know it; the genuine artwork always is something other than repetition to the extent that it is also "a thing among things," a thing of "which we do not fully know what it is" ("von dem wir nicht wissen, was es ist").[32] In the end, the critical moment of orientation, like the artwork itself, can retain the challenge that it embodies only by interminably working both to posit and to displace its own space of reference.

CHAPTER SEVEN

False Life, Living On
Adorno with Derrida

Thinking and thanking form an uneasy couplet. As Nietzsche, the great doubter and relentless interrogator of ingratitude, cautions us in *Human, All-Too-Human: A Book for Free Spirits*, "He who gives a great gift encounters no gratitude [*findet keine Dankbarkeit*]; for the recipient, simply by accepting it, already has too much of a burden [*denn der Beschenkte hat schon durch das Annehmen zu viel Last*]."[1] It is no coincidence, therefore, that Nietzsche later has Zarathustra say: "Great indebtedness does not make men grateful [*nicht dankbar*], but vengeful [*sondern rachsüchtig*]; and if a little charity is not forgotten, it turns into a gnawing worm [*Nage-Wurm*]."[2] There is a sense in which the thinking of thanking, and the act of thanking for thinking, are fraught with an irreducible overdetermination. The gift for which we are called upon to give thanks places a double burden on us: the fact of its magnitude (which may be out of all proportion to what we were prepared to receive) and the corresponding debt of gratitude that we come to owe to the one from whom we have received the gift. Perhaps we might say, *pace* Nietzsche, that the "gift," when thought in the context of thanking, becomes visible in both its English and its German senses—that is, as a present and as a poison. If Nietzsche's intuition is correct, our indebtedness also occasions something other than gratitude. It evokes resentment and persistent feelings of revenge, gnawing at us like a worm. There is no doubt about the pertinence of Nietzsche's sentiment.

Yet perhaps we should begin by taking a step back to contemplate specific circumstances that will cast the relationship between thinking and thanking into sharper relief. One such circumstance is the pivotal moment in which a thinker, poet, or artist receives the public honor of a prize and responds to this honor with a speech that records, and thinks through, his or her gratitude.

Delivering a public speech to mark such an occasion makes visible the imbrication of the honoree's own life and thinking with the life and thinking of an other. This *being-with* is a fundamental dimension of our being in the world. As creatures who dwell in *Mitsein,* we also think, speak, and write within more or less visible quotation marks. Even the thoughts that we, in moments of egoic grandeur, call our "own" tend to be mere evocations of other voices that participate in a spectral conversation inside of us. As such, the occasion of a prize speech invites the one whose life and work are being honored to reflect upon, and to make public, the traces of those others who have made the honoree's life and work what they are. Therefore, a prize acceptance speech also calls into presence the inextricable relation between thinking and thanking, which is to say, the relation between the call issued by an other's thinking and the gratitude that such an inheritance silently demands. This gratitude of and for thinking hardly can be reduced to the currency of an economic transaction, the mere repayment of an outstanding debt, which, once performed, would lift, from the one who has recorded this gratitude, the burden of debt and guilt (two interlaced concepts for which, as Nietzsche himself well knew, German tellingly employs but a single word, *Schuld*).[3] What is it about contemplating the relation between thinking and thanking in the rhetorical contexts of a prize acceptance speech that sheds new light on a thinking life that is both inherited and created for another time, a time to come, a time that is still to be lived? And—from the perspective of the fragility and radical finitude of the life in which thinking and thanking meet—how do thinking and thanking inflect our relation to the idea of damaged life, possible survival, and modes of living on?

Paul Celan's 1958 "Speech on the Occasion of Receiving the Literature Prize of the Free Hanseatic City of Bremen" bears the visible and invisible scars of a life lived on, a life of Shoah survival, and a life of mourning the loss of others, including the death of his father and mother, at the hands of the Nazis. Thirteen years after the end of World War II, Celan casts his life as "the efforts of someone who, overarced by the stars that are human handiwork, and who shelterless in this till now undreamt-of sense and thus most uncannily in the open, goes with his very being to language, stricken by and seeking reality."[4] The poet's attempts to locate damaged life and its possible futurities in language and in a language to come require a certain vigilant mindfulness and a relentlessly commemorative gratitude. It is not by chance, therefore, that Celan takes the imbrication of thinking and thanking as his point of departure, reminding his listeners in the opening words of his acceptance speech:

> Thinking and thanking in our language are words from one and the same source. Whoever follows out their meaning enters the semantic field of: "recollect," "bear in mind," "remembrance," "devotion." Permit me, from this standpoint, to thank you.[5]
>
> [Denken und Danken sind in unserer Sprache Worte ein und desselben Ursprungs. Werihrem Sinn folgt, begibt sich in den Bedeutungsbereich von: "gedenken", "eingedenk sein", "Andenken", "Andacht". Erlauben Sie mir, Ihnen von hier aus zu danken.][6]

Celan emphasizes the topography of thinking and thanking, giving particular thought to the site ("von hier aus") from which his thanking emanates. It is from this place, from this standpoint, from this poetic *hier*, that the thinking of thanking issues forth. He speaks of a thinking and thanking that will come to pass in language, a language that is shared by others, and therefore is multiple—not "in *meiner* Sprache" but always "in *unserer* Sprache." For Celan, to speak, to think, and to thank means to speak with, to think with, and to thank many others. He begins to speak by seeking permission from those others ("Erlauben Sie mir," permit me) to thank them from that particular precarious place where thinking and thanking intersect. His solicitation is necessitated by the fact that the other can be thanked only when the thinking of thanking has emerged as a site in its own right. The gratitude that comes to pass in the act of thanking thereby is staged in and as a certain doubling: as a form of thanking for the thinking that has led to the prize itself and as a form of thanking the other for enabling thinking as the locus ("von hier aus") from which thanking can occur.

Through allusion and quotation without quotation marks, Celan records his implicit indebtedness to German mysticism (whose archaic German formulations "Eingedenken" and "eingedenk sein" play a key role in a certain commemorative practice of remembrance and interiorization), to the poetry of Hölderlin (whose 1803 hymn "Andenken" is of special significance to him), as well as to the thinking of Heidegger. By the time Celan delivered his Bremen prize speech, he had been studying Heidegger's writings, including his lectures on Hölderlin, for several years (at least since 1951, when he read *Der Feldweg*), and he would continue to read Heidegger's work, eventually giving a reading in his presence, corresponding with him, engaging in a series of personal meetings with him, and writing a poem, "Taudtnauberg," about the vicissitudes of a complicated encounter in Heidegger's Black Forest hut.[7] To conjoin thinking and thanking at the outset of his prize speech is also to record, if only through allusion, Celan's complex debt to a thinker to whom he felt uneasily bound by an opaque and porous band. Throughout his life, Celan felt deeply troubled by Heidegger's erstwhile alliance with the National Socialist movement and his steadfast refusal to break his silence about it—much less to begin to think through it—after the end of the war. For Celan, the conjunction of thinking and thanking the other is also relevant to a damaged life, whose contours are cast into sharp relief by the poetically and intellectually compelling—even necessary—yet always unsettling gesture of giving thought and giving thanks.

The recalcitrant couplet *Denken* and *Danken*, thinking and thanking, evokes a reflection on the life in which the two occur—and other lives that are touched by this life in multiple ways. If Celan's implicit reference here is to Heidegger's meditations on what there is to be thought and to be thanked for, the reference is operative on several levels. The two words and concepts, separated only by a vowel, appear as early as Heidegger's 1929 inaugural lecture, "What Is Metaphysics?," a lecture that Celan, according to a penciled notation in his amply underlined copy of the book, read in August 1952.[8] There, Heidegger thematizes the connection between *Denken* and *Danken* in the realm of poetic writing (*Dichten*), in a way that surely would have caught the attention of a poet. Reflecting on the ways in which being can be thought to be imbricated in the shifting constellation of *Dichten*, *Denken*, and *Danken*, Heidegger suggests that "*Danken* and *Dichten*, in different ways, probably stem from primordial thinking, which they require but without being capable of being a *Denken* in themselves."[9] Heidegger later returns to these concerns in his interpretations of Hölderlin's poetry, which also are informed by the nexus of *Dichten*, *Denken*, and *Danken*—and which Celan received as a gift from his close friend, the Austrian poet Klaus Demus in 1953—and in the 1951–1952 lecture "What Is Called Thinking?" ("Was heißt Denken?") that Celan read in 1954.[10] In this lecture, Heidegger elaborates on the ways in which *Denken* and *Danken* enable each other. He asks: "What is it that is named with the words 'Denken,' 'Gedachtes,' 'Gedanke'? Toward what sphere of what is spoken do they point?" Heidegger continues: "Is *Denken* a *Danken*? What does *Danken* mean here? Or does *Dank* rest in *Denken*? What does *Denken* mean here? Is memory no more than a container for the *Gedachte* of *Denken*, or does *Denken* itself reside in *Gedächtnis*? How does *Dank* relate to

Gedächtnis?"[11] By situating thought (*der Gedanke*) and thanks (*der Dank*) in the shared etymological ancestor *der Gedanc*, we also hear echoes of *Gedächtnis*, or memory, and the Hegelian distinction between *Gedächtnis* and *Erinnerung*. The distinction here is between memory as a kind of reflective thinking (a *Gedächtnis* that relates to *Gedanke* and *Denken*) and memory as a nonthinking interiorization (*Erinnerung* as the mnemonic act of the one who interiorizes, "*Er innert*"). In Heidegger's model, *Dank* is the gift that *Denken* presents, insofar as something that requires thanks necessarily comes from an other and is given (*geben, gegeben*) by the other as a gift (*Gabe*). It is here—in the gift that comes from the other, the gift that reaches us from outside ourselves and requires an acknowledgment of the other—that we are confronted with our own dependence on, and fundamental interrelatedness with, the other. When we experience this thinking form of thanking that the other inspires in us, then—precisely in the act of receiving the other's gift, the gift that is the other—we also remark upon the ways in which we are called upon by the idea of the other more generally. That is to say, in and through the other we experience our fundamental relatedness to the other as our thinking opens onto the idea of *relation* itself. In this moment we can begin to think the thanks that are due for the talent with which our existence has been gifted, our personal *Begabung* that becomes visible in the *Gabe* when it illuminates the relation of *Denken* and *Danken* in the act of *Dichten*. Heidegger's reflections on life's inexorable imbrication of thinking, thanking, writing, and memorializing that dwells in language impose themselves, in an almost spectral way, on Celan as he accepts his prize.

In her lecture on the occasion of receiving the Theodor W. Adorno Prize of the City of Frankfurt on September 11, 2012, Judith Butler performs her own imbrication of thinking and thanking by reminding her audience of the political significance of Adorno's famous sentence "Es gibt kein richtiges Leben im falschen" or, in the published English translation, "Wrong life cannot be lived rightly" (not an unproblematic rendition, as we shall see).[12] Without making explicit reference to the genealogy of a legacy, she inscribes herself in a tradition of prize speeches—which, in the modern German context includes, among many others, such illustrious examples as Celan's Bremen and "Meridian" speeches, Hannah Arendt's Lessing Prize speech, and, more recently, Alexander Kluge's Schiller Memorial Prize speech—that employ the rhetorical moment of the prize acceptance speech to place the conjunction of thinking and thanking into syntactical relation with a larger reflection on the life in which this conjunction comes to pass. In Butler's prize speech, Adorno's dictum about the right life provides an occasion for reflecting on its connection to some of the themes that have occupied her own thinking, such as the concepts of resistance, the grievability or nongrievability of various lives, the distribution of different lives' vulnerability, and the plural—and therefore always shared—exposure to precarity. She reminds us that Adorno's concern embodies "a question that takes new form depending on the historical time in which it is formulated," while the "historical time in which we live" works to "condition and permeate the form of the question itself."[13] Although we cannot follow Butler's particular concerns in her Adorno Prize lecture through extensive commentary here, for our present purposes we will allow it to set the stage for our own consideration, with regard to the rhetorical and experiential moment that conjoins thinking and thanking—which is to say, the moment that makes them visible once again in their always already shared gestures—in a reflection on the very life in which they occur.

Let us approach this knot of problems through a series of fundamental questions that are provoked by Adorno's sentence. What is one to do if one has the feeling that the life in which one participates, or that has imposed itself on oneself, is somehow fundamentally wrong and that this falsity cannot merely be accepted, assimilated into one's psychical economy as natural or self-evident? This falsity could encompass, among other things, the perpetuation of needless suffering; an unjust and unsustainable global political economy such as late techno-finance capitalism; an ideological formation that mistakes its own untruth as corresponding to reality; an institutional crisis in which the very principles on which the institution was supposedly founded are systematically violated; an unthinking comportment toward the lifeworld in which other life-forms are intentionally or casually denigrated through daily ecocides; or, on a more experience-near level, the realization that our relations to others have been tacitly instrumentalized and ossified by the dominant epistemes of our times, in which our relations to others become ever more visible as one of the three major sources of suffering that Freud identifies.[14] To evoke Lenin's old question, what is to be done in such a situation? Should one fight for change or ignore the falsity one has identified? Or are resignation and acceptance more appropriate responses? For the one who requires clarification on the presumed falsity of his or her life, it may seem attractive to heed the well-known advice rendered in a laconically declarative mode and mood by the lyrical voice of Rilke's "Du mußt Dein Leben ändern"—"You must change your life," which we already encountered in chapter 6.[15] Saturated with both urgency and potentiality, Rilke's poetic command, one may now add, implies that such change is in fact possible and that the effects of that change could be measured, at least in principle, independently of the general *Lebenswelt*, to employ Husserl's old phenomenological term. In other words, a singular life's change takes place or at least is made an object of reflection and thus of potential change. The trajectories of a particular life and its lifeworld could then be measured in separation from each other, even as they necessarily intersect and serve as the condition of possibility for each other.

A powerfully contrapuntal mode of reflection can be found in facets of Adorno's moral philosophy. As a writer meticulously attuned to the movements of Celan's prose and poetry and as a thinker whose exchanges with Celan elicited, among other things, the wish to write a book about him (a wish never realized), Adorno produces sentences that often seem marked, even overdetermined, by the concerns with damaged life that permeate Celan's writing after Auschwitz. Adorno's apodictic statement occurs at the conclusion of thought-image 18, "Refuge for the Homeless," in part one of his *Minima Moralia: Reflections from Damaged Life:* "Es gibt kein richtiges Leben im falschen" (which, as opposed to the published English translation, means something closer to "There is no right life within the false one").[16] To be sure, the immediate context of this part of *Minima Moralia*, composed in American exile in 1944 (with part two added in 1945 and part three in 1946–1947), is the experience of a world-historical darkness. Celan, in his poem "Death Fugue," written between 1944 and early 1945, would call this experience the "thousand darknesses of death-bringing speech"—foisted on life by Hitler's National Socialism. Yet Adorno's concern with the question of life and living also opens onto a more general and conceptual level, one that transcends the experience of both the particularity of his life and its historical specificity, however much this double situatedness can neither be shucked nor ignored by the thinking that it produces.[17] For no matter how much a life may wish to change, no matter how much it may wish to heed Rilke's command to change, even a transformed life cannot transcend its own falsity, or merely propel itself out of this falsity through an act of determined consciousness, because the larger life or lifeworld in which a single life's change takes place is still predicated upon a fundamental falsity. From that perspective, life cannot carve out a niche for itself, a niche of rightness or goodness in a sea of falsity, the way a beautiful soul, as Goethe would call it, will not succumb to the postlapsarian darkness and baseness that seem to have befallen life. Among other things, Adorno's sentence is meant to caution us against what he rejects as "a tone of fresh and cheerful conviction" according to which "if only you change little things here and there, then perhaps everything will be better. I cannot accept this presupposition."[18] To mistake miniscule, superficial change—a merely reformist adjustment of what is—for an actual transformation of the false whole, can be a way, he seems to suggest, not only of creating the false impression that the iron collar of the currently prevailing conditions in principle could be cast off at will, but also of betraying the possibility of a true transformation to come. Such supposed change therefore deserves to be rejected as a premise for any transformative thought and praxis. Yet if Adorno's well-known statement about false life can be understood not merely as a form of resignation but, on the contrary, as an implicit call to think the conditions of possibility for a reexamination of that very "false life," it also points, through the negative dialectic it performs, toward the refractory possibility of a "right life," which itself, however, is not yet determined but rather remains to be thought. This fragile future-directedness of thinking always also subtends the uncoercive gaze, which will not remain demarcated by the present or the past but always also is attuned to its own possible futurity. To witness Adorno worry about the possible impossibility of a right life within a false life is to be reminded of the affirmative nature of negation, for to write a pessimistic text is a thoroughly optimistic act. It is not coincidental that the Blanchot of *The Writing of the Disaster* quotes Valéry's dictum "Optimists write badly," then adds: "But pessimists do not write."[19] Such, we might say, is Adorno's negatively dialectical perspective on the precariousness of living a life and on casting an uncoercive gaze upon that life.

"Es gibt kein richtiges Leben im falschen," Adorno says. How are we to translate this statement? As we have noted, the standard English translation, by Jephcott, offers: "Wrong life cannot be lived rightly."[20] To be sure, this is one legitimate way of glossing (or perhaps dubbing) this thorny sentence. But Adorno is too exacting a writer for us to remain indifferent to the precision and nuances of his language. "Es gibt kein richtiges Leben im falschen" mobilizes a self-consciously spatial rhetoric ("im," which is a contraction of the dative form "in dem") to pursue its thought ("richtiges im falschen"), a rhetoric that is elided in the English translation. After all, at stake in Adorno's formulation is not simply the possibility of a reversal (according to the terms of which a wrong life could be reversed by being lived rightly) but rather the question of whether, *within* the context of a larger wrongness or falsehood (what Adorno generally calls life's *Verblendungszusammenhang* or broad delusional context), it is possible to demarcate a form of life that differs enough from the wrong life that surrounds and even situates it, to be named a right life at all. It is interesting to note that, for instance, the standard Italian translation of Adorno's German sentence keeps the philosophical and political emphasis on spatiality alive through the contraction "nella" ("in" plus "la"): "Non si dà vera vita nella falsa."[21]

The official Spanish translation, too, maintains the spatial situatedness of Adorno's reflection: "No cabe la vida justa en la vida falsa."[22] The standard French translation, in turn, is an interesting case because, though it retains Adorno's "im" by rendering it as "dans," it is also highly problematic in that it inserts "monde" (world) for "life": "Il ne peut y avoir de vraie vie dans un monde qui ne l'est pas." In other words, through its misleading shift from life to world, the French translation acts as if Adorno had written "in einer Welt, die es nicht ist" ("in a world that is not [right or true]"), effectively rendering inoperative the oppositional pair of a right life versus a false life that is so central to Adorno's argumentation, while introducing another oppositional pair that is not Adorno's: "vie" versus "monde," *das Leben* versus *die Welt*, life versus world.[23]

How, then, does Adorno's "in" come to pass? In what light does the "in" present itself to the uncoercive gaze? Are we to conceive of a particular life (or way of life) that is demarcated from the larger life in which it is nevertheless immersed? What are the contours and conditions of possibility of this demarcation? How would the two lives on each side of this demarcation line, for all their differences, relate to each other? Are the two lives simply at odds with each other, or does each one, through a logic of irreducible supplementarity, stand in need of the other in order to become, precisely through difference, what it "itself" is—so that the "itself" on each side of the divide (and, by extension, "right" and "false") is no longer only itself? Or would the "in" rather designate a *single* life, but one that is internally divided into different regions or modes of living? Would Adorno's "in" imply a previous process of incorporation, the result of which was, precisely, the movement of one life or way of life into another? And if there is no right life "in" the wrong life, as the sentence argues, is there perhaps a right life that is not "in" the wrong life but that relates to the wrong life in a different modality—and therefore ultimately not through the preposition "in" but rather another preposition altogether, yet to be formulated? Why is it that Adorno's preposition "in" appears to mark the relation between two forms of life at all, rather than a form of life (the right life) in relation to a general falsity, that is not simply identical to a life or a form of life? After all, by simply capitalizing the "f" in the last word of the sentence, the one immediately following the preposition, which would have given us "Falschen" instead of "falschen," Adorno could have shifted the orientation of the sentence from being a statement about a false life to being a statement about the relationship between a life (the right life) and the general concept or state of falsity as such ("das Falsche"). In other words, he could easily have written "Es gibt kein richtiges Leben im Falschen" rather than "Es gibt kein richtiges Leben im falschen," especially since the nominalization of the adjective "falsch" as "das Falsche" is by no means foreign to his critical lexicon. Yet the "in" that Adorno wishes to begin to think calls for a consideration of the relation between (at least) two forms of life, a minimum of two possibilities that, even if only negatively or by way of a negative dialectics, perpetuate the promise of being able to think more than one life at once, more than one way of living a life, more than a mere resignation to (a) false life, which, in order even to become *visible as false* (rather than as natural, given, and self-evident—and therefore not visible at all), implies the theoretical possibility of a right life, however remote.

One might add that the spatial trope of the "in" lodged within "im falschen" also alludes to the noteworthy spatial trope in the subtitle of the book in which the sentence occurs, namely, "Reflexionen aus dem beschädigten Leben," which is to say, reflections not *on* or *about* damaged life but *from* or, most literally, *out of* ("aus") damaged life. The inverted parallelism between "in" and "aus," in and out, through which Adorno interlaces his infamous sentence with the book's title makes itself felt here. What is more, the perspective and directionality of the "aus" suggest a trajectory out of, and therefore *potentially* away from, that in which the reflections nevertheless always remain situated. Adorno's "aus" obliquely eschews the position of an implied difference from, or even mastery over something, that the equally idiomatic German preposition "über" ("on" or "over"), which the reader might have expected here, would have denoted.[24]

One could go further and ask if the "richtige Leben" perhaps is to be understood not as the "right life" but rather as "the good life," as the Aristotelian tradition might call it.[25] Either way, Adorno's sentence, through its insistence on the "in," asks us to cast an uncoercive gaze upon it by considering the question as to who or what could possibly make the distinction between a *richtiges Leben* and a *falsches Leben*, a right or good life and a wrong life, and according to what criteria. If the sentence "Es gibt kein richtiges Leben im falschen" originates within the orbit of false life—and how could it not?—what is it that tacitly refuses to render this sentence merely coextensive with the precepts of the wrong life in which it occurs and from which it presumably wishes to depart? Adorno's apodictic formulation calls upon us to reflect on whether the statement "Es gibt kein richtiges Leben im falschen" is true (*richtig*) or false (*falsch*) according to the parameters that it itself articulates. For, if it is false, it might be disregarded. Yet if it is true, and if it itself also was articulated within the presumed precincts of false life (*das falsche Leben*), then it is in principle possible at least to articulate true sentences (*richtige Sätze*) even within false life. In that case, false life cannot be *only* or *exclusively* false.[26] What then?

In his September 22, 2001, Frankfurt acceptance speech on the occasion of receiving the Adorno Prize—eleven years before Butler received hers and forty-three years after Celan's Bremen prize speech that commences with an allusion to Heidegger's thinking and thanking—Derrida, himself an astute reader of Heidegger, Celan, and Nietzsche, also reveals his debt of gratitude to the thinking of Adorno. He confides:

> For decades I have been hearing voices, as they say, in my dreams. They are sometimes friendly voices, sometimes not. They are voices in me. All of them seem to be saying to me: why not recognize, clearly and publicly, once and for all, the affinities between your work and Adorno's, in truth your debt to Adorno? Aren't you an heir of the Frankfurt School?[27]
>
> [Depuis des décennies, j'entends en rêve, comme on dit, des voix. Ce sont parfois des voix amies, parfois non. Ce sont des voix en moi. Toutes elles semblent me dire: pourquoi ne pas reconnaître, clairement et publiquement, une fois pour toutes, les affinités entre ton travail et celui d'Adorno, en vérité ta dette envers Adorno? N'es-tu pas un héritier de l'école de Francfort?][28]

Even though the "response to this will always be complicated, of course, and partially virtual," Derrida continues by evoking his gratitude—"and for this I say 'thank you' once again"—for the fact that, because of the Adorno Prize, "I can no longer act as if I were not hearing these voices."[29] He affirms the relation between thinking and thanking Adorno by confirming that "I can and must say 'yes' to my debt to Adorno, and on more than one count, even if I am not yet capable of responding adequately to it or taking up its responsibilities."[30] Delivered only days after the 9/11 terrorist attacks on the United States, the speech, entitled *"Fichus,"* not only engages a lifeworld in which life has become damaged or even extinct; it also reflects on—again through the implicit imbrication of thinking and thanking—the impossible possibilities of a life to come, a life still in the future and yet already touched by finitude. We might say that here, in the particular moment of thinking and thanking that the receiving of a prize calls into presence, the one who speaks feels closer to his own finitude than he ever has before, yet at the same time further away from that finitude than he ever will be again. The book that Derrida dreams of writing about his complicated debt to Adorno and the Frankfurt School would, he imagines, comprise at least seven chapters, with the first chapter, a comparative reading of the French and German legacies of Hegel and Marx, already consisting of "about ten thousand pages [*à peu près dix mille pages*]."[31] Could we, in turn, imagine Derrida, in the course of his hypothetical book on Adorno, also shedding light on the latter's sentiment that "Es gibt kein richtiges Leben im falschen"? Could we imagine Derrida, whose gesture of thinking and thanking Adorno already includes commentary on other sentences from *Minima Moralia*, also gloss—somewhere in the course of the tens of thousands of pages on Adorno that Derrida dreams of writing—this particular one, even if only indirectly?

To be sure, Derrida, who passed away three years after delivering his Adorno Prize speech, never completed such a work. But perhaps one might say that what a preliminary deconstructive thinking of the problem of a false life entails in fact becomes visible across the entire trajectory of Derrida's corpus. Let us here focus on two salient ideas or representative moments that may help us to begin to conceptualize the problem of living a false or a right life in a Derridean sense: "living on" and "negotiation."

As Derrida asks repeatedly in his hundred-page essay from 1979, "Living On: Border Lines," in a phrase that hauntingly imposes itself on his work like a leitmotif or refrain, "But who's talking about living?"[32] His text, already at odds with itself, splits itself into two bands running parallel to each other on every page, with the upper part of the page occupied by the textual band entitled "Living On." Here, Derrida meditates on the ways in which the life of a text and the text of a life refer primarily to themselves and simultaneously, in a gesture of radical other-directedness, always disconcertingly to other texts and other languages. Placing into syntactical constellation two narratives by Blanchot (*La Folie du jour* and *L'Arrêt de mort*) with Shelley's last major poem, "*The Triumph of Life*," Derrida develops, in the course of a highly self-conscious and vigilant argument that interweaves a series of different conceptual and thematic threads, a notion of life as survival. "Several pairs of quotation marks," Derrida suggests, "may enclose one or two words: 'living on' ['*survivre*'], 'on' living ['*sur' vivre*], 'on' 'living,' on 'living,' producing each time a different . . . effect." Pointing out that he still has "not exhausted the list," Derrida asks us to be "alert to these invisible quotation marks, even within a word: *survivre*, living on. Following the triumphal procession of an 'on,' they trail more than one language behind them."[33] If there is no one language, no single language that could hope to come to terms with what conjoins living and living on, life and (its) survival, it is because the very question as to who or what among the living and the dead has been authorized by the act of living itself to pose questions about life and its survival, its living on, has been posed and momentarily suspended. The question circulates among both the living and the specters—of life itself, of language, but also of history, perpetually returning to haunt them. As Derrida puts it,

> "But who's *talking about living*?": in other words, who can really speak about living? Who is in a position to? Who is already on the other side [*bord*], little enough alive, or alive enough, to dare to speak about living, not about one life, not even about life, but about living, the immediate, present, even impersonal act of living that nevertheless guarantees even the spoken word that it conveys and that it thus defies to *speak on living*: it is impossible to use living speech to speak of living—unless it is possible *only* within living speech, which would make the aporia even more paralyzing.[34]

If living a life, and speaking of and out of this life, always also is to confront the experience of living on, along with the permanent possibility of the termination of that very living on—that is, the interruption, silencing, or even cessation of survival itself—then the question concerning a right or false living would require that it be understood as a potentially right or false mode of life whose value and interpretability cannot be thought, spoken of, and lived in separation from a consideration of how this life resists its own assimilation into a determined meaning. The question of a false life would have to be framed by a thinking of life as surviving, living on, a survival that finds itself inheriting a haunting set of legacies that cannot be fully understood. The inheritance and multiple legacies of living on cannot be separated from a certain fundamental mode of reversal that permeates that inheritance. This relentless unworking of apparently self-identical structures of living and of life is performed in the name of something else, the otherness of a life that is unnamable and nevertheless always yet to come. To think and to thank this otherness we call a life would mean coming to terms with an as-yet-unnamable futurity of living on.

When seen from this perspective, it is perhaps no accident that Derrida, only about a year and half before his own death, returns to the question of living on and its relation to the legacies of finitude one more time. In his final seminar, "*The Beast and the Sovereign*," he speaks of finitude—conceived as an imbrication of the living and the dead—as a kind of "survivance." If Derrida mobilizes an unusual, even idiosyncratic term here, it is because, in his wish to think "a sur-vivance that lends itself to neither comparative nor superlative," he prefers "the middle voice 'survivance' to the active voice of the active infinitive 'to survive' or the substantializing substantive *survival*."[35] Survivance, then, should be understood "in the sense of survival that is neither life nor death pure and simple, a sense that is not thinkable on the basis of the opposition between life and death, a survival that is not, in spite of the apparent grammar of the formation of the word (*überleben* or *fortleben*, living on or to survive, survival)" primarily something that is superior or above life or even "something extra" added to life. As Derrida writes,

> No, the survivance I am speaking of is something other than life death, but a groundless ground from which are detached, identified, and opposed what we think we can identify under the name of death or dying (*Tod, Sterben*), like death properly so-called as opposed to some life properly so-called. It [*Ça*] begins with survival. And that is where there is some other that has me at its disposal; that is where any self is defenseless. That is what the self is, that is what I am, what the *I* is, whether I am there or not. The other, the others, that is the very thing that survives me that is called to survive me and that I call the other inasmuch as it is called, in advance, to survive me, structurally my survivor. Not my survivor, but the survivor of me, the *there* beyond my life.[36]

According to this logic, the question of my survival or survivance is always also a question posed to, for, and by the other, the other or otherness that outlives me and to which I relate, already before my actual death, as that which will outlive me, survive me—already in life, during my lifetime. Life here is no mere property, no mere possession held by the living or, more precisely, by those who, for the moment, are living on; rather, life unfolds on what may be termed a groundless ground, a treacherous terrain that demarcates life's radical vulnerability, exposedness, and dependency on an unaccounted-for survivance that is always predicated upon the other as the survivor of me. In this survivance, the other survives me even before my death, and, as such, it is the other that countersigns the very possibility of my living and my life. In fact, it is as though the structure of survivance did not require me to be present for it to be operative—it is at work or sets itself to work, as Derrida reflects, "whether I am there or not." Survivance makes itself felt; it beckons and is itself called forth. Whatever the question of leading a right life or of living in a right manner may demand of me, it will have been formulated within the experiential and conceptual space of this precarious survivance.[37]

A complementary perspective on the question of living a life, a life that is survivance, rightly or falsely—and of living on while thinking and thanking this life as survivance—is opened up by Derrida's insistence, throughout much of his later work, on the significance of the concept and practice of "negotiation." As becomes evident for instance in a 1987 interview conducted by his then-students at Yale, Deborah Esch and Thomas Keenan, "negotiation" comes from "neg-otium," meaning notease, not-quiet, no leisure, pointing toward a restlessness or unease that will impose itself always one more time.[38] If the later Derrida prefers the word "negotiation" to "more noble words," even though it is "no more perfect and no more univocal out of context than any other" and even though the mobilization and usage of "negotiation" itself demands to be negotiated, it is because there is "always something about negotiation that is a little dirty, that gets one's hands dirty . . . something is being trafficked, . . . relations of force."[39] To the extent that negotiation refuses to disguise anxiety with nobility, and to the extent that it involves compromise and an equivocal purity-impurity, it can be said simultaneously to be both "more mediocre" and more unexpectedly disclosive than many other terms. When considering the question pertaining to a right or a false life, to a living on and the multiple living legacies that are implied in the question, this living also needs to confront its own "impossibility of stopping, of settling into a position. Whether one wants it or not, one is always working in the mobility between several positions, stations, places, between which a shuttle is needed."[40] If, as Derrida argues, one "must always go from one to the other," then negotiation is inexorably inscribed in "the impossibility of establishing oneself anywhere." For him, this negotiation of even the nonnegotiable, which touches, within the precincts of moral philosophy, on the relation between the categorical and the hypothetical imperative, also "is a feeling, an affective relation I have to myself of being someone who cannot stop anywhere."[41] According to this logic, one "cannot separate this concept and this practice of negotiation from the concept of the *double bind*, that is, of the double duty." This is so because there is "a negotiation when there are two incompatible imperatives that appear to be incompatible but are equally imperative. One does not negotiate between exchangeable and negotiable things. Rather, one negotiates by engaging the nonnegotiable in negotiation."[42] In other words, negotiation in the strong sense is not oriented toward any means-end calculation, much less an operation performed under the dictates of what Adorno and Horkheimer memorably reject as instrumental reason, in which, under the calculative pull of pure instrumentality, reason itself may emerge as profoundly unreasonable, but precisely, and therefore all the more fatefully, in the name of reason. On the contrary, the without-rest that negotiation names cannot be a program to be followed by the living, a living suspension of certain imperatives and precepts that would allow a thinking of the Husserlian *epoché* to transform, within the space of a suspension, reflective experience into understanding.

Does not Derrida's insistence on life as living on and as negotiation also touch upon the status of the "in" or, better, the "within"—the relation of something or someone being both and at the same time with and in an other—housed so precariously and provocatively in Adorno's "Es gibt kein richtiges Leben im falschen"? If the possibility of thinking, speaking, or, indeed, dreaming of a *richtiges Leben*—and of giving thanks for it in the register of philosophical thought or of poetic speech—is not a priori foreclosed by the conditions of the wrong life in which it is articulated, then perhaps the kind of feeling of life, the *Lebensgefühl*, associated with a thinking that relentlessly confronts its own limits in the name of an unarticulated otherness that is yet to come, is one in which the borders between inside and outside, between the contours of the right life and those of a wrong life, are perpetually negotiated. The challenge then no longer would lie primarily in being able to tell a right life from an ostensibly wrong life, or in ascertaining the impossibility of living a right life within that wrong life, but rather in recognizing and affirming the survival of life itself, of life as life, of living as living on, precisely in the kind of restless and vigilant negotiation that living itself occasions. The question of the right life would then have to be renegotiated and rearticulated with every new historical and personal situation, with every uncoercive gaze cast, and with every new way of feeling life, that is, with every new act of thinking—within damaged life—a thankful yet precarious survival, however improbable.

The question concerning the right life and, indeed, of living as such, always touches upon the question of the prize. The prize celebrates a life and its trajectories thus far, but it also anticipates a mourning to come—a death that is yet to occur yet has already inscribed itself silently into the very commemoration that the bestowing of a prize upon a life occasions. The prize, as a mode of temporary survival that is also a memento mori, interweaves the thinking of life with the thinking of finitude.

The ceaseless negotiation of the right life and its anticipated commemoration, possible only in its impossibility, is the price we are asked to pay, yet also the prize we stand to receive. Is it a mere etymological coincidence that, in both modern German and French, there is only one word for the contemporary English terms "price" and "prize" (*der Preis* and *le prix*)? Will not the negotiation of what we call life ultimately have been a matter of thinking, and giving thanks for, this uneasy *prix*, this unsettling *Preis*?

CONCLUSION

A Kind of Leave-Taking

We have come a long way, traversing a good segment of what Benjamin termed Adorno's "ice-desert of abstraction." Along the way, we have made stops at critical signposts that helped to orient us in the midst of the uncharted terrain, from Adorno's reconceptualization of the concept of tradition to his self-conscious inheritance of Hegelian thought, from questions of judgment and of orientation in the work of art to the irreducible difference between literal and figurative dimensions of a literary text as exemplified by Kafka, from the rethinking of political resistance on the basis of a negative dialectics to the problem of how to live a right life within a damaged one, and beyond. By pausing at these outposts in Adorno's ice-desert and by allowing him to be in meaningful dialogue with other writers and thinkers, we have comprehended that this terrain is neither inhospitable nor ossified; on the contrary, it has proven, precisely in the uncoercive gaze, to be very much alive. We have come to appreciate the ways in which Adorno's texts resist systematic appropriation in the name of this or that preestablished agenda, and we experienced, I hope, some of their singular and intractable beauty. In other words, we have begun to learn to *think with* Adorno, not following him pedantically or accepting his thought piously and uncritically, but rather allowing him, through the practice of the uncoercive gaze, to set the stage for a rigorous, transformative, and critically vigilant thinking to come.

Thinking with Adorno and through the uncoercive gaze requires us to confront seminal questions of our experience anew, even—and especially—if that experience is threatened by deformation and destruction. It is thus perhaps no accident that in the 1950s and 1960s, after Adorno had returned to Germany from his American exile, readers from all walks of life felt compelled to write to him to share their concerns and to seek his advice. These readers may have read one of his widely circulated books such as *Minima Moralia: Reflections from Damaged Life*, or they may have listened to him during one of the many radio appearances, in which he addressed highbrow topics—such as how to read Hegel, the notion of "culture," education after Auschwitz, the contradictions inherent in utopian longing, or the challenge of Proust—in a way that sought to make them accessible and teachable to a large postwar audience of German listeners eager for education, reflection, and cultural redefinition. Adorno received, and often answered at length, intensive and searching correspondence from despondent graduate students, isolated teachers in small German towns, a perplexed baroness, music lovers desirous of his views on Mahler, an entrepreneur-turned-monk, former grade-school classmates, and a young Austrian art student struggling with his homosexuality, among many others.[1] These readers felt that for all the apparent icy-ness that they, too, must have encountered in Adorno's abstractions, there persisted in his writing and thinking something profoundly pertinent to life as we experience it, something affirmative even in the manifold diagnoses of hopelessness, something forward-looking and liberatory even in the seemingly most exasperatingly abstract turns of the dialectical screw.

If, in our encounters with the Adornean ice-desert, we have focused—at times explicitly, at others implicitly—on the figure of the uncoercive gaze that fastens upon an object and enters a relation of critical intimacy with it, we have foregrounded a certain "snuggling up to the object," a certain "Anschmiegen" that causes critical thought to cling to, and nestle against, the object, concept, or phenomenon. Yet no method, no manual, no recipe can teach the critic how to employ this uncoercive gaze or how, exactly, to snuggle up to an object and enter a relation of critical intimacy with it. As the experience of our readings has shown, only the singular and each-time unique demands of the particular object, concept, or phenomenon under investigation can teach us how to cast this critical gaze upon it. What the critical acts demand is that the uncoercive gaze be recalibrated each time it fastens upon a new object of reflection. If critical intimacy is to emerge, it must, as we have seen in the course of the preceding chapters, grow out of a felt contact with the singularity of the object's unique materials.

It may now seem as though the critical intimacy that the uncoercive gaze fosters had determined the position that Adorno's texts ultimately work to construct. Yet we would do well to heed the dialectical flip side of this critical intimacy as well: the insurmountable distance that is retained in the critical act despite any achieved proximity. Adorno makes vivid the experience of this irreducible divide—inscribed in the heart of any critical intimacy—in the melancholic language of a certain leave-taking or *Abschiednehmen*. In a letter to the philosopher and sociologist Helmuth Plessner on February 11, 1958, Adorno confides: "But it is evidently my fate to have to coax my entire production from my life by a gradual process, and that may well be far from the worst way to work. I could imagine that this is connected with another peculiarity that I have observed in what I cobble together—that in truth every text of mine is a kind of leave-taking [*daß eigentlich jeder Text von mir eine Art von Abschiednehmen ist*]."[2] What could Adorno have meant by this remarkable statement? If it seems to him as though each of his texts were somehow wrenched or wrested from life through a kind of ruse or special cunning ("meinem Leben abzulisten")—as if life in truth did not want him to have or to create these texts, somehow conspiring against his creative production of works—then the peculiar process by which his texts came into being deserves reflection. What is it that connects the practice of textual creation to the idea of a leave-taking?

With every text he wrote—whether explicitly philosophical, musicological, literary, sociological, political, or autobiographical—Adorno experienced a kind of leave-taking or departure, "eine Art von Abschiednehmen." One might suggest that this experience of leave-taking is operative on several levels: on a most basic level, a finished text signals the end, preliminary or actual, of a period of intense preoccupation with a certain object, concept, or phenomenon. Yet the leave-taking that a text calls into being also may be tied to the idea that, in the wake of this newly composed text, a previously held idea or assumption no longer can be upheld, because it has been refuted or significantly altered by the new text and its arguments. In this sense the completion of the text requires that the critic, along with his readers, now take leave of an old idea or assumption. A further requirement for the composition of a text, especially one of the level of density and complexity of Adorno's, is that the writer take leave of the quotidian world for a substantial amount of time, living, as one says, in his own head for the duration of its composition, largely saying goodbye to the things that surround him in his lifeworld and that normally lay claim to his concern and attention. In that case, the text acts as a double marker: it embodies the record of a former leave-taking even as it augurs the end of that leave-taking and the beginning of a reentry into the world that, during the creation of a text, has simply raged on.

Yet something else is at stake in Adorno's assertion "that in truth every text of mine is a kind of leave-taking," "daß jeder Text von mir eine Art von Abschiednehmen ist," as well. What if this phrase also conjured a more existential leave-taking, such as the primordial *Abschiednehmen* that normally accompanies the thought of death? Is the leave-taking that all of Adorno's texts perform not also a way of marking the transition from presence to absence, from life to death? To be sure, a writer sometimes is thought to "live on" in his texts even after death—so that "thy eternal summer shall not fade," as Shakespeare has it in Sonnet 18. Yet could we not also conclude that the leave-taking or *Abschiednehmen* of which Adorno speaks pertains to the moment in which the writer releases his text into the world, where it will be interpreted, in separation from its author's intentions, in this way or that, where it will be understood or misunderstood, read or ignored, celebrated or maligned, kept alive or forgotten, archived or destroyed? These structural possibilities obtain even before the writer's actual death; in fact, one might say that they prepare their author for his death, prior to his actual passing. One's texts, already during one's lifetime, will come to stand in for oneself, even when one is still alive, the way they will when one has passed on. They are on the order of what the Austrian writer Robert Musil might call a *Nachlaß zu Lebzeiten*, the posthumous papers of a living author. One relinquishes control of one's creations, takes leave of them in order, ultimately, to take leave of oneself—that is, to become the mournful object of one's own *Abschiednehmen*.

If Adorno is to be believed that "in truth every text of mine is a kind of leave-taking," that "jeder Text von mir eine Art von Abschiednehmen ist," then the leave-taking of which he speaks is not limited to the production of this or that text; rather, it bespeaks the critical act itself. Even the uncoercive gaze—and the critical intimacy that the critic entertains with the objects to which he snuggles up—are touched by the double movements of its welcoming attraction and its leave-taking. Such a movement of "Willkommen und Abschied," a "Welcome and Leave-Taking," as the title of Goethe's well-known early poem has it, structures the critical act. This genuinely critical act is characterized by a passionately affirmative, even ecstatic engagement with its object—and, by extension, with the setting in which it dwells—coincident with a melancholic leave-taking from that object and its setting, a double gesture that acknowledges, tacitly or explicitly, the critic's physical and temporal limitations—in a word, his radical finitude.

Is the practice of critical theory itself not always also a kind of leave-taking, an Adornean *Abschiednehmen*? As we ourselves take leave of and with this book, we are mindful of the idiosyncratic ways in which Adorno's uncoercive gaze holds open a transformative perspective on the manifold consequences of that very possibility. No afterlife, no heirs, no other-directedness, no welcoming, no futurity without this leave-taking.

ACKNOWLEDGMENTS

Most of the present book appears here in English for the first time, and about half of the pages are entirely new in any language. Earlier versions of chapters 4 and 5 were included in *Palgrave Handbook of Critical Theory*, ed. Michael J. Thompson (London: Palgrave Macmillan, 2017), and in *Kafka's* The Trial: *Philosophical Perspectives*, ed. Espen Hammer (Oxford: Oxford University Press, 2018), respectively. Prior versions of chapters 6 and 7 were published in the journal *MLN* (Johns Hopkins University Press), as was an earlier and shorter version of chapter 3 that appeared in German. It is published here in English for the first time, adroitly translated by Kristina Mendicino. The index was prepared by Karen Embry.

NOTES

INTRODUCTION: THE ART OF READING

    1. Theodor W. Adorno, "Who Is Afraid of the Ivory Tower? A Conversation with Theodor W. Adorno," translated, edited, and with an introduction by Gerhard Richter, in *Language without Soil: Adorno and Late Philosophical Modernity*, ed. Gerhard Richter (New York: Fordham University Press, 2010), 227–238, here 232; "Keine Angst vor dem Elfenbeinturm. Ein 'Spiegel'-Gespräch." *Gesammelte Schriften*, vol. 20, ed. Rolf Tiedemann (Frankfurt am Main: Suhrkamp, 1997), 402–409, here 402.

    Throughout this book, standard English translations of non-English texts on occasion have been adjusted to enhance their fidelity to the original or to emphasize a particular dimension of meaning present in an original text that may not be readily apparent in the existing translation. In cases in which no translator is indicated, translations are my own.

    2. William Faulkner, *Requiem for a Nun* (New York: Vintage, 2012), 73.

    3. Alban Berg is cited in Hartmut Scheible, *Theodor W. Adorno* (Reinbek bei Hamburg: Rowohlt, 1993), 152.

    4. Theodor W. Adorno, *Alban Berg: Master of the Smallest Link*, trans. Juliane Brand and Christopher Hailey (Cambridge: Cambridge University Press, 1991), xviii; *Mahler. Meister des kleinsten Übergangs, Gesammelte Schriften*, ed. Rolf Tiedemann, vol. 13 (Frankfurt am Main: Suhrkamp, 1997), 321–494, here 324. In this context, also consider the correspondence collected in Theodor W. Adorno and Alban Berg, *Correspondence 1925–1935*, trans. Wieland Hoban

(Cambridge: Polity, 2005); *Briefwechsel 1925–1935*, ed. Henri Lonitz (Frankfurt am Main: Suhrkamp, 1997).

5. Theodor W. Adorno, *Minima Moralia: Reflections from Damaged Life*, trans. E. F. N. Jephcott (London: Verso, 1974), 132; *Minima Moralia. Reflexionen aus dem beschädigten Leben*, *Gesammelte Schriften*, ed. Rolf Tiedemann, vol. 4 (Frankfurt am Main: Suhrkamp, 1997), 150.

6. These include, among others, investigations of the relation between Adorno's late modernism and the problem of painting (Bernstein); the as-yet-little-understood relays between Adorno's negative dialectics and Heidegger's fundamental ontology (Macdonald and Ziarek); the residual promise of Adorno's category of the aesthetic (Hohendahl); the possible convergences of Adorno's thought with developments in contemporary philosophy (Bowie); Adorno's modernism in relation to the experience of catastrophe (Hammer); Adorno's aesthetics of negativity in relation to Blanchot (Allen); the relevance of Adorno's unweaving of "Germanness" to our contemporary political challenges (Trawny); Adorno's complex relation to the existentialist tradition of Kierkegaard and others (Gordon); and certain strategies of "aestheticizing" theoretical thought as practiced in Adorno and Nietzsche (Endres et al.). See J. M. Bernstein, *Against Voluptuous Bodies: Later Modernism and the Meaning of Painting* (Stanford, CA: Stanford University Press, 2006); Iain Macdonald and Krzysztof Ziarek (eds.), *Adorno and Heidegger: Philosophical Questions* (Stanford, CA: Stanford University Press, 2008); Peter Uwe Hohendahl, *The Fleeting Promise of Art: Adorno's Aesthetic Theory Revisited* (Ithaca, NY: Cornell University Press, 2013); Andrew Bowie, *Adorno and the Ends of Philosophy* (Cambridge: Polity, 2013); Espen Hammer, *Adorno's Modernism: Art, Experience, and Catastrophe* (Cambridge: Cambridge University Press, 2015); William S. Allen, *Aesthetics of Negativity: Blanchot, Adorno, and Autonomy* (New York: Fordham University Press, 2016); Peter Trawny, *Was ist deutsch? Adornos verratenes Vermächtnis* (Berlin: Matthes & Seitz, 2016); Peter Gordon, *Adorno and Existence* (Cambridge, MA: Harvard University Press, 2016); and Martin Endres, Axel Pichler, and Claus Zittel (eds.), *Text/Kritik: Nietzsche und Adorno* (Berlin: De Gruyter, 2017).

7. Theodor W. Adorno, *Negative Dialectics*, trans. E. B. Ashton (London: Continuum, 1973), xix; *Negative Dialektik*, *Gesammelte Schriften*, ed. Rolf Tiedemann, vol. 6 (Frankfurt am Main: Suhrkamp, 1997), 9.

8. Adorno, *Minima Moralia: Reflections from Damaged Life*, 219; *Minima Moralia. Reflexionen aus dem beschädigten Leben*, 250.

9. Theodor W. Adorno, "Aus einem Schulheft ohne Deckel. Bar Harbor, Sommer 1939," *Frankfuter Adorno Blätter* 4 (1995): 7.

10. Theodor W. Adorno, *Ontologie und Dialektik* (1960/61), ed. Rolf Tiedemann (Frankfurt am Main: Suhrkamp, 2008).

11. Adorno, *Minima Moralia: Reflections from Damaged Life*, 101; *Minima Moralia. Reflexionen aus dem beschädigten Leben*, 114.

12. Theodor W. Adorno, "Skoteinos, or, How to Read Hegel," *Hegel: Three Studies*, trans. Shierry Weber Nicholsen (Cambridge, MA: MIT Press, 1993), 89–148, here 94ff; "Skoteinos oder Wie zu lesen sei," *Drei Studien zu Hegel, Gesammelte Schriften*, ed. Rolf Tiedemann, vol. 5 (Frankfurt am Main: Suhrkamp, 1997), 326–375, here 330.

13. Theodor W. Adorno, "Notes on Philosophical Thinking," *Critical Models: Interventions and Catchwords*, trans. Henry Pickford (New York: Columbia University Press, 2005), 127–134, here 130; "Anmerkungen zum philosophischen Denken," *Gesammelte Schriften*, ed. Rolf Tiedemann, vol. 10 (Frankfurt am Main: Suhrkamp, 1997), 599–607, here 602.

14. Adorno, "Notes," 129; "Anmerkungen," 602.

15. Adorno, "Notes," 126; "Anmerkungen," 598.

16. Adorno, "Notes," 131; "Anmerkungen," 604.

17. Adorno, "Notes," 133ff; "Anmerkungen," 607.

18. Adorno, *Negative Dialectics*, 18; *Negative Dialektik*, 29.

19. Henry David Thoreau, *Writings, Journal, 1837–1846*, ed. Bradford Torrey (Boston: Houghton Mifflin, 1906), 24.

20. Adorno, *Minima Moralia: Reflections from Damaged Life*, 107; *Minima Moralia. Reflexionen aus dem beschädigten Leben*, 121.

1. ADORNO AND THE UNCOERCIVE GAZE

1. Theodor W. Adorno and Siegfried Kracauer, *Briefwechsel 1923–1966*, ed. Wolfgang Schopf (Frankfurt am Main: Suhrkamp, 2008), 482.

2. Theodor W. Adorno, "On the Question: 'What Is German?,'" *Critical Models: Interventions and Catchwords*, trans. Henry Pickford (New York: Columbia University Press, 2005), 205–214, here 212; "Auf die Frage: Was ist deutsch," *Gesammelte Schriften*, ed. Rolf Tiedemann, vol. 10 (Frankfurt am Main: Suhrkamp, 1997), 691–701, here 699ff.

3. Adorno, "What Is German," 212ff; "Was ist deutsch," 700ff.

4. Adorno, "What Is German," 213; "Was ist deutsch," 701.

5. Theodor W. Adorno, *Negative Dialectics*, trans. E. B. Ashton (London: Continuum, 1973), 18; *Negative Dialektik, Gesammelte Schriften*, ed. Rolf Tiedemann, vol. 6 (Frankfurt am Main: Suhrkamp, 1997), 29. Adorno here implicitly alludes also to Walter Benjamin's conviction, memorably expressed in the opening line of his *Trauerspiel* book, that it "is the peculiarity of philosophical writing to stand, with each turn or trope, in front of the question of presentation anew [*Es ist dem philosophischen Schrifttum eigen, mit jeder Wendung erneut vor der Frage der Darstellung zu stehen*]." Walter Benjamin, *Ursprung des deutschen Trauerspiels, Gesammelte Schriften*, vol. 1, eds. Rolf Tiedemann and Hermann Schweppenhäuser (Frankfurt am Main: Suhrkamp, 1991), 207.

6. Adorno, *Negative Dialectics*, 56; *Negative Dialektik*, 65ff.

7. Adorno, *Negative Dialectics*, 55; *Negative Dialektik*, 65.

8. Ibid. Here, as so often, the standard published English translation of *Negative Dialektik* gets Adorno's meaning completely wrong. Adorno writes: "Sie [die Rhetorik] behauptet sich in den Postulaten der Darstellung, durch welche Philosophie von der Kommunikation bereits erkannter und fixierter Inhalte sich unterscheidet." The translator, Ashton, inexplicably renders this sentence as "It holds a place among the postulates of contents already known and fixed." The translation thus makes Adorno say the opposite of what he actually says—namely, that rhetoric holds its place by considering the problems of presentation and, as such, differs from the mere communication of known and fixed contents favored by the kind of philosophy for which language and presentation are not issues of great importance. In order to make Adorno appear to say the opposite of what he in fact says, it was necessary for the translator to repress (that is, not to include in the translation at all) several elements of Adorno's sentence, including such key words as "Philosophie," "Kommunikation," "unterscheiden (to differ or differentiate)." Why?

9. Stanley Corngold, "Adorno's 'Notes on Kafka': A Critical Reconstruction," *Monatshefte* 94 (2002), special issue: *Rereading Adorno*, ed. Gerhard Richter, 24–42, here 24ff.

10. Robert Hullot-Kentor, "Translator's Introduction," in Theodor W. Adorno, *Aesthetic Theory*, trans. Robert Hullot-Kentor (Minneapolis: University of Minnesota Press, 1997), xi–xxi, here xv.

11. Samuel Weber, "Translating the Untranslatable," Introduction to Theodor W. Adorno, *Prisms*, trans. Samuel and Shierry Weber (Cambridge, MA: MIT Press, 1981), 9–15, here 11ff.

12. Rolf Tiedemann's suggestion that the "Theses" date from the early 1930s is to be found in his "Editorische Nachbemerkung," the editorial afterword, to volume 1 of Adorno, *Gesammelte Schriften*, ed. Rolf Tiedemann (Frankfurt am Main: Suhrkamp, 1997), 379–384, here 383. For a consideration of Adorno's essays "The Actuality of Philosophy" and "Why Still Philosophy" in the context of programmatic and linguistic concerns, see Peter Uwe Hohendahl, "The Discourse of Philosophy and the Problem of Language," *Prismatic Thought: Theodor W. Adorno* (Lincoln: University of Nebraska Press, 1995), 217–242.

13. Theodor W. Adorno, "Notes on Philosophical Thinking," *Critical Models: Interventions and Catchwords*, trans. Henry Pickford (New York: Columbia University Press, 2005), 127–134, here 125; "Anmerkungen zum philosophischen Denken," *Gesammelte Schriften*, ed. Rolf Tiedemann, vol. 10 (Frankfurt am Main: Suhrkamp, 1997), 599–607, here 597.

14. Translator's note 1, Adorno, "Introduction" to *Catchwords*, *Critical Models: Interventions and Catchwords*, 352.

15. Adorno, "Notes," 127.

16. Adorno, *Negative Dialectics*, 408; *Negative Dialektik*, 400.

17. Adorno, *Aesthetic Theory*, trans. Robert Hullot-Kentor (Minneapolis: University of Minnesota Press, 1997), 3; *Ästhetische Theorie, Gesammelte Schriften*, ed. Rolf Tiedemann, vol. 7 (Frankfurt am Main: Suhrkamp, 1997), 10.
18. Adorno, "Anmerkungen," 599.
19. Adorno, "What Is German," 210; "Was ist deutsch," 697.
20. Adorno, "Notes," 127; "Anmerkungen," 599.
21. Adorno, "Notes," 127ff; "Anmerkungem," 599.
22. Adorno, "Notes," 128; "Anmerkungen," 600.
23. Ibid.
24. Adorno, "Notes," 129; "Anmerkungen," 601.
25. Adorno, "Notes," 133; "Anmerkungen," 606.
26. Adorno, "Notes," 134; "Anmerkungen," 607.
27. The most sustained engagement with the untrackability of stupidity in its relation to cognition, in which stupidity emerges as a repressed condition of knowledge, is to be found in Avital Ronell, *Stupidity* (Urbana: University of Illinois Press, 2002).
28. Adorno, "Notes," 132.
29. Adorno, "Anmerkungen," 605.
30. Translator's note, Adorno, "Notes," 356n24.
31. Adorno, "Notes," 132; "Anmerkungen," 605.
32. Adorno, "Notes," 131ff; "Anmerkungen," 604.
33. Theodor W. Adorno, *Minima Moralia: Reflections from Damaged Life*, trans. E. F. N. Jephcott (London: Verso, 1974), 192; *Minima Moralia. Reflexionen aus dem beschädigten Leben, Gesammelte Schriften*, ed. Rolf Tiedemann, vol. 4 (Frankfurt am Main: Suhrkamp, 1997), 218. Compare further my analysis of this phrase in Gerhard Richter, "Nazism and Negative Dialectics: Adorno's Hitler in *Minima Moralia*," *Thought-Images: Frankfurt School Reflections from Damaged Life* (Stanford, CA: Stanford University Press, 2007), 147–190, here 171ff.
34. Adorno, "Notes," 130; "Anmerkungen," 602.
35. Adorno, "Notes," 130; "Anmerkungen," 602ff.
36. Adorno, "Notes," 130; "Anmerkungen," 603.
37. Ibid.
38. Adorno, "Notes," 133; "Anmerkungen," 606.
39. Readers of Derrida take heed.
40. Sigmund Freud, *Civilization and Its Discontents*, trans. James Strachey (New York: Norton, 1989), 25.
41. Adorno, "Notes," 132; "Anmerkungen," 605.
42. Ibid.
43. A far-reaching discussion of Adorno's and Benjamin's conceptions of experience in the context of the larger philosophical and historical problem of experience can be found in Martin Jay, "Lamenting the Crisis of Experience: Benjamin and Adorno," in *Songs of Experience: Modern American and European*

Variations on a Universal Theme (Berkeley: University of California Press, 2005), 312–360.

44. Adorno, *Negative Dialectics*, 183–186; *Negative Dialektik*, 184–193.

45. Adorno, *Minima Moralia: Reflections from Damaged Life*, 247; *Minima Moralia. Reflexionen aus dem beschädigten Leben*, 283. For a focused reading of this thought-image, "Zum Ende," see Gerhard Richter, "Aesthetic Theory and Nonpropositional Truth Content in Adorno," *New German Critique* 97 (Winter 2006): 119–135.

46. Adorno, "Notes," 129; "Anmerkungen," 602.

47. Theodor W. Adorno and Gershom Scholem, *Briefwechsel 1939–1969*, ed. Asaf Angermann (Berlin: Suhrkamp, 2015), 414.

48. Adorno, *Negative Dialectics*, 408; *Negative Dialektik*, 399.

49. Gilles Deleuze and Félix Guattari, *What Is Philosophy?*, trans. Hugh Tomlinson and Graham Burchell (New York: Columbia University Press, 1994), 5.

50. Adorno, "Notes," 130; "Anmerkungen," 602.

51. Ibid.

52. Ibid.

53. Ibid.

54. Georg Wilhelm Friedrich Hegel, *Encyclopedia of the Philosophical Sciences in Basic Outline, Part 1: Logic of Science*, trans. and ed. Klaus Brinkmann and Daniel O. Dahlstrom (Cambridge: Cambridge University Press, 2010), 127; *Enzyklopädie der philosophischen Wissenschaften im Grundrisse, Erster Teil: Die Wissenschaft der Logik*, eds. Eva Moldenhauer and Karl Markus Michel, *Werke*, vol. 8 (Frankfurt am Main: Suhrkamp, 1986), 170.

55. Adorno, "Notes," 131; "Anmerkungen," 603.

56. Adorno, "Notes," 130; "Anmerkungen," 602.

57. Theodor W. Adorno, *Ontologie und Dialektik (1960/61)*, ed. Rolf Tiedemann (Frankfurt am Main: Suhrkamp, 2008), 14.

2. BURIED POSSIBILITY: ADORNO AND ARENDT ON TRADITION

1. Only relatively recently have attempts been made to submit Arendt and Adorno to more sustained and contextualized comparative readings. See, for instance, *Arendt und Adorno*, eds. Dirk Auer, Lars Rensmann, and Julia Schulze Wessel (Frankfurt am Main: Suhrkamp, 2003); Alfons Söllner, "Der Essay als Form politischen Denkens. Die Anfänge von Hannah Arendt und Theodor W. Adorno nach dem Zweiten Weltkrieg," *Text & Kritik* 166/167 (2005): 79–91; *Affinität wider Willen? Hannah Arendt, Theodor W. Adorno und die Frankfurter Schule*, ed. Liliane Weissberg (Frankfurt am Main: Campus Verlag, 2011); and *Arendt and Adorno: Political and Philosophical Investigations*, eds. Lars Rensmann and Samir Gandesha (Stanford, CA: Stanford University Press,

2012). Arendt's and Adorno's respective concepts of tradition have, as far as I can tell, not figured in these comparative readings.

2. Steven Aschheim, "Introduction: Hannah Arendt in Jerusalem," in *Hannah Arendt in Jerusalem*, ed. Steven Aschheim (Berkeley: University of California Press, 2001), 1–15, here 2. Aschheim goes on to suggest that much of Arendt's "acuity derived from the fact that she embodied the tensions and contradictions that fueled so much of its [German culture's] creativity, especially as they manifested themselves in the productive turbulence of the Weimar Republic, in which she spent her formative years. Her Weimar friends, lovers, and adversaries—including Karl Jaspers and Martin Heidegger, Kurt Blumenfeld, Theodor Adorno, Gershom Scholem, and Walter Benjamin—were all incarnations of its manifold, yet related sensibilities" (2). More recently, Jerome Kohn—Arendt's former student and research assistant, now her literary executor—engages with the question of a Jewish dimension in Arendt's thinking by suggesting that we emphasize "experience" rather than "identity" when considering intellectual and political problems related to her Jewishness: "Hannah Arendt's Jewish Experience: Thinking, Acting, Judging," in *Thinking in Dark Times: Hannah Arendt on Ethics and Politics*, eds. Roger Berkowitz, Jeffrey Katz, and Thomas Keenan (New York: Fordham University Press, 2010), 179–194.

3. Theodor W. Adorno, *Negative Dialectics*, trans. E. B. Ashton (London: Continuum, 1973), 365; *Negative Dialektik, Gesammelte Schriften*, ed. Rolf Tiedemann, vol. 6 (Frankfurt am Main: Suhrkamp, 1997), 358.

4. Hannah Arendt, *The Origins of Totalitarianism* (San Diego: Harcourt, 1985), ix.

5. This general definition of tradition is offered by the legal scholar and historian Douglas Klusmeyer in "Hannah Arendt on Authority and Tradition," in *Hannah Arendt: Key Concepts*, ed. Patrick Hayden (London: Routledge, 2014), 138–152, here 138. His essay offers a circumspect reconstruction of the relationship between certain elements of Arendt's thinking of tradition and the refractory concept of political, social, and ethical authority. Historical overviews of the contested notion of tradition in general may be found in Josef Pieper, *Über den Begriff der Tradition* (Cologne: Westdeutscher Verlag, 1958) and *Überlieferung. Begriff und Anspruch* (Munich: Kösel, 1970); Edward Shils, *Tradition* (Chicago: University of Chicago Press, 1981); David Gross, *The Past in Ruins: Tradition and the Critique of Modernity* (Amherst: University of Massachusetts Press, 1992); and, more recently, Mark Salber Phillips and Gordon Schochet (eds.), *Questions of Tradition* (Toronto: University of Toronto Press, 2004).

6. Robert Pogue Harrison, *The Dominion of the Dead* (Chicago: University of Chicago Press, 2003), ix.

7. Harrison, ix ff.

8. Harrison, x.

9. A useful collection of texts by Arendt and Benjamin documenting the intellectual relationship between the two has been assembled by Detlev Schöttker and Erdmut Wizisla, *Arendt und Benjamin. Texte, Briefe, Dokumente* (Frankfurt am Main: Suhrkamp, 2006).

10. Hannah Arendt, "Walter Benjamin: 1892–1940," trans. Harry Zohn, in *Men in Dark Times* (New York: Harcourt, Brace, 1968), 201; *Walter Benjamin, Bertolt Brecht. Zwei Essays* (Munich: Piper, 1971), 57.

11. Gershom Scholem, *Walter Benjamin: The Story of a Friendship*, trans. Harry Zohn (Philadelphia: Jewish Publication Society of America, 1981), 217.

12. Arendt, *Dark Times*, 193; *Zwei Essays*, 49.

13. As Peg Birmingham points out in her discussion of Arendt's reading of Benjamin in relation to Arendt's theoretical and political understanding of natality, the "transcendent force of citability makes the present a moment of deflection whereby the past becomes a projective force of the unknown and the unfamiliar; that is, a projective force of the new. Citability, therefore, offers a notion of historical narrative that is not descriptive but inaugurative. Its inaugurative force is derived precisely from its decontextualization, from its break with a prior content" so that citability "in the deflected present makes graphic a moment of transformation, not merely the continuum of history." *Hannah Arendt and Human Rights: The Predicament of Common Responsibility* (Bloomington: Indiana University Press, 2006), 21.

14. Arendt, *Dark Times*, 195; *Zwei Essays*, 51.

15. Ibid.

16. Arendt, *Dark Times*, 198ff; *Zwei Essays*, 54ff.

17. Arendt, *Dark Times*, 199; *Zwei Essays*, 55.

18. Ibid.

19. Adorno, *Negative Dialectics*, 53; *Negative Dialektik*, 63.

20. Adorno, *Negative Dialectics*, 54; *Negative Dialektik*, 63.

21. Ibid.

22. Ibid.

23. Ibid.

24. Adorno, *Negative Dialectics*, 54ff; *Negative Dialektik*, 64.

25. Adorno, *Negative Dialectics*, 55; *Negative Dialektik*, 64.

26. Walter Benjamin, *Das Passagen-Werk, Gesammelte Schriften*, eds. Rolf Tiedemann and Hermann Schweppenhäuser, vol. 5 (Frankfurt am Main: Suhrkamp, 1991), 578.

27. Étienne Balibar, "(De)constructing the Human as Human Institution: A Reflection on the Coherence of Hannah Arendt's Practical Philosophy," in *Hannah Arendt: Verborgene Tradition—Unzeitgemäße Aktualität?*, ed. Heinrich-Böll-Stiftung (Berlin: Akademie Verlag, 2007), 261–268, here 261.

28. Arendt later also included a German version of the essay, in the translation by her friend Charlotte Beradt, under the title "Tradition und die

Neuzeit" in her German collection of essays *Fragwürdige Traditionsbestände im politischen Denken der Gegenwart* (Frankfurt am Main: Europäische Verlagsanstalt, 1957), 9–45.

29. That Arendt considered *Between Past and Future* her best book is pointed out by her former doctoral student at the New School, Elisabeth Young-Bruehl, in her biography *Hannah Arendt: For the Love of the World*, 2nd ed. (New Haven, CT: Yale University Press, 2004), 473.

30. Hannah Arendt, "Tradition and the Modern Age," in *Between Past and Future: Eight Exercises in Political Thought* (New York: Penguin, 1993), 13ff.

31. Hannah Arendt, *The Life of the Mind*, vol. 1: *Thinking* (New York: Harcourt Brace Jovanovich, 1978), 212.

32. Arendt, *Between Past and Future*, 3.

33. Arendt, *Between Past and Future*, 14.

34. See, for instance, her remarks in the 1964 German television interview with Günter Gaus, "Fernsehgespräch mit Günter Gaus," in *Ich will verstehen. Selbstauskünfte zu Leben und Werk*, by Hannah Arendt, ed. Ursula Ludz (Munich: Piper, 1996), 44–70, here 44ff.

35. Arendt, "Tradition," 17.

36. Arendt, "Tradition," 18.

37. Agnes Heller, "Hannah Arendt on Tradition and New Beginnings," in *Hannah Arendt in Jerusalem*, ed. Steven Aschheim (Berkeley: University of California Press, 2001), 19–32, here 20. Heller proceeds to explore the role that stories and, by extension, the notion of narrative play in Arendt's conception of a philosophical and political beginning. However, the idea that there is, for Arendt, a "redemptive power" in narrative, as critics such as Seyla Benhabib imagine, remains debatable. Seyla Benhabib, "Hannah Arendt and the Redemptive Power of Narrative," in *Hannah Arendt: Critical Essays*, eds. Lewis Hinchman and Sandra Hinchman (Albany: State University of New York Press, 1994), 111–137.

38. Hannah Arendt, "No Longer and Not Yet," in *Essays in Understanding, 1930–1940*, ed. Jerome Kohn (New York: Harcourt, Brace, 1993), 158–162. Compare chapter 11, "Afterness and Empty Space: No Longer and Not Yet," on Arendt's reading of Broch in this essay, in Gerhard Richter, *Afterness: Figures of Following in Modern Thought and Aesthetics* (New York: Columbia University Press, 2011), 199–205.

39. Arendt, "Tradition," 19.

40. Arendt, "Tradition," 20ff.

41. Arendt, "Tradition," 21.

42. Arendt, "Tradition," 21ff.

43. Arendt, "Tradition," 23.

44. Arendt, "Tradition," 25.

45. Ibid. Arendt's intuition here—that one does not need to be conscious of the fundamental metaphysical impulses and assumptions that guide one's

thinking for them to have a profound impact on one's being—can be seen as belonging to her investment in a certain post-metaphysical comportment and mode of questioning. From this perspective, Albrecht Wellmer, in his analysis of Arendt's specific relation to political and philosophical liberalism, is certainly right to suggest that Arendt's critique "rests on a deconstruction of the whole 'metaphysical' tradition of political thought starting with Plato and Aristotle" and that, by extension, "her re-reading and critique of the Western tradition of political philosophy is therefore radical in Heidegger's sense, even as it attempts to set his deconstruction of metaphysics on its feet, and to turn it around politically." Albrecht Wellmer, "Arendt on Revolution," in *The Cambridge Companion to Hannah Arendt*, ed. Dana Villa (Cambridge: Cambridge University Press, 2000), 220–241, here 225.

This view is corroborated by Arendt herself, who confesses, in the section of *The Life of the Mind* that revisits the question of the gap between the past and the future, "I have clearly joined the ranks of those who for some time now have been attempting to dismantle metaphysics, and philosophy with all its categories, as we have know them from their beginning in Greece until today. Such dismantling is possible only on the assumption that the thread of tradition is broken and that we shall not be able to renew it. Historically speaking, what actually has broken down is the Roman trinity that for thousands of years united religion, authority, and tradition." Arendt, *The Life of the Mind*, 212.

46. Arendt, "Tradition," 25.

47. Ibid.

48. Jerome Kohn makes this point in "The Loss of Tradition," in *Hannah Arendt: Verborgene Tradition—Unzeitgemäße Aktualität?*, ed. Heinrich-Böll-Stiftung (Berlin: Akademie Verlag, 2007), 37–47, here 38.

49. For Heidegger, this transition from Greek to Roman culture was fateful because the Romans were not intellectually prepared to receive the complex Greek tradition on its own terms but rather misunderstood and misappropriated it. For instance, in the 1936 "The Origin of the Work of Art," he emphasizes that "the translation of the Greek names into the Latin language is not at all the inconsequential process it is considered to this day. Rather, beneath the seemingly literal and thus preserving translation hides a translation or carrying-across [*Über-setzen*] of Greek experience into a different way of thinking. Roman thought takes over the Greek words with the equi-primordial experience [*ohne die gleichursprüngliche Erfahrung*] of what they say, without the Greek word. The groundlessness [*Bodenlosigkeit*] of Western thought begins with this translation or carrying-across." Martin Heidegger, "Der Ursprung des Kunstwerks," *Holzwege* (Frankfurt am Main: Klostermann, 1980), 1–72, here 7.

50. Arendt thinks in a similar direction in the course of her "thought-diary," her *Denktagebuch*. There, several of the fragmentary entries concern the

ways in which Roman thought and practice called the notion of tradition into presence. In March 1953, for instance, she remarks, under the heading "Ad Tradition," that the Roman manner of "shifting authority into tradition (instead of the divine messiah, who is the idea)" meant "seeing the divine at work in the founding of the cities. The beginning [*Der Anfang*] received its a priori standing, which it had never had in a *historical* sense with the Greeks, from this political experience." *Denktagebuch 1950–1973*, eds. Ursula Ludz and Ingeborg Nordmann (Munich: Piper, 2002), vol. 1, 334.

51. Arendt, "Tradition," 25.
52. Arendt, *Dark Times*, 194; *Zwei Essays*, 50.
53. Arendt, "Tradition," 26.
54. Ibid.
55. Ibid.
56. Arendt, "Tradition," 28.
57. Ibid.
58. Arendt, "Tradition," 35.
59. Arendt, "Tradition," 36.
60. Arendt, "Tradition," 38.
61. Arendt, "Tradition," 39.
62. Arendt, "Tradition," 40.
63. Theodor W. Adorno, "Resignation," in *Critical Models: Interventions and Catchwords*, trans. Henry Pickford (New York: Columbia University Press, 2005), 289–293, here 293; "Resignation," in *Gesammelte Schriften*, ed. Rolf Tiedemann, vol. 10 (Frankfurt am Main: Suhrkamp, 1997), 794–799, here 798.
64. Adorno, "Resignation" (*Critical Models*), 293.
65. Adorno, "Resignation" (*Gesammelte Schriften*), 798.
66. Theodor W. Adorno, "On Tradition," no translator specified ("collaborative translation"), *Telos* 94 (Winter 1992–93): 75–82, here 75; "Über Tradition," *Gesammelte Schriften*, ed. Rolf Tiedemann, vol. 10 (Frankfurt am Main: Suhrkamp, 1997), 310–320, here 310.
67. One might say that the question of the hand here also belongs to Adorno's larger interest in the question of gesturing and in the concept of the gesture as such. For a brief discussion of Adorno's attentiveness to the notion of the gesture in relation to the specific problem of leave-taking as it comes to pass in his essay on tradition, see Eva Geulen, "Theodor Adorno on Tradition," in *The Actuality of Adorno: Critical Essays on Adorno and the Postmodern*, ed. Max Pensky (Albany: State University of New York Press, 1997), 183–193.
68. Adorno, "On Tradition," 78.
69. Adorno, "Über Tradition," 315.
70. Adorno, "On Tradition," 79; "Über Tradition," 315ff.
71. Adorno, "On Tradition," 79; "Über Tradition," 316.

72. On the concept of rescuing (*Rettung*) as it is inflected by Adorno and Benjamin more broadly, see Gerhard Richter, "Can Anything Be Rescued by Defending It? Benjamin with Adorno," *differences* 31: 3 (2010): 34–35.

73. Adorno, "On Tradition," 79; "Über Tradition," 316.

74. Ibid.

75. The number, dates, and locations of these meetings between Adorno and Beckett are provided by Stefan Müller-Doohm, *Adorno. Eine Biographie* (Frankfurt am Main: Suhrkamp, 2003), 863.

76. Theodor W. Adorno, "Trying to Understand *Endgame*," in *Notes to Literature*, trans. Shierry Weber Nicholsen, vol. 1 (New York: Columbia University Press, 1991), 241–275, here 259; "Versuch, das Endspiel zu verstehen," *Noten zur Literatur, Gesammelte Schriften*, ed. Rolf Tiedemann, vol. 11 (Frankfurt am Main: Suhrkamp, 1997), 281–321, here 303.

77. Adorno, "On Tradition," 80; "Über Tradition," 317.

78. Adorno, "On Tradition," 81; "Über Tradition," 318.

79. Adorno, "On Tradition," 82.

80. Adorno, "Über Tradition," 320.

3. THE INHERITANCE OF THE CONSTELLATION: ADORNO AND HEGEL

1. This chapter was translated by Kristina Mendicino.

2. See Catherine Malabou, *L'avenir de Hegel: Plasticité, temporalité, dialectique* (Paris: Vrin, 1996); Rebecca Comay, *Mourning Sickness: Hegel and the French Revolution* (Stanford, CA: Stanford University Press, 2010); and Slavoj Žižek, *Less Than Nothing: Hegel and the Shadow of Dialectical Materialism* (London: Verso, 2012).

3. Hans-Georg Gadamer, "The Heritage of Hegel," trans. Frederick G. Lawrence, in *The Gadamer Reader: A Bouquet of the Later Writings*, ed. Richard E. Palmer (Evanston, IL: Northwestern University Press, 2007), 322–344, here 326.

4. Georg Wilhelm Friedrich Hegel, *Vorlesungen über die Geschichte der Philosophie, Werke*, vol. 18, ed. Eva Moldenhauer and Karl Markus Michel (Frankfurt am Main: Suhrkamp, 1986), 36.

5. Gadamer, "The Heritage of Hegel," 334.

6. Ibid.

7. Gadamer, 335.

8. Gadamer, 336.

9. Gadamer, 335.

10. Georg Wilhelm Friedrich Hegel, *The Difference between Fichte's and Schelling's System of Philosophy*, trans. and ed. H. S. Harris and Walter Cerf (Albany: State University of New York Press, 1977), 87.

11. Theodor W. Adorno, *Letters to His Parents, 1939–1951*, trans. Wieland Hoban (Cambridge: Polity, 2006); *Briefe an die Eltern 1939–1951*, ed. Christoph Gödde and Henri Lonitz (Frankfurt am Main: Suhrkamp, 2003).

12. Consider, for example, the image of the rat that Adorno develops in *Negative Dialectics* and in connection with psychoanalysis, in order to stage the dialectic of enlightenment. See Gerhard Richter, "Nazism and Negative Dialectics: Adorno's Hitler in *Minima Moralia*," in *Thought-Images: Frankfurt School Writers' Reflections from Damaged Life* (Stanford, CA: Stanford UP, 2007), 147–190, here 176–184.

13. Theodor W. Adorno, *Quasi una Fantasia: Essays on Modern Music*, trans. Rodney Livingstone (London and New York: Verso, 1998), 33–34; *Quasi una fanatasia. Musikalische Schriften II, Gesammelte Schriften*, vol. 16, ed. Rolf Tiedemann (Frankfurt am Main: Suhrkamp, 1997), 281.

14. Ibid.

15. Ibid.

16. Theodor W. Adorno, "What Does Coming to Terms with the Past Mean?," in *Bitburg in Moral and Political Perspective*, ed. Geoffrey Hartman, trans. Timothy Bahti and Geoffrey Hartmann (Bloomington: Indiana University Press, 1986), 114–129, here 123; "Was bedeutet: Aufarbeitung der Vegangenheit," *Gesammelte Schriften*, vol. 10, ed. Rolf Tiedemann (Frankfurt am Main: Suhrkamp, 1997), 555–572, here 566.

17. Theodor W. Adorno, "Television as Ideology," in *Critical Models: Interventions and Catchwords*, trans. Henry W. Pickford (New York: Columbia University Press, 2005), 59–70, here 62; "Fernsehen als Ideologie," *Gesammelte Schriften*, vol. 10, ed. Rolf Tiedemann (Frankfurt am Main Suhrkamp, 1997), 321–494, here 334.

18. Theodor W. Adorno, *Alban Berg: The Master of the Smallest Link*, trans. Juliane Brand and Christopher Hailey (Cambridge: Cambridge University Press, 1997), 8; *Berg. Der Meister des kleinsten Übergangs, Gesammelte Schriften*, vol. 13, ed. Rolf Tiedemann (Frankfurt am Main: Suhrkamp, 1997), 321–494, here 334.

19. Theodor W. Adorno, *Philosophy of New Music*, trans. Robert Hullot-Kentor (Minneapolis: University of Minnesota Press, 2006), 12; *Philosophie der neuen Musik, Gesammelte Schriften*, vol. 12, ed. Rolf Tiedemann (Frankfurt am Main: Suhrkamp, 1997), 18.

20. If one devotes oneself to a many-layered question such as that of inheritance in Adorno's work, one would be well-advised to enter into this enterprise by facing the general horizon of interpretation, which presents itself and gives orientation by confronting readers with the irreducible aporias of Adorno's texts. Alexander García Düttmann has emphasized this foundational aporetic structure in his critical commentary on Adorno's *Minima Moralia*: "Thinking leads ultimately into aporias, not out from them. But only through the argument is

the aporia discovered. And once the aporia is discovered, there remains nothing other than a 'that's how it is'—a confirmation of how there is no way out, which nonetheless shows the way that one wants to go, although the argument also cannot mark that way as an exit, as a tried and true practice, or a universally valid solution to the aporia. Should it be more than a mere prejudice, the 'that's how it is' requires the highest and most continuous attentiveness to the world, for which there is no prescribed measure. It consequently marks the imbrication of knowledge and morality." *So ist es: Ein philosophischer Kommentar zu Adornos* Minima Moralia (Frankfurt am Main: Suhrkamp, 2004), n.p. No reading of Adorno can circumvent such a simultaneously productive and interruptive aporia.

21. This is not to say that, besides his engagement with Hegel's legacy, the process of working through the legacy of Kant does not stand at the center of Adorno's attention, especially in the writings explicitly concerned with aesthetics. In this respect, one might share J. M. Bernstein's assessment when he emphasizes that although "there are many possibilities for characterizing Adorno's philosophy in relation to Kant and Hegel—as post-Nietzschean Hegelianism or as re-kantified Lukács—the least that must be said is that he situates his philosophy between Kant and Hegel, whereby the 'between' demarcates the space that was opened and needed in the wake of all that happened after Hegel. That is to say: after Marx, after Nietzsche, after the failure of the Revolution, after Auschwitz." "Negative Dialektik: Begriffe und Kategorien III. Adorno zwischen Kant und Hegel," trans. Anje Korsmeier, *Klassiker Auslegen: Negative Dialektik* (Berlin: de Gruyter, 2005), 89–118, here 91. Peter Uwe Hohendahl has also pursued the question of whether Adorno, in the realm of aesthetics, knows himself to be indebted to the Hegelian tradition that presupposes a tight intertwinement between concept and artwork, and thus points beyond the formalism associated with Kant. See Hohendahl, "The Ephemeral and the Absolute," in *Language without Soil: Adorno and Late Philosophical Modernity*, ed. Gerhard Richter (New York: Fordham University Press, 2010), 206–226.

22. See J. M. Bernstein, "Negative Dialectic as Fate: Adorno and Hegel," in *The Cambridge Companion to Adorno*, ed. Tom Huhn (Cambridge: Cambridge University Press, 2004), 19–50, esp. 20 and 46. Compare Simon Jarvis, "The 'Unhappy Consciousness' and Conscious Unhappiness: On Adorno's Critique of Hegel and the Idea of an Hegelian Critique of Adorno," in *Hegel's Phenomenology of Spirit: A Reappraisal*, ed. Gary Browning (Dordrecht: Kluwer, 1997), 57–72.

23. Ernst Bloch, "Aussprache über Hegel," *Werkausgabe*, vol. 10 (Frankfurt am Main: Suhrkamp, 1985), 420–423, here 420.

24. If the question of intellectual heritage stands in the foreground of his thought, Adorno is also thoroughly aware of the general discussion of inheritance that shaped the cultural politics of the GDR shortly after his return from exile to West Germany. For example, he writes in the text that he composed

between 1954 and 1958, the "Essay as Form," that the widely promoted "neutralization of cultural works to commodities" was a "process . . . in recent intellectual history [that] has irresistibly taken hold of what the Eastern bloc ignominiously calls 'the heritage.'" "The Essay as Form," in *Notes to Literature*, trans. Shierry Weber Nicholsen, vol. 1 (New York: Columbia University Press, 1991), 3–23, here 6; "Der Essay als Form," *Gesammelte Schriften*, vol. 11, ed. Rolf Tiedemann (Frankfurt am Main: Suhrkamp, 1997), 9–33, here 12. The question of what from the so-called bourgeois tradition could still endure as an inheritance for socialism was controversially discussed. On one side stood those, such as Franz Mehring and Georg Lukács, who wanted, under the auspices of a humanistic heritage, to make way for the bourgeois tradition of classicism (especially Goethe and Schiller), Heine, as well as the brothers Thomas and Heinrich Mann, to enter the officially promoted culture of socialism. At the same time, however, they wished to permit no entrance for the works of the Romantics such as Friedrich Schlegel, which they classified as too formalistic or even negative, not to mention the art of expressionism and the somber oeuvres of Proust, Joyce, or Kafka. Although there were also important counter-appeals (e.g., those of Bloch, Brecht, Anna Seghers, and Hans Meyer) against the problematic unspoken assumptions of this exclusionary mechanism, the assessments represented by Mehring and Lukács insisted upon a rigorous differentiation between a purportedly progressive heritage and a reactionary one. This differentiation, however, necessarily entailed reducing the question of meaning and understanding to something presupposed as stable and already perceived, something that needed only to be classified according to criteria based on current convictions. In his polemical essay from 1958 on the late Lukács—which not least of all engages with the latter's understanding of Hegel—Adorno finds fault with an approach "that believes itself to be objective, as long as it merely neglects self-reflection." This approach "only succeeds in concealing the fact that it has purified the dialectical process of its objective, as well as subjective, value. Dialectics are paid lip-service, but for such a thinker all has been decided in advance. The writing becomes undialectical." Theodor W. Adorno, "Reconciliation under Duress: On Georg Lukács," trans. Rodney Livingstone, in *Aesthetics and Politics*, ed. Ronald Taylor (London: Verso, 1980), 151–176, here 154; "Erpreßte Versöhnung. Zu Georg Lukács: 'Wider den mißverstandenen Realismus,'" *Gesammelte Schriften*, vol. 11, ed. Rolf Tiedemann (Frankfurt am Main: Suhrkamp, 1997), 251–280, here 255. The radically constellative model that Adorno attempts to think regarding Hegel's inheritance and for inheritance *per se* cannot be satisfied with decisions made in advance over it. Rather, its evidence emerges first from the potentially infinite engagement with what can never be decided in advance, and from the constantly threatening fragility of stable meanings and of understanding itself.

25. Theodor W. Adorno, *Hegel: Three Studies*, trans. Shierry Weber Nicholsen (Cambridge: MIT Press, 1993), 1; *Drei Studien zu Hegel, Gesammelte*

Schriften, vol. 5, ed. Rolf Tiedemann (Frankfurt am Main; Suhrkamp, 1997), 247–381, here 251.

26. Ibid.

27. Adorno, *Hegel: Three Studies*, 2; *Drei Studien zu Hegel*, 251.

28. Ibid.

29. Theodor W. Adorno, *Philosophische Terminologie*, vol. 1., ed. Rudolf zur Lippe (Frankfurt am Main: Suhrkamp, 1973), 7.

30. Adorno's own description of his purpose points in this direction, where it is precisely a question of the *positioning* of something toward something else and thus shows itself to be motivated by Hegelian thinking: "What I have in mind is closer to what Hegel, in the introduction to his *System of Philosophy*, calls the 'positioning of thought toward objectivity.'" *Hegel: Three Studies*, 54; *Drei Studien zu Hegel*, 296. This *positioning toward something* is—as is the relation—a question of the constellation.

31. Walter Benjamin, *Ursprung des deutschen Trauerspiels*, in *Gesammelte Schriften*, vol. 1, ed. Rolf Tiedemann and Hermann Schweppenhäuser (Frankfurt am Main: Suhrkamp, 1991), 203–430.

32. It would, for instance, be time to distinguish the radicality of Adorno's negative-dialectical model of the constellation from the field that the philosopher Dieter Henrich has named "constellation-research," which he developed in order to investigate certain currents of German Idealism via models of influence. A recent overview of this field can be found in the volume *Konstellationsforschung*, eds. Martin Mulsow and Marcelo Stamm (Frankfurt am Main: Suhrkamp, 2005).

33. Adorno, *Hegel: Three Studies*, 139; *Drei Studien zu Hegel*, 368.

34. Adorno, *Hegel: Three Studies*,163; *Drei Studien zu Hegel*, 353.

35. Georg Wilhelm Friedrich Hegel, *Phänomenologie des Geistes*, *Werke*, eds. Eva Moldenhauer and Karl Markus Michel, vol. 3 (Frankfurt am Main: Suhrkamp, 1986), 65.

36. Theodor W. Adorno, *Negative Dialectics*, trans. E. B. Ashton (London and New York: Routledge, 2004), 162; *Negative Dialektik, Gesammelte Schriften*, vol. 6, ed. Rolf Tiedemann (Frankfurt am Main: Suhrkamp, 1997), 164ff.

37. Recently, Jochen Hörsch has reminded us of the ways in which the productive moment of Hegelian negation doubles as affirmation: "To conceive of negation as affirmative—that means nothing other than this: it is good that there are negations, for without determinate negations there would be nothing graspable and sensually experienceable. Negations are affirmative and productive not only because speculative philosophy has, with sophistic lust, fallen in love with them, but because they are real, because they issue precisely not into 'nothingness' as a sort of 'ultimum,' but rather because mental and communicative acts of negation allow, conversely, a clever and commensurate understanding of

being, existence, time and infinity." *Bedeutsamkeit: Über den Zusammenhang von Zeit, Sein und Medien* (Munich: Hanser, 2009), 138. It would also be important to pursue, in another context, the question as to how Adorno's notions of negation and the negative relate to recent attempts to grasp the restlessness of negativity in Hegel, such as Jean-Luc Nancy's *Hegel: L'inquiétude du negatif* (Paris: Hachette, 1997).

38. Theodor W. Adorno, "Theses on the Language of the Philosopher," in *Adorno and the Need in Thinking: New Critical Essays*, eds. Donald Burke et al. (Toronto: University of Toronto Press, 2007), 35–40, here 36; "Thesen über die Sprache des Philosophen," *Gesammelte Schriften*, vol. 1, ed. Rolf Tiedemann (Frankfurt am Main: Suhrkamp, 1997), 366–371, here 367.

39. See also the determination of "language" as the "organ of theory" in Theodor W. Adorno, "Aus einem Schulheft ohne Deckel: Bar Harbor, Sommer 1939," *Frankfurter Adorno Blätter* 4 (1995): 7.

40. Mirko Wischke, "'Keine Erkenntnis von Dingen': Adorno über das Begrifflose am Begriff," *Zeitschrift für kritische Theorie* 17 (2003): 73–88, here 79.

41. Ibid.

42. Friedrich Nietzsche, "On Truth and Lie in an Extra-Moral Sense," in *Friedrich Nietzsche: Rhetoric and Language*, ed. and trans. Sander L. Gilman, Carole Blair, and David J. Parent (Oxford: Oxford University Press, 1989), 249–250.

43. On the multiply mediated relation between self and other as the problem of the possibility and the thought of history, culture, and reason, see Terry Pinkard, *Hegel's Phenomenology: The Sociality of Reason* (Cambridge: Cambridge University Press, 1996).

44. Hegel formulates it in the following way: "To the contrary, in that the result, as it is in truth, is taken up as *determinate* negation, a new form will have arisen immediately and made the transition in negation, through which progress yields itself, as of itself, through the full series of shapes." Hegel, *Phänomenologie des Geistes*, 74.

45. In precisely this counter-striving between experience and concept, the hermeneutic problem-structure becomes visible at the same time, out of which the relation of experience and the concept of understanding itself come to expression for Hegel. On this, see Werner Hamacher's exposition: "Hegel does not dissolve the aporia of understanding. On the contrary, for him, the aporia constitutes the resistance from which experience must rebound and turn back upon itself. By supposing that the incomprehensible has a meaning, spirit understands it as its object and understands itself as its positing." Hamacher, *Premises: Essays on Philosophy and Literature from Kant to Celan*, trans. Peter Fenves (Stanford, CA: Stanford University Press, 1999), 7.

46. Hegel, *Phänomenologie des Geistes*, 72.

47. Adorno, *Hegel: Three Studies*, 55; *Drei Studien zu Hegel*, 297.

48. Adorno, *Hegel: Three Studies*, 56; *Drei Studien zu Hegel*, 297.
49. Adorno, *Hegel: Three Studies*, 83; *Drei Studien zu Hegel*, 320.
50. See, for example, Otto Pöggeler, "Die Komposition der *Phänomenologie des Geistes*," in *Materialien zu Hegels* Phänomenologie des Geistes, eds. Hans Fulda and Dieter Henrich (Frankfurt am Main: Suhrkamp, 1973), 276–327; Robert B. Pippin, "You Can't Get There from Here: Transition Problems in Hegel's *Phenomenology of Spirit*," in *The Cambridge Companion to Hegel*, ed. Frederick Beiser (Cambridge: Cambridge UP, 1993), 52–85; as well as Jon Stewart's attempt to glimpse a concealed unity behind the seemingly incoherent structure of the text: *The Unity of Hegel's Phenomenology of Spirit* (Evanston, IL: Northwestern University Press, 2000). On the question of the structure and composition of the text, see also Eckart Förster's essay, "Hegels Entdeckungsreisen: Entstehung und Aufbau der Phänomenologie des Geistes," in *Hegels* Phänomenologie des Geistes: *Ein kooperativer Kommentar zu einem Schlüsselwerk der Moderne*, eds. Wolfgang Welsch and Klaus Vieweg (Frankfurt am Main: Suhrkamp, 2008), 37–56.
51. Pippin, "You Can't Get There from Here," 78.
52. Adorno, *Hegel: Three Studies*, 2; *Drei Studien zu Hegel*, 252.
53. Adorno, *Hegel: Three Studies*, 51; *Drei Studien zu Hegel*, 294.
54. Walter Benjamin, "Literaturgeschichte und Literaturwissenschaft," in *Gesammelte Schriften*, vol. 3, ed. Hella Tiedemann-Bartels (Frankfurt am Main: Suhrkamp, 1991), 283–290, here 286.
55. Adorno, *Hegel: Three Studies*, xxxv ff; *Drei Studien zu Hegel*, 249.
56. Adorno, *Hegel: Three Studies*, xxxvi; *Drei Studien zu Hegel*, 249.
57. Adorno, *Hegel: Three Studies*, 89; *Drei Studien zu Hegel*, 326.
58. Adorno, *Hegel: Three Studies*, 109; *Drei Studien zu Hegel*, 342.
59. Friedrich Schlegel, *Friedrich Schlegel's* Lucinde and the Fragments, trans. Peter Firchow (Minneapolis: University of Minnesota Press, 1971), 167.
60. Adorno, *Hegel: Three Studies*, 91; *Drei Studien zu Hegel*, 327.
61. Adorno, *Hegel: Three Studies*; 91; *Drei Studien zu Hegel*, 328.
62. Adorno, *Hegel: Three Studies*, 104; *Drei Studien zu Hegel*, 339.
63. Adorno, *Hegel: Three Studies*, 99; *Drei Studien zu Hegel*, 334.
64. Adorno, "Notes on Philosophical Thinking," *Critical Models: Interventions and Catchwords*, trans. Henry W. Pickford (New York: Columbia University Press, 2005), 127–134, here 131; "Anmerkungen zum philosophischen Denken," *Gesammelte Schriften*, vol. 10, ed. Rolf Tiedemann (Frankfurt am Main: Suhrkamp University Press, 1997), 599–607, here 604.
65. Ibid.
66. Friedrich Hölderlin, "Mnemosyne (Entwurf)," in *Sämtliche Werke und Briefe*, vol. 1, ed. Michael Knaupp (Munich: Hanser, 1992), 436–437, here 436.

4. JUDGING BY REFRAINING FROM JUDGMENT: ADORNO'S ARTWORK AND ITS *EINORDNUNG*

1. Theodor W. Adorno, "Cultural Criticism and Society," in *Prisms*, trans. Samuel and Shierry Weber (Cambridge, MA: MIT Press, 1981), 17–34, here 32; "Kulturkritik und Gesellschaft," *Gesammelte Schriften*, vol. 10, ed. Rolf Tiedemann (Frankfurt am Main: Suhrkamp, 1997), 9–30, here 27.

2. Theodor W. Adorno and Thomas Mann, *Correspondence 1943–1955*, trans. Nicholas Walker (Cambridge: Polity, 2006), 93; *Briefwechsel 1943–1955*, eds. Christoph Gödde and Thomas Sprecher (Frankfurt am Main: Fischer, 2003), 122.

3. Rüdiger Bubner, "Kann Theorie ästhetisch werden? Zum Hauptmotiv der Philosophie Adornos," *Materialien zur Ästhetischen Theorie Theodor W. Adornos. Konstruktionen der Moderne*, eds. Burkhardt Lindner and Martin Lüdke (Frankfurt am Main: Suhrkamp, 1980), 108–137.

4. Norbert Bolz, "Gnosis and Systems Theory: A Conversation between Norbert Bolz and Michael Hirsch," trans. Steven Lindberg, in *Adorno: The Possibility of the Impossible*, eds. Nicolaus Schafhausen, Vanessa Joan Müller, and Michael Hirsch, vol. 1. (Berlin: Sternberg, 2003), 93–108, here 105.

5. Agamben here implicitly, and in a highly mediated way, takes up aspects of his earlier interpretation of Benjamin's and Adorno's differences in the chapter "The Prince and the Frog: The Question of Method in Adorno and Benjamin" of his study, originally published in Italian in 1978: *Infancy and History: The Destruction of Experience*, trans. Liz Heron (London: Verso, 1993).

6. Giorgio Agamben, *The Time That Remains: A Commentary on the Letter to the Romans*, trans. Patricia Dailey (Stanford, CA: Stanford University Press, 2005), 38.

7. Agamben, *The Time That Remains*, 38ff.

8. Alexander García Düttmann, *Was weiß Kunst? Für eine Ästhetik des Widerstands* (Konstanz: Konstanz University Press, 2015), 37–65.

9. Christoph Menke, *Die Kraft der Kunst* (Berlin: Suhrkamp, 2013), 56–81.

10. Theodor W. Adorno, *Ästhetische Theorie. Gesammelte Schriften*, vol. 7, ed. Rolf Tiedemann (Frankfurt am Main: Suhrkamp, 1997), 187ff.

11. Theodor W. Adorno, *Aesthetic Theory*, trans. Robert Hullot-Kentor (Minneapolis: University of Minnesota Press, 1997), 123ff.

12. Adorno, *Aesthetic Theory*, 124; *Ästhetische Theorie*, 188.

13. This epistolary exchange between Heidegger and Staiger on Mörike can now be found under the title "Zu einem Vers von Mörike. Ein Briefwechsel mit Martin Heidegger von Emil Staiger (1951)," in Martin Heidegger, *Aus der Erfahrung des Denkens* (1910–1976), *Gesamtausgabe*, vol. 13 (Frankfurt am Main: Klostermann, 2002), 93–109.

14. Adorno, *Ästhetische Theorie*, 188.

15. Friedrich Hölderlin, "Being and Judgment," in *Essays and Letters on Theory*, trans. Thomas Pfau (Albany: State University of New York Press, 1988), 37; "Seyn, Urtheil, Modalität," *Sämtliche Werke und Briefe*, vol. 2, ed. Michael Knaupp (Munich: Hanser, 1992), 50.

16. Adorno, *Aesthetic Theory*, 87; *Ästhetische Theorie*, 135.

17. Adorno, *Aesthetic Theory*, 126ff; *Ästhetische Theorie*, 192f.

18. Adorno, *Aesthetic Theory*, 128; *Ästhetische Theorie*, 193. Adorno here implicitly returns to a train of thought from his earlier essay on Thomas Mann, first published in "Die Neue Rundschau" in 1962. There he writes, "However rigorously Thomas Mann's oeuvre separates itself in its linguistic form from its origins in the individual, pedagogues . . . revel in it because it encourages them to take out of it as its substance [*als Gehalt herauszuholen*] what the author put into it. . . . Instead, however, I believe that the substance [*Gehalt*] of a work of art begins precisely where the author's intention stops; the intention is extinguished in the substance." Theodor W. Adorno, "Toward a Portrait of Thomas Mann," in *Notes to Literature*, vol. 2, trans. Shierry Weber Nicholson (New York: Columbia University Press, 1992), 12–19, here 12ff; "Zu einem Portrait Thomas Manns," *Gesammelte Schriften*, vol. 11, ed. Rolf Tiedemann (Frankfurt am Main: Frankfurt, 1997), 335–344, here 335ff. Both this thought from Adorno's Mann essay and the passage from *Aesthetic Theory* are strongly indebted to Benjamin's anti-intentionalist conception of truth as outlined in the epistemo-critical prologue to his book on the German *Trauerspiel*. Adorno was very familiar with Benjamin's text, which was first published in 1928 and became the subject of a seminar that Adorno taught at the University of Frankfurt in the early 1930s—most likely the first university seminar on Benjamin ever. In the *Trauerspiel* book, Benjamin argues: "Truth is an intentionless state of being, made up of ideas. The proper approach to it is not therefore one of intention and knowledge, but rather of total immersion and absorption in it. Truth is the death of intention. . . . The structure of truth, then, demands a mode of being which in its lack of intentionality resembles the simplest existence of things, but which is superior in its permanence." *The Origin of the German Tragic Drama*, trans. John Osborne (London: Verso, 1998), 36.

19. Adorno, *Aesthetic Theory*, 128; *Ästhetische Theorie*, 193.

20. Walter Benjamin, "Goethe's Elective Affinities," trans. Stanley Corngold, in *Selected Writings*, vol. 1, eds. Marcus Bullock and Michael W. Jennings (Cambridge, MA: Harvard University Press, 1996), 297–360.

21. *Der Gehalt*, which as a masculine noun signifies import, substance, or significance, is not be confused with the neuter version of the same noun, *das Gehalt*, which means "salary."

22. This is the case even though the translator of *Aesthetic Theory* is aware that there is a difference between *Inhalt* and *Gehalt* and that this difference

ought to have implications for the translation as a whole. But one might say that the practical conclusions the translator draws from this state of affairs are hard to accept. Adorno, *Aesthetic Theory*, 368, translator's note.

23. Adorno, *Aesthetic Theory*, 225ff; *Ästhetische Theorie*, 335.
24. Adorno, *Aesthetic Theory*, 59; *Ästhetische Theorie*, 93.
25. Theodor W. Adorno, "Short Commentaries on Proust," trans. Shierry Weber Nicholsen, in *Notes to Literature*, vol. 1 (New York: Columbia University Press, 1991), 174–184, here 175; "Kleine Proust-Kommentare," *Gesammelte Schriften*, vol. 11, ed. Rolf Tiedemann (Frankfurt am Main: Suhrkamp, 1997), 203–215, here 204.
26. Martin Walser, *A Gushing Fountain*, trans. David Dollenmayer (New York: Arcade, 2015), 3. In the original German, Walser's remarkable passage reads: "Solange etwas ist, ist es nicht das, was es gewesen sein wird. Wenn etwas vorbei ist, ist man nicht mehr der, dem es passierte. Allerdings ist man dem näher als anderen. Obwohl es die Vergangenheit, als sie Gegenwart war, nicht gegeben hat, drängt sie sich jetzt auf, als habe es sie so gegeben, wie sie sich jetzt aufdrängt. Aber solange etwas ist, ist es nicht das, was es gewesen sein wird. Wenn etwas vorbei ist, ist man nicht mehr der, dem es passierte. Als das, von dem wir jetzt sagen, daß es gewesen sei, haben wir nicht gewußt, daß es ist. Jetzt sagen wir, daß es so und so gewesen sei, obwohl wir damals, als es war, nichts von dem wußten, was wir jetzt sagen." *Ein springender Brunnen* (Frankfurt am Main: Suhrkamp, 1998), 9.
27. Adorno, *Aesthetic Theory*, 124; *Ästhetische Theorie*, 188.
28. Adorno, *Aesthetic Theory*, 124; *Ästhetische Theorie*, 189.
29. Philip Roth, *The Dying Animal* (Boston: Houghton Mifflin, 2001), 98.
30. Ibid., 100.
31. Julian Barnes, *The Sense of an Ending* (New York: Vintage, 2011), 115.
32. Jacques Derrida, *Learning to Live Finally: An Interview with Jean Birnbaum*, trans. Pascale-Anne Brault and Michael Naas (Hoboken, NJ: Melville House, 2007), 24ff.
33. Barnes, 113.
34. Barnes, 163.
35. Theodor W. Adorno and Walter Benjamin, *The Complete Correspondence 1928–1940*, trans. Nicholas Walker (Cambridge, MA: Harvard University Press, 1999), 54; *Briefwechsel 1928–1940*, ed. Henri Lonitz (Frankfurt am Main: Suhrkamp, 1994), 74.
36. Adorno, *Aesthetic Theory*, 2; *Ästhetische Theorie*, 11.
37. Adorno, *Aesthetic Theory*, 3; *Ästhetische Theorie*, 12.
38. Adorno, *Ästhetische Theorie*, 10.
39. Adorno, *Aesthetic Theory*, 3.
40. Alexander Nehamas, *Only a Promise of Happiness: The Place of Beauty in a World of Art* (Princeton, NJ: Princeton University Press, 2007), 35.

41. Karl Kraus, *Aphorismen. Schriften*, vol. 8, ed. Christian Wagenknecht (Frankfurt am Main: Suhrkamp, 1986), 283.

5. THE LITERARY ARTWORK BETWEEN WORD AND CONCEPT: ADORNO AND AGAMBEN READING KAFKA

1. W. H. Auden, "The Wandering Jew," in *The Complete Works of W. H. Auden*, vol. 2: Prose, 1939–1948, ed. Edward Mendelson. (Princeton, NJ: Princeton University Press, 2002), 110–113, here 110.

2. Franz Kafka, *The Trial*, trans. Mike Mitchell (Oxford: Oxford University Press, 2009), 3; *Der Proceß*, ed. Malcolm Pasley. *Kritische Ausgabe* (Frankfurt am Main: Fischer, 2002), 7.

3. Martin Walser, "Description of a Form," trans. James Rolleston, in *Twentieth Century Interpretation of* The Trial*: A Collection of Critical Essays*, ed. James Rolleston (Englewood Cliffs, NJ: Prentice-Hall, 1976), 21–35, here 21.

4. Franz Kafka, *Dearest Father and Other Writings*, trans. Ernst Kaiser and Eithne Wilkins (New York: Schocken, 1954), 87.

5. Franz Kafka, *Nachgelassene Schriften und Fragmente II*, ed. Jost Schillemeit. *Kritische Ausgabe* (Frankfurt am Main: Fischer, 2002), 75–76.

6. Gayatri Chakravorty Spivak, *A Critique of Postcolonial Reason: Toward a History of the Vanishing Present* (Cambridge, MA: Harvard University Press, 1999), 145n49.

7. Franz Kafka, *Dearest Father and Other Writings*, 40; *Nachgelassene Schriften und Fragmente II*, 59.

8. Franz Kafka, *Letters to Felice*, trans. James Stern and Elisabeth Duckworth (New York: Schocken, 1973), 265; *Briefe an Felice*, ed. Erich Heller and Jürgen Born (Frankfurt am Main: Fischer, 1983), 394.

9. I borrow the remainder of this paragraph as well as a couple of sentences of the next from my essay "Aesthetic Theory and Nonpropositional Truth Content in Adorno," *New German Critique* 97 (Winter 2006): 119–135.

10. Theodor W. Adorno, *Aesthetic Theory*, trans. Robert Hullot-Kentor (Minneapolis: University of Minnesota Press, 1997), 72; *Ästhetische Theorie. Gesammelte Schriften*, vol. 7, ed. Rolf Tiedemann (Frankfurt am Main: Suhrkamp, 1997), 113.

11. Theodor W. Adorno, *Lectures on Negative Dialectics: Fragments of a Lecture Course 1965/1966*, trans. Rodney Livingstone (Cambridge: Polity, 2008), 77; *Vorlesung über Negative Dialektik. Nachgelassene Schriften*, vol. 16, ed. Rolf Tiedemann (Frankfurt am Main: Suhrkamp, 2003), 115.

12. Theodor W. Adorno, "Words from Abroad" in *Notes to Literature*, vol. 1, trans. Shierry Weber Nicholsen (New York: Columbia University Press, 1991), 185–199, here 189; "Wörter aus der Fremde," *Noten zur Literatur. Gesammelte*

Schriften, vol. 11, ed. Rolf Tiedemann (Frankfurt am Main: Suhrkamp, 1997), 216–232, here 221.

13. Theodor W. Adorno, "Notes on Kafka," in *Prisms*, trans. Samuel and Shierry Weber (Cambridge, MA: MIT Press, 1981), 243–271, here 247; "Aufzeichnungen zu Kafka." *Kulturkritik und Gesellschaft I. Gesammelte Schriften*, vol. 11, ed. Rolf Tiedemann (Frankfurt am Main: Suhrkamp, 1997). 254–287, here 256. It is important to recall that Adorno's Kafka essay stands in permanent spectral conversation with the Kafka essays of two of his most important interlocutors and friends, Siegfried Kracauer's 1931 "Franz Kafka," first published in the *Frankfurter Zeitung*, and Walter Benjamin's 1934 "Franz Kafka. Zur zehnten Wiederkehr seines Todestages" ("Franz Kafka: On the Tenth Anniversary of His Death"), which first appeared in the *Jüdische Rundschau*. Equally significant in this context are Adorno's extensive epistolary exchanges with Benjamin on the topic of Kafka from the time Benjamin's Kafka essay appeared in 1934 to Benjamin's death in 1940. See Theodor W. Adorno and Walter Benjamin, *Briefwechsel 1928–1940* (Frankfurt am Main: Suhrkamp, 1994). For a reading of Benjamin's Kafka essay from the perspective of an intellectual inheritance, compare Gerhard Richter, "*Erbsünde*: A Note on Paradoxical Inheritance in Benjamin's Kafka Essay," in *Inheriting Walter Benjamin* (London: Bloomsbury, 2016), 15–33.

14. I will focus in my reading of Adorno's Kafka essay almost exclusively on the significance of this distinction between literality and figurality for the theoretical or philosophical interpretation of a (literary) work of art. For an incisive reading that focuses on other key elements of Adorno's richly textured essay, including the logic of an inverse theology that Adorno, *pace* Freud and Marx, observes at work in Kafka's writing, see Stanley Corngold, "Adorno's 'Notes on Kafka': A Critical Reconstruction," *Monatshefte* 94 (2002), Special Issue: *Rereading Adorno*, ed. Gerhard Richter, 24–42. For a probing consideration of Adorno's Kafka essay that places the question of literality in relation to Orson Welles's film adaptation of *The Trial* as well as to J. M. Coetzee's novel *Elizabeth Costello*, see Alexander García Düttmann, *Was weiß Kunst? Für eine Ästhetik des Widerstands* (Konstanz: Konstanz University Press, 2015), 111–125.

15. Adorno, "Notes on Kafka," 247; "Aufzeichnungen," 257.
16. Adorno, "Notes on Kafka," 247; "Aufzeichnungen," 257.
17. Adorno, "Notes on Kafka," 247; "Aufzeichnungen," 257.
18. Adorno, "Notes on Kafka," 247; "Aufzeichnungen," 257.
19. Adorno, "Notes on Kafka," 247; "Aufzeichnungen," 257.
20. Kafka, *Der Proceß*, 7.
21. To formulate it in a somewhat pointed manner, while Kafka's German sentence literally and figuratively opens the trial, its English translation is forced to close it from the start.
22. Franz Kafka, *The Diaries of Franz Kafka, 1910–1913*, trans. Joseph Kresh and ed. Max Brod (New York: Schocken, 1948), 9; *Tagebücher*, eds.

Hans-Gerd Koch, Michael Müller, and Malcolm Pasley, *Kritische Ausgabe* (Frankfurt am Main: Fischer, 2002), 9.

23. Adorno, "Notes on Kafka," 245; "Aufzeichnungen," 255.
24. Adorno, "Notes on Kafka," 246; "Aufzeichnungen," 256.
25. Adorno, "Notes on Kafka," 246; "Aufzeichnungen," 255.
26. The premise that any interpretation of Kafka should quite literally begin on the level of the individual sentence and linger with it is pursued by the recent collection *Kafkas Sätze*, ed. Hubert Spiegel (Frankfurt am Main: Fischer, 2009). In it, some seventy well-known critics and writers each present their single favorite sentence in Kafka and submit it, in short essays, to renewed interpretation. One of the questions that remains is whether or not the totality of sentences with a given Kafkan text can be said to amount to a literary form that invites inclusion of the text in a particular genre (and, by extension, that genre's particular histories and conceptual problems). For a structural discussion of *The Trial* from the perspective of genre, see Gerhard Neumann, "'Blinde Parabel' oder Bildungsroman? Zur Struktur von Kafkas 'Proceß'-Fragment," *Jahrbuch der deutschen Schillergesellschaft* 41 (1997): 399–427.
27. Friedrich Nietzsche, *Beyond Good and Evil*, trans. Walter Kaufmann, in *Basic Writings* (New York: Modern Library, 2000), 178–435, here 279.
28. Adorno, "Notes on Kafka," 248; "Aufzeichnungen," 258f. For a recent analysis of how the theatrical logic of the tension between words and gestures structures the entire opening scene of *The Trial*, see Stanley Corngold, "Medial Interventions in *The Trial*; or, *Res* in Media," in *Lambent Traces: Franz Kafka* (Princeton, NJ: Princeton University Press, 2004), 51–66.
29. Adorno, "Notes on Kafka," 248; "Aufzeichnungen," 258.
30. Jacques Derrida, "White Mythology: Metaphor in the Text of Philosophy," *Margins of Philosophy*, trans. Alan Bass (Chicago: University of Chicago Press, 1982), 207–229; Paul de Man, "Semiology and Rhetoric," in *Allegories of Reading: Figural Language in Rousseau, Nietzsche, Rilke, and Proust* (New Haven, CT: Yale University Press, 1979), 3–19.
31. De Man, "Semiology and Rhetoric," 10.
32. Jacques Derrida, "Before the Law," trans. Avital Ronell and Christine Roulston, in *Acts of Literature*, ed. Derek Attridge (New York: Routledge, 1992), 181–220, here 211.
33. Derrida, "Before the Law," 213.
34. Kafka, *The Trial*, 155; *Der Proceß*, 295.
35. Kafka, *The Trial*, 155; *Der Proceß*, 295.
36. Kafka, *The Trial*, 157; *Der Proceß*, 298.
37. Kafka, *The Trial*, 156; *Der Proceß*, 297.
38. Heinz Politzer, "The Trial against the Court," in *Franz Kafka: Parable and Paradox* (Ithaca, NY: Cornell University Press, 1962), 163–217.
39. Kafka, *Diaries 1914–1923*, 33–34; *Tagebücher*, 517.

40. Giorgio Agamben, "K.," in *Nudities*, trans. David Kishik and Stefen Pedatella (Stanford, CA: Stanford University Press, 2011), 20–36, here 20. I will bracket here the discussion of Kafka in relationship to the concept of sovereignty that Agamben undertakes in his earlier work, *Homo Sacer: Sovereign Power and Bare Life*, trans. Daniel Heller-Roazen (Stanford, CA: Stanford University Press, 1998), specifically in the chapter "Form of Law," 49ff.

41. Agamben, "K.," 21.

42. Agamben, "K.," 21.

43. Kafka, *The Trial*, 160; *Der Proceß*, 304.

44. Agamben, "K.," 21.

45. Agamben, "K.," 24.

46. Agamben, "K.," 25.

47. Agamben, "K.," 21.

48. As readers who have spent a lifetime engaging with Kafka's work—such as the late Walter H. Sokel, one of Kafka's most circumspect interpreters—will attest, even though Kafka's writing represents "the ever-renewed attempt to push toward . . . an explanation," the fact remains that a "final evaluative meaning, expressing a definite and definable intentionality in his work," is "impossible." After all, the "fundamental ambivalence of Kafka's writing precludes an ultimate judgment that could be called an 'explanation.'" Walter H. Sokel, "Beyond Self-Assertion: A Life of Reading Kafka," in *A Companion to the Works of Franz Kafka*, ed. James Rolleston (Rochester, NY: Camden House, 2002), 33–59, here 56. Reading Kafka's writing from a philosophical perspective would therefore have to entail an openness to hearing a different kind of demand. Among other things, this different kind of demand as it is mediated by the Kafkan text can be named an "imperative to write," as Jeff Fort has recently put it, an imperative that also encompasses a persistent element of textual self-reflection in which remnants of a failed or dispersed Kantian sublimity lingers on among the ruins of writing itself. Jeff Fort, *The Imperative to Write: Destitutions of the Sublime in Kafka, Blanchot, and Beckett* (New York: Fordham University Press, 2014).

49. Maurice Blanchot, *The Writing of the Disaster*, trans. Ann Smock. (Lincoln: University of Nebraska Press, 1995), 144f. Blanchot pursues some of the implications of this insight in his variegated essays on Kafka collected in *De Kafka à Kafka* (Paris: Gallimard, 1981).

50. Franz Kafka, *The Diaries of Franz Kafka, 1914–1923*, trans. Martin Greenberg, with Hannah Arendt, ed. Max Brod (New York: Schocken, 1949), 200–201; *Tagebücher*, 875. In a different context, it would be fruitful to investigate the implications of the fact that this passage on metaphor from Kafka's diaries also constitutes the one reference to Kafka that finds its way into Derrida's early seminal work *De la grammatologie*, where it is introduced at a crucial juncture: in the discussion, contained in "Deuxieme Partie: Nature, Culture,

Écriture," of how the supplement and the source relate in the space of writing. Jacques Derrida, *De la grammatologie* (Paris: Les Éditions de Minuit, 1967), 383–384.

The question concerning the volatile status of metaphor as a pivotal rhetorical figure traversing Kafka's writing has received much attention in the scholarship. For an exemplary reading of how, in the test case of *The Metamorphosis*, an "entire story is organized around a figure whose entire sense is to demystify and truly to deconstruct metaphor" precisely "by tampering with its normal operations" through a "chiastic movement," see Stanley Corngold and Benno Wagner, "Thirteen Ways of Looking at a Vermin (*The Metamorphosis*)," in *Franz Kafka: The Ghosts in the Machine* (Evanston, IL: Northwestern University Press, 2011), 57–73, here 73.

51. Rainer Stach, *Kafka. Die Jahre der Entscheidungen* (Frankfurt am Main: Fischer, 2004), 537.

52. One might add that the "law" of this irreducible hermeneutic lawlessness also stands in the way of any attempt to "rescue" *The Trial* and its doorkeeper episode from the threats of undecidability that have been assigned, in apparent moments of critical discomfort, designations such as "lawless reading [*gesetzloses Lesen*]," as in Hartmut Binder. Hartmut Binder, *"Vor dem Gesetz": Einführung in Kafkas Welt* (Stuttgart: Metzler, 1993), 3. And can one really speak of a redemptive "defense of writing" or a "defense of the text" if one chooses to see in *The Trial* primarily a ciphered "process of reflection" that merely requires hermeneutic unlocking and cultural retranslation in order to reveal its tacitly veiled, but in principle stable and accessible, meaning? This is the assumption made by studies such as *Verteidigung der Schrift. Kafkas Prozeß*, ed. Frank Schirrmacher (Frankfurt am Main: Suhrkamp, 1987). Yet is such an alleged defense, a *Verteidigung*, of the novel not in reality a way of making it superfluous—precisely by showing that what it says and how it says it could have been said another way as well (that is, in the language of critical commentary and explanation), without essential loss?

6. THE ARTWORK WITHOUT CARDINAL DIRECTION: NOTES ON ORIENTATION IN ADORNO

1. Niklas Luhmann, *Social Systems*, trans. John Bednarz, Jr., with Dirk Baecker (Stanford, CA: Stanford University Press, 1995), l.

2. Georg Lukács, *The Theory of the Novel: A Historico-Philosophical Essay on the Forms of Great Epic Literature*, trans. Anna Bostock (Cambridge, MA: MIT Press, 1971), 41.

3. Michel Foucault, "Of Other Spaces," trans. Jay Miskowiec, *Diacritics* 16 (Spring 1986): 22–27, here 22.

4. J. Hillis Miller, "Paul de Man at Work: In These Bad Days, What Good Is an Archive?" In *Theory and the Disappearing Future: On de Man, On*

Benjamin, eds. Tom Cohen, Claire Colebrook, and J. Hillis Miller (London: Routledge, 2012), 55–88, here 55.

5. Fredric Jameson, *Postmodernism, or, The Cultural Logic of Late Capitalism* (Durham, NC: Duke University Press, 1991), 54.

6. For a history of the concept of orientation since its entry into Western philosophy in the eighteenth century through the work of Moses Mendelsohn and Kant, see Werner Stegmaier, "Weltorientierung, Orientierung," *Historisches Wörterbuch der Philosophie*, eds. Joachim Ritter et al., vol. 12 (Basel: Schwabe, 2004), columns 498–507. A representative variety of recent philosophical perspectives—from both "Continental" and "analytic" traditions of thought—on the concept of orientation can be found, for instance, in *Orientierung: Philosophische Perspektiven*, ed. Werner Stegmaier (Frankfurt am Main: Suhrkamp, 2005). For the most part, such perspectives on orientation tend to exclude questions of aesthetics and the work of art.

7. Herbert Schnädelbach, "Dialektik der Vernunftkritik. Zur Konstruktion des Rationalen bei Adorno," in *Adorno-Konferenz 1983*, eds. Ludwig von Friedeburg and Jürgen Habermas (Frankfurt am Main: Suhrkamp, 1983), 66–93, here 90.

8. Martin Seel, *Adornos Philosophie der Kontemplation* (Frankfurt am Main: Suhrkamp, 2004), 19.

9. Rolf Tiedemann, "Der Philosoph vor dem Mikrophon," *Adorno und Benjamin noch einmal. Erinnerungen, Begleitworte, Polemiken* (Munich: Edition Text & Kritik, 2011), 164–174, here 173.

10. J. M. Bernstein, *Adorno: Disenchantment and Ethics* (Cambridge: Cambridge University Press, 2001); Thierry de Duve, "Resisting Adorno, Revamping Kant," *Art and Aesthetics after Adorno*, The Townsend Papers in the Humanities No. 3, ed. Anthony Cascardi (Berkeley: University of California Press, 2010), 249–299. Such approaches will need to be modulated by an attentiveness to the ways in which Adorno's apparent untimeliness today, especially in the area of his philosophy of art, may almost paradoxically open up new critical possibilities, as argued most recently by Peter Uwe Hohendahl, *The Fleeting Promise of Art: Adorno's Aesthetic Theory Revisited* (Ithaca, NY: Cornell University Press, 2013).

11. Theodor W. Adorno, "Introduction," in *The Positivist Dispute in German Sociology*, by Theodor W. Adorno, Hans Albert, Ralf Dahrendorf, Jürgen Habermas, Harald Pilot, and Karl R. Popper, trans. Glyn Adey and David Frisby (New York: Harper & Row, 1976), 1–67, here 14; "Einleitung zum *Positivismusstreit in der deutschen Soziologie*," *Gesammelte Schriften*, ed. Rolf Tiedemann (Frankfurt am Main: Suhrkamp, 1997), vol. 8, 280–353, here 294.

12. Theodor W. Adorno, "Culture Industry Reconsidered," trans. Anson Rabinbach, in *The Culture Industry: Selected Essays on Mass Culture*, ed. J. M. Bernstein (London: Routledge, 1991), 98–106, here 103; "Résumé über Kultur-

industrie," *Gesammelte Schriften*, ed. Rolf Tiedemann (Frankfurt am Main: Suhrkamp, 1997), vol. 10, 337–345, here 342.

13. Jacques Derrida, "*Fichus*: Frankfurt Address," in *Paper Machine*, trans. Rachel Bowlby (Stanford, CA: Stanford University Press, 2005), 164–181, here 166.

14. Friedrich Hölderlin, *Essays and Letters*, trans. Jeremy Adler and Charlie Louth (London: Penguin, 2009), 118.

15. Immanuel Kant, "What Is Orientation in Thinking?," trans. H. B. Nisbet, in *Political Writings*, ed. Hans Reiss (Cambridge: Cambridge University Press, 1991), 237–249, here 238.

16. Kant, "Orientation," 239.

17. Kant, "Orientation," 240.

18. Ibid.

19. Kant, "Orientation," 247.

20. Kant, "Orientation," 249.

21. Martin Heidegger, *Being and Time*, trans. John Macquarrie and Edward Robinson (New York: Harper Perennial, 2008), 144.

22. Martin Heidegger, "The Thinker as Poet," trans. Albert Hofstadter, in *Poetry, Language, Thought* (New York: Harper Perennial, 2001), 1–15, here 4; *Aus der Erfahrung des Denkens* (Stuttgart: Klett-Cotta, 2005), 7.

23. Theodor W. Adorno, "Ohne Leitbild: Anstelle einer Vorrede," in *Gesammelte Schriften*, ed. Rolf Tiedemann (Frankfurt am Main: Suhrkamp, 1997), vol. 10, 291–301, here 297.

24. Ibid.

25. One might add that it is along the lines of this *eigene Bewegung*, too, that the logic of Adorno's nonpropositional thinking in relation to the work of art would have to be traced.

26. Franz Kafka, "'Ach, sagte die Maus,'" in *Zur Frage der Gesetze und andere Schriften aus dem Nachlaß* (Frankfurt am Main: Fischer, 1994), 163.

27. Theodor W. Adorno, "Notes on Kafka," in *Prisms*, trans. Samuel and Shierry Weber (Cambridge, MA: MIT Press, 1983), 243–271, here 246; "Aufzeichnungen zu Kafka," *Gesammelte Schriften*, ed. Rolf Tiedemann (Frankfurt am Main: Suhrkamp, 1997), vol. 11, 254–287, here 255.

28. Rainer Maria Rilke, "Archaic Torso of Appolo," in *The Selected Poetry of Rainer Maria Rilke*, bilingual English and German edition, ed. and trans. Stephen Mitchell (New York: Vintage, 1989), 61.

29. Reinhard Lettau, *Zur Frage der Himmelsrichtungen* (Munich: Hanser, 1988).

30. Theodor W. Adorno, "Who's Afraid of the Ivory Tower? A Conversation with Theodor W. Adorno," translated, edited, and with an introduction by Gerhard Richter, in *Language without Soil: Adorno and Late Philosophical Modernity*, ed. Gerhard Richter (New York: Fordham University Press, 2010), 227–238,

here 233; "'Keine Angst vor dem Elfenbeinturm': Ein *Spiegel*-Gespräch," in *Gesammelte Schriften*, ed. Rolf Tiedemann (Frankfurt am Main: Suhrkamp, 1997), vol. 20, 402–409, here 403.

31. "Ivory Tower," 238; "Elfenbeinturm," 408.

32. Theodor W. Adorno, "Art and the Arts," trans. Rodney Livingstone, in *Can One Live after Auschwitz? A Philosophical Reader*, ed. Rolf Tiedemann (Stanford, CA: Stanford University Press, 2003), 368–387, here 385; "Die Kunst und die Künste," *Gesammelte Schriften*, ed. Rolf Tiedemann (Frankfurt am Main: Suhrkamp, 1997), vol. 10, 432–453, here 450.

7. FALSE LIFE, LIVING ON: ADORNO WITH DERRIDA

1. Friedrich Nietzsche, *Human, All-Too-Human: A Book for Free Spirits*, trans. Marion Faber, with Stephan Lehmann (Lincoln: University of Nebraska Press, 1996), 180.

2. Friedrich Nietzsche, *Thus Spoke Zarathustra: A Book for All and None*, trans. Walter Kaufmann (New York: Modern Library, 1995), 89.

3. In section 20 of the Second Essay, "'Guilt,' 'Bad Conscience,' and the Like" ("'Schuld,' 'schlechtes Gewissen' und Verwandtes") of the *Genealogy of Morals*, Nietzsche even goes so far as to inflect his genealogical account of morality itself by a consideration of the nexus between the "consciousness of being in debt" ("Bewußtsein, . . . Schulden zu haben") and the concept of guilt ("Schuld") as the two appear in a "feeling of guilty indebtedness" ("Schuldgefühl"). *On the Genealogy of Morals*, trans. Walter Kaufmann and R. J. Hollingdale, in *On the Genealogy of Morals and Ecce Homo* (New York: Vintage, 1989), 90–91.

4. Paul Celan, "Speech on the Occasion of Receiving the Literature Prize of the Free Hanseatic City of Bremen," in *Selected Poems and Prose*, trans. John Felstiner (New York: Norton, 2001), 395–396, here 396; "Ansprache anläßlich der Entgegennahme des Literaturpreises der Freien Hansestadt Bremen," *Der Meridian und andere Prosa* (Frankfurt am Main: Suhrkamp, 1994), 37–39, here 39.

5. Celan, "Speech," 395.

6. Celan, "Ansprache," 37.

7. A meticulous philological record of Celan's readings of Heidegger—including the specific texts he read and the dates when he marked them as read—can be found in a volume listing the titles of the philosophical books contained in Celan's personal library, his annotations in these books, as well as notebooks pertaining to his readings of these works. Paul Celan, *La bibliothèque philosophique/Die philosophische Bibliothek: Catalogue raisonné des annotations*, eds. Alexandra Richter, Patrik Alac, and Bertrand Badiou (Paris: Éditions Rue d'Ulm, 2004). My references to dates of Celan's readings of specific Heideggerean texts are based on this edition.

8. I borrow the remaining sentences in this paragraph, in revised form, from my *Thought-Images: Frankfurt School Writers' Reflections from Damaged Life* (Stanford, CA: Stanford University Press, 2007), 162.

9. Martin Heidegger, *Was ist Metaphysik?* (Frankfurt am Main: Vittorio Klostermann, 1992), 51.

10. See Martin Heidegger, *Elucidations of Hölderlin's Poetry*, trans. Keith Hoeller (Amherst, NY: Humanity, 2000); *Erläuterungen zu Hölderlins Dichtung*, 4th edition (Frankfurt am Main: Vittorio Klostermann, 1971).

11. Martin Heidegger, *What Is Called Thinking?*, trans. Fred Wieck and J. Glenn Gray (New York: Harper and Row, 1968), 138ff; *Was heißt Denken?* (Tübingen: Niemeyer, 1954), 91.

12. Judith Butler, "Can One Lead a Good Life in a Bad Life? Adorno Prize Lecture," *Radical Philosophy* 176 (2012): 9–18. Established in 1977, the Adorno Prize is awarded by the City of Frankfurt every three years to a scholar, writer, or artist of international significance who exemplifies the transdisciplinary orientation of Frankfurt School critical thought.

13. Butler, "Adorno Prize Lecture," 9.

14. The other two are our own body and the external world. As Freud explains, "We are threatened with suffering from three directions: from our own body, which is doomed to decay and dissolution and which cannot even do without pain and anxiety as warning signals; from the external world, which may rage against us with overwhelming and merciless forces of destruction; and finally from our relation to other men. The suffering which comes from this last source is perhaps more painful to us than any other. We tend to regard it as a kind of gratuitous addition, although it cannot be any less fatefully inevitable than the suffering which comes from elsewhere." *Civilization and Its Discontents*, trans. James Strachey (New York: Norton, 1961), 26.

15. Rainer Maria Rilke, "Archaischer Torso Apollos," in *Die Gedichte* (Frankfurt am Main: Insel, 2006), 483.

16. Theodor W. Adorno, *Minima Moralia: Reflexionen aus dem beschädigten Leben, Gesammelte Schriften*, ed. Rolf Tiedemann, vol. 4 (Frankfurt am Main: Suhrkamp, 1997), 43.

17. For a consideration of Adorno's text within the orbit of its thinking "after Auschwitz" that strives to take into account the impossibility of its own undertaking, see Gerhard Richter, "Nazism and Negative Dialectics: Adorno's Hitler in *Minima Moralia*," in *Thought-Images: Frankfurt School Writers' Reflections from Damaged Life* (Stanford, CA: Stanford University Press, 2007), 147–190.

18. Theodor W. Adorno, "Who's Afraid of the Ivory Tower? A Conversation with Theodor W. Adorno," translated, edited, and with an introduction by Gerhard Richter, in *Language without Soil: Adorno and Late Philosophical Modernity*, ed. Gerhard Richter (New York: Fordham University Press, 2010), 227–238, here

233; "Keine Angst vor dem Elfenbeinturm. Ein 'Spiegel'-Gespräch." *Gesammelte Schriften*, vol. 20, ed. Rolf Tiedemann (Frankfurt am Main: Suhrkamp, 1997), 402–409, here 403.

19. Maurice Blanchot, *The Writing of the Disaster*, trans. Ann Smock (Lincoln: University of Nebraska Press, 1995), 113.

20. Theodor W. Adorno, *Minima Moralia: Reflections from Damaged Life*, trans. E. F. N. Jephcott (London: Verso, 1974), 39.

21. Theodor W. Adorno, *Minima Moralia: Meditazione della vita offesa*, trans. Renato Solmi (Turin: Einaudi, 1994), 35.

22. Theodor W. Adorno, *Minima Moralia: Reflexiones desde la vida dañada*, trans. Joaquin Chamorro Mielke (Madrid: Akal Ediciones, 2004), 44.

23. Theodor W. Adorno, *Minima Moralia: Réflexions sur la vie mutilée*, trans. Éliane Kaufholz and Jean-René Ladmiral (Paris: Éditions Payot & Rivages, 2006), 48.

24. We might say that, from the perspective offered here, the revised title under which an English publisher recently reissued Adorno's text, *Minima Moralia: Reflections on a Damaged Life* (London: Verso, 2005) is no improvement over the title of the original English translation (*Minima Moralia: Reflections from Damaged Life*). On the contrary, the change of prepositions from "from" to "on" implies a difference from, and potential mastery of, life that are at odds with the more objective or general forms of damaged life that Adorno attempts to think. His thinking is imbricated in the life that he attempts to think; his philosophy assumes no vantage point outside a damaged life that would allow one to reflect "on" it, as if it were a discrete, separate object of inquiry. Furthermore, the introduction of the indefinite article "a" before the word "life" betrays something of a misconstrual, at least to my way of thinking, of the relation between life and thought that Adorno hopes to forge—as if Adorno had written "aus einem beschädigten Leben," rather than "aus dem beschädigten Leben." The difference is important because, for him, *Minima Moralia*, even though it also is anchored undeniably in a personal and therefore contingent form of subjective experience, is by no means "merely" an autobiography or a record of the working through of a personal trauma. The text engages not simply "a life" (say, Adorno's) but rather—precisely through the idiomaticity of a particular life—damaged life itself under the framing conditions of a certain world-historical, political, and philosophical episteme. In it, the impersonal pull—and therefore certain general life conditions—of what Adorno would often call "die Objektivität der Sache" makes itself felt.

25. This Aristotelean possibility is one that Butler weighs in her Adorno Prize speech.

26. This performative tension is pursued in Jochen Hörisch's extended essay, *Es gibt (k)ein richtiges Leben im falschen* (Frankfurt am Main: Suhrkamp, 2003).

27. Jacques Derrida, "*Fichus*: Frankfurt Address," in *Paper Machine*, trans. Rachel Bowlby (Stanford, CA: Stanford University Press, 2005), 164–181, here 176.

28. Jacques Derrida, *Fichus: Discours de Francfort* (Paris: Galilée, 2002), 43.

29. Derrida, "*Fichus*: Frankfurt Address," 176; *Fichus: Discours de Francfort*, 43–44.

30. Derrida, "*Fichus*: Frankfurt Address," 176; *Fichus: Discours de Francfort*, 44.

31. Derrida, "*Fichus*: Frankfurt Address," 177; *Fichus: Discours de Francfort*, 45. In a different context, it would prove fruitful to take Derrida's Frankfurt speech on Adorno as the occasion for a more systematic interrogation of how writers associated with the Frankfurt School of critical theory were read (or not read) by French thinkers of Derrida's generation more broadly. While the legacy of Heidegger in the French context is much better understood—see, for instance, the remarkable intellectual history by Dominique Janicaud, *Heidegger in France*, trans. François Raffoul and David Pettigrew (Bloomington: Indiana University Press, 2015)—the role played by thinkers associated with the Frankfurt School still waits to be thought in its full complexity. One thinks here, for example, of remarks made by Michel Foucault in a late interview with Gérard Raulet. There, Foucault suggests that in the France of his intellectual formation, "the Frankfurt School was practically unheard of. This, by the way, raises a minor historical problem which fascinates me and which I have not been able to resolve at all. It is common knowledge that many representatives of the Frankfurt School came to Paris in 1935, seeking refuge, and left very hastily, sickened presumably—some even said as much—but saddened anyhow not to have found more of an echo. Then came 1940, but they had already left for England and the U.S., where they were actually much better received. The understanding that might have been established between the Frankfurt School and French philosophical thought . . . never occurred. And when I was a student, I can assure you that I never once heard the name of the Frankfurt School mentioned by any of my professors." And Foucault adds, perhaps in a slightly ironic mode but certainly with a gesture commemorating a missed opportunity for thinking and thanking, that "if I had been familiar with the Frankfurt School, if I had been aware of it at the time, I would not have said a number of stupid things that I did say and I would have avoided many of the detours which I made while trying to pursue my own humble path—when, meanwhile, avenues had been opened up by the Frankfurt School. It is a strange case of non-penetration between two very similar types of thinking which is explained, perhaps, by that very similarity. Nothing hides the fact of a problem in common better than two similar ways of approaching it." Michel Foucault, "Critical Theory/Intellectual History," trans. Jeremy Harding, in *Politics, Philosophy, Culture: Interviews and*

Other Writings, 1977–1984, ed. Lawrence Kritzman (London: Routledge, 2003), 17–46, here 26.

32. Jacques Derrida, "Living On: Border Lines," trans. James Hulbert, in *Deconstruction and Criticism*, by Harold Bloom, Paul de Man, Jacques Derrida, Geoffrey Hartman, and J. Hillis Miller (New York: Seabury, 1979), 75–176, here 75.

33. Derrida, "Living On," 76.

34. Derrida, "Living On," 78.

35. Jacques Derrida, *The Beast and the Sovereign*, vol. 2, trans. Geoffrey Bennington (Chicago: University of Chicago Press, 2011), 131.

36. Ibid.

37. Just how precarious this survivance is for Derrida powerfully emerges in his last interview, conducted shortly before his death. There, he confides, implicitly taking up the question of survival from his final seminar: "When it comes to thought, the question of survival has taken on absolutely unforeseeable forms. At my age, I am ready to entertain the most contradictory hypotheses in this regard: I have simultaneously—I ask you to believe me on this—the *double feeling* that, on the one hand, to put it playfully and with a certain immodesty, one has not yet begun to read me, that even though there are, to be sure, many very good readers (a few dozen in the world perhaps, people who are also writer-thinkers, poets), in the end it is later on that all this has chance of appearing; but also, on the other hand, and thus simultaneously, I have the feeling that two weeks or a month after my death *there will be nothing left*. Nothing except what been copyrighted and deposited in libraries. I swear to you, I believe sincerely and simultaneously in these two hypotheses." Jacques Derrida, *Learning to Live Finally: The Last Interview*, trans. Pascale-Anne Brault and Michael Naas (Hoboken, NJ: Melville House, 2007), 33ff.

38. Jacques Derrida, "Negotiations," in *Negotiations: Interventions and Interviews 1971–2001*, ed. and trans. Elizabeth Rottenberg (Stanford, CA: Stanford University Press, 2002), 11–40, here 11.

39. Derrida, "Negotiations," 12–13.

40. Derrida, "Negotiations," 12.

41. Ibid.

42. Derrida, "Negotiations," 13.

CONCLUSION: A KIND OF LEAVE-TAKING

1. See the account of this aspect of Adorno's public persona in postwar Germany by Philip Felsch, *Der lange Sommer der Theorie. Geschichte einer Revolte, 1960–1990* (Munich: Beck, 2015), 37–42.

2. This as-yet-unpublished letter from Adorno to Plessner is housed in the archives of the Institut für Sozialforschung in Frankfurt; the passage quoted here is cited in Alex Demirovic, *Der nonkonformistische Intellektuelle. Die Entwicklung der Kritischen Theorie zur Frankfurter Schule* (Frankfurt am Main: Suhrkamp, 1999), 673; and in Stefan Müller-Dohm, *Adorno. Eine Biographie* (Frankfurt am Main: Suhrkamp, 2003), 730; *Adorno: A Biography*, trans. Rodney Livingstone (Cambridge: Polity, 2005), 481.

INDEX

Adorno, Theodor W.: American exile, 18, 31, 150, 162; on "after Auschwitz," 2, 40, 77, 134, 150, 162, 182n21, 198n17; and animal motifs, 76; on the distracted gaze, 36–38; on *Enthaltung*, 100, 103–104, 110; on *das Gedachte*, 22–23, 31; on *der Gehalt*, 103–105, 107, 110–111, 188nn18,21; and instrumental reason, 9, 37, 89, 92, 102, 134–135, 149, 158; and *Nachdenken*, 28–29; on presentation (*Darstellung*), 4–6, 10, 18–21, 82, 84–86, 90, 91, 93, 131, 171n5, 172n8; on "primacy of the object," 7, 33–38, 44–45, 61–66; on *richtiges Leben*, 14, 148–155, 157, 159, 161; on *skoteinos*, 6, 12, 79, 90, 94; on thinking as constellation, 8, 12, 16, 70–94, 110, 183n24, 184nn30,32; on thinking as interruption, 1, 29–30, 37, 81, 88, 156, 182n20; and thinking as nonidentical, 30, 32, 59, 63, 64, 79, 81, 83–84, 133; on thinking thinking, 4, 23–36; thinking with, 6, 9, 10–11, 145, 162; on trace (*Spur*), 31–32, 61, 62; on tradition, 11–12, 39–43, 45–47, 58–69; on truth content (*Wahrheitsgehalt*), 13, 63, 68, 87, 92, 97, 102–103, 105 118, 134

Adorno, Theodor W., negative dialectics: and the "as if" mode, 111; as constellation, 184n32; within the German philosophical tradition, 19; and Heidegger's fundamental ontology, 170n6; inheritance of Hegel, 12; lecture course on, 22; as nonidentical thinking, 30, 79, 81–84; and "right life," 151, 153, 161; against systematicity, 15, 27–28, 32, 96–97

Adorno, Theodor W., uncoercive gaze: Adorno on, 7, 37–38; and aesthetic theory, 118–120; constellation of inheritance, 77; as critical art, 13; in the face of tradition, 59–60, 68–69; as a form of life, 14–15; and *Gehalt*, 105, 110–111; Hegelian inheritance, 12, 70–71,

Adorno, Theodor W. *(continued)* 83; as inheriting, reading, interpreting, 83; and judgment, 95–97, 105, 114; and orientation in thinking, 133–134, 142–143; as perpetual engagement, 9–11; and presentation, 10; as relation to things and concepts, 80; as rescuing, 63–64; and "right life," 159; as "snuggling up to an object" (*Anschmiegen*), 7–8, 33–38, 61, 162; as transformative thinking to come, 151–153, 161–165

Adorno, Theodor W., works by: "The Actuality of Philosophy," 22, 102, 172n12; *Aesthetic Theory*, 13, 24, 28, 97–98, 103, 111, 118, 136, 142, 188–189n22; *Alban Berg: Master of the Smallest Link*, 3, 169n4, 181n18; "Aus einem Schulheft ohne Decke," 170n9, 185n39; Bar Harbor notebook, 5; "Cultural Criticism and Society," 186n1; "Culture Industry Reconsidered," 195n12; *Dialectic of Enlightenment* (with Max Horkheimer), 23, 76–77, 134–135, 181n12; "Essay as Form," 183n24; *Hegel: Three Studies*, 12, 79, 82, 90, 184n30; "Improvisations," 76; "Die Kunst und die Künste," 143; *Letters to His Parents*, 180n11; "Lyric Poetry and Society," 99, "Meditations on Metaphysics," 40; *Minima Moralia*, 4–5, 14, 28, 30, 33, 96–97, 136, 150, 155, 162, 174n45, 181–182n20, 199n24; *Negative Dialectics*, 4, 10, 12, 19, 22, 24, 28, 30, 33, 35, 40, 45, 60, 81–82, 136, 172n8, 181n12, 182n21; "Notes on Kafka," 119, 191nn13–14; "Notes on Philosophical Thinking," 7–8, 21–22, 33–34, 61–62; *Notes to Literature*, 105, 119, 136, 183n24, 188n18; *Ohne Leitbild. Parva Aesthetica*, 42, 139, 143; "On the Question: 'What Is German?,'" 18–19, 172n19; *Ontologie und Dialektik* (Lecture Course), 5, 38; "On Tradition," 11, 42–43, 45, 60, 66, 179n67; *Philosophical Terminology*, 80; *The Philosophy of New Music*, 78, 136; "Toward a Portrait of Thomas Mann," 188n18; *Prisms*, 21; *Quasi una fantasia*, 76; "Reconciliation under Duress," 183n24; "Remarks on Philosophical Thinking," 93; "Resignation," 58; "Resumé Concerning the Culture Industry," 135; "Scientific Experiences of a European Scholar in America," 33; "Short Commentaries on Proust," 105; "Skoteinos, or, How to Read," 6, 12, 79, 90, 94; *Stichworte*, 8, 22; "Television as Ideology," 181n17; "Theses on the Language of the Philosopher," 22, 83; "Tradition und Erkenntnis," 45; "Trying to Understand *Endgame*," 180n76; "What Does Coming to Term with the Past Mean?" 181n16; "Who Is Afraid of the Ivory Tower?," 169n1; "Words from Abroad," 190n12; "Why Still Philosophy?," 22, 172n12

Agamben, Giorgio, 11, 14, 96, 115, 126–128, 187n5, 193n40

Allen, William S., 170n6

Améry, Jean, 96

Anselm of Canterbury, 32

Arendt, Hannah: and Adorno, 11–12, 39–43, 45–47, 58, 60–65, 68–69; and Benjamin, 11–12, 42–46, 54, 176nn9,13; *Between Past and Future*, 11, 42, 48–50, 177n29; comparative readings on Arendt and Adorno, 174–175n1; deconstruction of metaphysics, 177–178n45; German television

interview, 177n34; on the Greeks, 53–54; and Judaism, 175n2; Lessing Prize speech, 148; *The Life of the Mind*, 178n49; and Marx, 42, 50, 51–53, 55–57, 60, 62, 63; on the Romans, 48–49, 53, 178–179n50; on Romanticism, 54; on tradition, 11–12, 39–65, 68–69, 175n5, 176–177n28, 177n37; and Weimar culture, 175n2
Aristotle, 50, 52, 178
Aschheim, Steven, 175n2
Ashton, E. B., 172n8
Auden, W. H., 115
Auer, Dirk, 174n1

Balibar, Étienne, 47–48
Balzac, Honoré de, 103, 105
Barnes, Julian, 105, 108, 109
Bauer, Bruno, 71
Bauer, Felice, 117
Beckett, Samuel, 65, 66–67, 77, 102, 104, 105, 118, 119, 180n75
Benhabib, Seyla, 177n37
Benjamin, Walter: within Adorno's "Notes on Philosophical Thinking," 33; on Adorno's works as "ice-desert of abstraction," 4, 161; Agamben on, 96, 187n5; *Arcades Project*, 47; Bolz on, 96; on constellation, 90; on culture and barbarism, 76; dialectic at a standstill, 81; on experience, 173n43; on *das Gedachte*, 23; on the German Baroque, 44; on Goethe's *Elective Affinities*, 102; on the image of the "little hunchback," 99; influence on Adorno, 10–12, 21, 39, 42–43, 45–47, 67, 188n18; influence on Arendt, 39, 42–46, 54, 175n2, 176nn9,13; on Kafka, 140, 191n13; and Karl Krauss, 113; letter from Adorno on the role of politics in writing, 110; *Origin of the German Mourning Play*, 81, 171n5, 188n18; on rescuing, 180n72; on thinking and stupidity, 28; on tradition, 45–47, 54
Berg, Alban, 3–4, 78, 118
Beethoven, Ludwig van, 3, 104
Beradt, Charlotte, 176n28
Bernstein, J. M., 134, 170n6, 182nn21–22
Binder, Hartmut, 194n52
Birmingham, Peg, 175n13
Blanchot, Maurice, 31, 129, 151, 155, 170n6, 193n49
Bloch, Ernst, 71, 79, 112, 183n24
Blumenfeld, Kurt, 175n2
Bolz, Norbert, 96
Borchardt, Rudolf, 63
Bowie, Andrew, 170n6
Brecht, Bertolt, 183n24
Broch, Hermann, 51, 177n38
Brod, Max, 124, 126, 140
Bubner, Rüdiger, 96
Butler, Judith, 148–149, 154, 198n12, 199n25

Celan, Paul, 77, 104, 145, 197n7
Char, René, 49
Cicero, 108
Coetzee, J. M., 191n14
Comay, Rebecca, 71, 180n2
Corngold, Stanley, 191n14, 192n28, 194n50
Croce, Benedetto, 70, 79

Dante, Alighieri, 115
De Man, Paul, 123–124
Demirovic, Alex, 202n2
Demus, Klaus, 147
Dickens, Charles, 119
Deleuze, Gilles, 35
Derrida, Jacques: and Arendt, 57; inheriting Adorno, 11, 14, 136, 154, 200n31; on Kafka, 124, 193–194n50;

Derrida, Jacques *(continued)*
on the literal and figurative in philosophical texts, 123; on "living on," 155–156; on negotiation, 158–159; on philosophy as learning how to die, 108–109; on survivance, 156–157, 201n37; on trace, 173n39

Descartes, René (Cartesian method), 11, 31, 77, 87, 92

Düttmann, Alexander García, 97, 181n20, 191n14

Duver, Thierry de, 134, 195n10

Eggers, Dave, 103

Eichendorff, Joseph Freiherr von, 119

Endres, Martin, 170n6

Esch, Deborah, 157–158

Faulkner, William, 2

Felsch, Philip, 201n1

Feuerbach, Ludwig, 71

Fichte, Johann Gottlieb, 74, 86

Fischer, Kuno, 71

Freud, Sigmund, 32, 73, 76, 109, 149, 191n14, 198n14

Fontane, Theodor, 66–67

Förster, Eckart, 186n50

Fort, Jeff, 193n48

Foucault, Michel, 27, 109, 132, 200n31

Frankfurt School, 1, 33, 42, 58, 70, 113, 136–137, 142, 154, 198n12, 200n31

Gadamer, Hans-Georg, 72–73

Gandesha, Samir, 174n1

Gans, Eduard, 71

Gaus, Günter, 177n34

George, Stefan, 105

George Circle, 63

German Idealism, 17, 74–75, 77, 84, 86, 136, 184n32

Geulen, Eva, 179n67

Goethe, Johann Wolfgang von, 15, 36–37, 102, 105, 115, 119, 121, 150, 164, 183n24

Gordon, Peter, 170n6

Gross, David, 175n5

Guattari, Félix, 35

Hamacher, Werner, 185n45

Hammer, Espen, 170n6

Harrison, Robert Pogue, 40–41

Hegel, Georg Wilhelm Friedrich: Adorno's inheritance of, 6; 11, 12, 21, 25, 41, 70–71, 75–76, 78–94, 136, 182n21, 183n24, 184n30; Adorno's *Three Studies* on, 12, 79, 82, 90, 161, 162, 184n30; Arendt's inheritance of, 51–52, 55–56, 57; Bloch on, 79; on the constellation, 8, 80–94; Derrida on legacy of, 155; *The Difference between Fichte's and Schelling's System of Philosophy*, 74; on experience and concept, 185n45; Gadamer on legacy of, 72–74; on *Gedächtnis* and *Erinnerung*, 148; Hegelian negation as affirmation, 184–185n37, 185n44; influence on Marx, 78; *Lectures on the History of Philosophy*, 72; on the need for thinking to limit itself, 36–37; *Phenomenology of Spirit*, 18, 27, 71, 74, 80, 84, 86, 89, 186n50

Heidegger, Martin: and Adorno, 19, 134, 170n6; Arendt on Benjamin and, 42; and Celan, 146–147, 154, 197n7; correspondence with Staiger, 187n13; on *Denken* and *Danken*, 147–148, 154; and *das Gedachte*, 23; Hölderlin, 146; influence on Arendt, 53–54, 175n2, 178n45; influence on Derrida and the French tradition, 200n31; influence on Gadamer, 72; on Kantian orientation, 138–139; on Mörike, 99, 187n13; on *Nachden-*

ken, 28; "The Origin of the Work of Art," 178n49; "Was heißt Denken?," 2, 147–148
Heine, Wilhelm, 105, 119, 183n24
Heller, Agnes, 51, 177n37
Henrich, Dieter, 184n32
Hitler, Adolf, 40, 150
Hohendahl, Peter Uwe, 170n6, 172n12, 182n21, 195n10
Hofmannsthal, Hugo von, 63
Hölderlin, Friedrich, 93, 100–101, 105, 119, 137, 146–147
Horkheimer, Max, 42, 76, 158
Hörisch, Jochen, 184n37, 199n26
Husserl, Edmund, 46, 77, 135–136, 150, 158

Jacobi, Friedrich Heinrich, 136
Jameson, Fredric, 133
Janicaud, Dominique, 200n31
Jarvis, Simon, 182n22
Jaspers, Karl, 175n2
Jay, Martin, 173n43
Jephcott, E. F. N., 151
Joyce, James, 63, 183n24
Judaism, 39, 44, 96, 120, 175n2
Judeo-Christian Bible, 72, 96

Kafka, Franz: Adorno on Beckett and, 66; Adorno's inheritance of, 6, 11, 77, 118, 123, 161, 191n13; Agamben on *The Trial*, 126–128, 193n40; allegorical style, 140–142; Benjamin on, 44, 140, 191n13; Blanchot on, 129, 193n49; *The Castle*, 120, 126; Corngold on, 191n14, 192n28, 193–194n50; Derrida on, 193–194n50; on "etwas Böses," 120–121; Kantian sublimity in, 193n48; Kracauer on, 191n13; the literal and the figurative in his works, 122–125, 191nn14,21, 192n26; "Little Fable," 140–141; *The Metamorphosis*, 115, 194n50; and Nietzsche, 122; in *Notes to Literature*, 105; place in literary tradition, 115, 183n24; *The Trial*, 13–14, 115–117, 119–130, 194n52
Kant, Immanuel: Adorno's inheritance of, 3, 11, 79, 84–86, 100, 103, 134, 182n21; on aesthetic judgement, 100, 103; on the concept, 84–86, 137; *Critique of Pure Reason*, 27; on the *Ding an sich*, 34; on orientation in thinking, 14, 136–139, 195n6; post-Kantian categorical imperative, 134; on the primacy of the object, 34; in relation to Hegel's absolute idealism, 74, 86; and the sublime in Kafka, 193n48; and the tradition of critique, 46, 62, 97, 137
Keenan, Thomas, 157–158
Kierkegaard, Søren, 55–56, 57, 62, 136, 170n6
Kluge, Alexander, 148
Klusmeyer, Douglas, 175n5
Kohn, Jerome, 175n2, 178n48
Kojève, Alexandre, 71
Kracauer, Siegfried, 17–18, 33, 67, 136, 191n13
Kraus, Karl, 113

Leibniz, Gottfried, Wilhelm, 11
Lenin, Vladimir, 62, 149
Lessing, Gotthold Ephraim, 136
Lessing Prize, 148
Lettau, Reinhard, 142
Luhmann, Niklas, 131, 136
Lukács, Georg, 89, 132, 182n21, 183n24
Lyotard, Jean-François, 55

Macdonald, Iain, 170n6
Mahler, Gustav, 104, 162
Malabou, Catherine, 71, 180n2
Mann, Heinrich, 183n24

Mann, Thomas, 96, 118, 183n24, 188n18
Marcuse, Herbert, 22, 142
Marx, Karl (Marxian thought): Arendt on, 50, 51–53, 55–58, 60–63; Derrida on, 155; and the Frankfurt
Marx, Karl *(continued)* School, 42; Hegelian legacy, 71, 72–73, 78; and the limits of thinking, 72–73; in relation to Adorno, 182n21, 191n14
Mehring, Franz, 183n24
Melville, Herman, 1
Mendelsohn, Moses, 136, 195n6
Menke, Christoph, 97
Meyer, Hans, 183n24
Miller, J. Hills, 132
Modigliani, Amedeo, 107
Montaigne, Michel de, 108
Mörike, Eduard, 12–13, 97–102, 110, 187n13
Müller-Dohm, Stefan, 180n75, 202n2
Musil, Robert, 164

Nancy, Jean-Luc, 185n37
National Socialism, 105–106, 150
Nehamas, Alexander, 112–113
Neumann, Gerhard, 192n26
Nietzsche, Friedrich: on the abyss, 122; Adorno on, 19; Adorno's inheritance of, 21, 170n6, 182n21; Arendt on, 55–57, 62; critique of concepts, 35, 85, 110; on debt and gratitude, 144–145, 197n3; *Genealogy of Morals*, 89; Hegelian influence, 71, 78; influence on Derrida, 154; and Kafka, 122; and the limits of thinking, 72–73; on the work of art, 109
Novalis, 132

Phillips, Mark Salber, 175n5
Pichler, Axel, 170n6
Pieper, Josef, 175n5
Pippen, Robert B., 89, 186n50
Pinkard, Terry, 185n43
Plato, 50–52, 55–58, 60, 108–109, 178n45
Plessner, Helmuth, 163, 202n2
Pöggeler, Otto, 186n50
Politzer, Heinz, 126
Pound, Ezra, 89
Proust, Marcel, 89, 105, 119, 162, 183n24

Raulet, Gérard, 200n31
Rensmann, Lars, 174n1
Richter, Gerhard (painter), 103
Rilke, Rainer Maria, 141, 149–150
Ronell, Avital, 173n27
Roth, Philip, 105, 107, 108
Rorty, Richard (Rortian pragmatism), 20

Schelling, Friedrich Wilhelm Joseph, 74, 86
Schiller, Friedrich, 183n24
Schiller Memorial Prize, 148
Schlegel, Friedrich, 92, 183n24
Schnädelbach, Herbert, 133
Schochet, Gordon, 175n5
Scholem, Gershom, 34, 42, 44, 175n2
Schönberg, Arnold, 66, 77, 104, 118
Schopenhauer, Arthur, 71
Schöttker, Detlev, 176n9
Schröder, Rudolf Alexander, 63
Seel, Martin, 134
Seghers, Anna, 183n24
Shakespeare, William, 51, 106, 116, 164
Shelley, Percy Bysshe, 155
Shils, Edward, 175n5
Shoah, 40, 48, 78, 145
Sokel, Walter H., 193n48
Söllner, Alfons, 174n1
Spiegel, Hubert, 192n26
Spinoza, Baruch, 136

Spivak, Gayatri, 116
Stach, Reiner, 129–130
Staiger, Emil, 99, 187n13
Stegmaier, Werner, 195n6
Stewart, Jon, 186n50
Strauß, David Friedrich, 71

Taubes, Jacob, 96
Taylor, Charles, 71
Thoreau, Henry David, 15–16
Tiedemann, Rolf, 22, 134, 172n12
Trawny, Peter, 170n6

Valéry, Paul, 105, 151

Wagner, Richard, 3
Walser, Martin, 105–107, 108, 116, 189n26

Weber, Samuel, 21
Wedekind, Frank, 119
Weimar Republic, 33, 39, 67, 175n2
Weissberg, Liliane, 174n1
Welles, Orson, 191n14
Wellmer, Albrecht, 178n45
Wessel, Julia Schulze, 174n1
Wharton, Edith, 103
Wittgenstein, Ludwig, 89
Wizisla, Erdmut, 176n9
Wolf, Hugo, 99

Yeats, W. B., 123
Young-Bruehl, Elisabeth, 176n29

Ziarek, Krzysztof, 170n6
Zittel, Claus, 170n6
Žižek, Slavoj, 71, 180n2

Gerhard Richter is Professor of German Studies and Comparative Literature at Brown University. His most recent books include *Inheriting Walter Benjamin* and *Afterness: Figures of Following in Modern Thought and Aesthetics*.

IDIOM: INVENTING WRITING THEORY

SERIES EDITORS: JACQUES LEZRA AND PAUL NORTH

Werner Hamacher, *Minima Philologica*. Translated by Catharine Diehl and Jason Groves

Michal Ben-Naftali, *Chronicle of Separation: On Deconstruction's Disillusioned Love*. Translated by Mirjam Hadar. Foreword by Avital Ronell

Daniel Hoffman-Schwartz, Barbara Natalie Nagel, and Lauren Shizuko Stone, eds., *Flirtations: Rhetoric and Aesthetics This Side of Seduction*

Jean-Luc Nancy, *Intoxication*. Translated by Philip Armstrong

Márton Dornbach, *Receptive Spirit: German Idealism and the Dynamics of Cultural Transmission*

Sean Alexander Gurd, *Dissonance: Auditory Aesthetics in Ancient Greece*

Anthony Curtis Adler, *Celebricities: Media Culture and the Phenomenology of Gadget Commodity Life*

Nathan Brown, *The Limits of Fabrication: Materials Science, Materialist Poetics*

Jay Bernstein, Adi Ophir, and Ann Laura Stoler, eds., *Political Concepts: A Critical Lexicon*

Laurent Dubreuil, *Poetry and Mind: Tractatus Poetico-Philosophicus*

Peggy Kamuf, *Literature and the Remains of the Death Penalty*

Gerhard Richter, *Thinking with Adorno: The Uncoercive Gaze*

www.ingramcontent.com/pod-product-compliance
Lightning Source LLC
Chambersburg PA
CBHW020109020526
44112CB00033B/1101